CELEBRATING DIFFERENCE, STAYING FAITHFUL

Also by Andrew Wingate

FREE TO BE

CELEBRATING DIFFERENCE, STAYING FAITHFUL

How to Live in a Multi-faith World

Andrew Wingate

DARTON · LONGMAN + TODD

First published in 2005 by
Darton, Longman and Todd Ltd
1 Spencer Court
140–142 Wandsworth High Street
London SW18 4JJ

Reprinted 2008

ISBN 978–0–232–52532–8

A catalogue record for this book is available from the British Library.

Unless otherwise stated, the Scripture quotations in this publication are
taken from the New Revised Standard Version © 1989, 1995. Division
of Christian Education of the National Council of the Churches of
Christ in the United States of America.

Designed and produced by Sandie Boccacci
Set in 10/12.25pt Minion
Printed and bound in Great Britain by
Intype Libra Ltd

Contents

Preface

This book will be released at a time when we are in the process of launching a new project in Leicester. This is to be known as St Philip's Centre, and is for study and engagement in a multi-faith society. It is an ecumenical project, and its primary aim is to help Christians feel confident to live out their lives in a multi-faith world, and to celebrate that reality. It aims to strengthen them in their witness to the love of God, as revealed in Jesus Christ, and to share that love with others. At the same time, it is a project designed to enable understanding across faiths, as people meet people in a search for truth and ways to work together for the common good. The centre, along with one in Bradford (for details see the Resources section), will offer courses and other opportunities of engagement to people locally, from different parts of the country, from mainland Europe and beyond.

This book gives a feel of the agenda of these new centres. It offers the kind of material which, I hope, will enable readers to do what the title suggests: to celebrate, and not just tolerate, difference, and at the same time to remain faithful to the Christian gospel. It is that very centring in the gospel that enables us to rejoice in difference. Much of the gospel, and indeed of Christian distinctiveness, is focused on Holy Week and Easter, which we have just finished celebrating as I write.

I would like to dedicate this book to two groups. The first group is the friends of various faiths who enable life to be so rich for me in Leicester. Without them, and without Muslim, Hindu, Sikh, Buddhist, Jewish and other friends from earlier times, this book could not have been written, nor our new centre have been made possible. The other group is the small congregation at St Philip's, Evington Road, and our priest Diane Johnson. It is their support, and our work with Diane, that has led to the realisation of the new centre, to which they have made a considerable financial contribution, as well as allowing us to make use of their fine buildings. Others are now joining with their help.

I would like to thank Brendan Walsh, editorial director at Darton, Longman and Todd, and his staff, for their advice and care. Brendan chose the title, having read the material, and I agreed immediately, so well does it describe what the book is trying to do. I would especially like to thank my wife Angela. She went through the text in a meticulous way, and perhaps could have a second career as a copy-editor! She also puts up with the intense and unpredictable schedule that lies behind the encounters that have laid the foundations for this book. It is not easy being the wife of a clergyman. It is particularly difficult if it is someone involved so heavily in interfaith relations!

ANDREW WINGATE
Easter 2005

INTRODUCTION: WHY SHOULD CHRISTIANS BOTHER ABOUT OTHER FAITHS?

The roots of this book go back three decades in my experience, but since September 11, 2001 there has been an urgency about all questions related to inter-religious relations. The attack on the Twin Towers has led to an enormous increase in interest in questions of religion and its influence on international issues. Religion, or at least religious rhetoric, has been one of the key factors, not only in 9/11, but in major conflicts around the world in recent years – in Afghanistan, Iraq, Kashmir, Israel/Palestine, Gujarat, Sri Lanka, Indonesia, the Philippines, Nigeria and Kosovo, to name but a few. Communism and colonialism are no longer the central factors. This raises a challenge to all religious people, Christians amongst them, which the Chief Rabbi Jonathan Sacks has expressed in this way, 'If religion is not part of the solution, it will certainly be part of the problem.'[1] Or, as Jonathan Freedland wrote in *The Guardian* on 4 September 2002, the world has changed decisively since last September but not in the way perhaps expected: 'The anticipated wave of spectacular, follow-up horrors did not come, we do not live in the permanent shadow we feared, constantly waiting for al-Qaida's next strike.' Rather the transformation has come in the reassertion of religion. He goes on:

> The thought that an act of such horror could be fuelled by religious anger sent people rushing back to texts they had once ignored. The Koran became a US bestseller, as people learned anew that religion was not just a private matter for individuals but one with grave public implications. In our own country, the appointment of a new Archbishop of Canterbury became a question of great, national moment ... The Booker-nominated novel, *Life of Pi*, centres on faith. Religion is back.

This has also happened at the local level. The riots in British cities in the summer of 2001, in which religion was a significant factor, gave a new impulse to the need to address their causes. The British National Party now target not Black or Asian people, but Muslims. In Oldham, Burnley and other places their antipathy focused on Muslims, while Hindus and others were left free from their attacks and even encouraged to join an anti-Muslim movement. In July 2004 a secretly filmed BBC programme clearly exposed their hatred of Islam. Recently I preached in Hinckley – a town where there are few Muslims – on Muslim-Christian relations. At the end, a man refused to shake my hand at the door and commented, 'Why did you not mention the Twin Towers? There is only one word for Muslims – murderers.'

More positively, there is a clear understanding at central government and local authority level that religious groups have a defined and often pivotal role in the area of social cohesion and city regeneration. At the educational level, since 9/11 demand for courses or day programmes on interfaith relations or Islam has mushroomed, not only in cities but across the country. In an age of globalisation, mass media and the Internet, there is a realisation that the international and the local deeply influence each other. Christians cannot easily live in an insulated capsule of piety. In addition, there has been an increased vigour in theological debate about faiths, about truth, salvation, grace, and the question of who 'my neighbour' is. An example is the report *The Mystery of Salvation* produced by the Doctrine Commission of the Church of England in 1995.[2] I drafted the chapter 'Christ and World Faiths' (Ch. 7). Its publication prior to 9/11 indicates that there was a clear understanding of the importance of the theology of religions before the attack occurred. In fact, these questions have been considered in Europe ever since adherents of those religions have lived on the continent. But they have always been central in Asia, in the so-called 'mission field'. That field is now here. It is important that we learn from those Christians who have had centuries of experience in Asia, while recognising the rather different context now in Europe.

This book is written primarily for Christians who seek guidance in how to live in our multi-religious world; who would like to talk with those of other faiths with whom they live and work, and seek the confidence to do so; who meet the issues through family, social, employment or community situations; who want to reflect on biblical and theological questions in this field; or who are concerned about what the mission of the Church should be in our multi-faith society. It is for clergy, future clergy, those in leadership roles such as readers or local preachers, and the many lay Christians who are excited, puzzled, concerned or energised by this area of learning, and wish to understand more. It ranges widely, to provide, within one book, material for reflection on a whole variety of issues. It also includes booklists, website links, case studies and questions, which make it of use for groups in training, as well as for private reading.

I shall be drawing primarily on my experience in Britain, in India and other parts of South Asia. I was a lecturer at the Tamilnadu Theological Seminary, South India, where I lived for seven years with my wife and two daughters, who were joined by our Indian-born son. I was also a Prison Chaplain there. I have kept up contact by regular return visits there and to Sri Lanka ever since. As Principal of the West Midlands Ministerial Course at Queen's College Birmingham, I enabled a programme by which all future clergy were engaged in dialogue and reflection, from wherever they came.[3] There followed ten years as Principal of the United College of the Ascension, Selly Oak Colleges, Birmingham, where I was involved in the setting up of the Centre for the Study of Asian Religions at Birmingham University. Here Christian students from all over the world taught me about the enormous variety of contexts in which faiths interact together. This is also emphasised worldwide by the Network for Interfaith Concerns of the Anglican Communion (NIFCON) which I have been part of for ten years, and within Britain by my membership of the Interfaith Consultative Group of the Church of England.

We moved to Leicester in 2000, where I have been involved in training work with clergy and lay people. I am Adviser to the Bishop on Interfaith Relations and Canon Theologian of Leicester Cathedral. In all these posts I have been involved ecumenically in theological education, both for lay and ordained people, and it is out of that educational experience that I write in the hope of encouraging others to embark on this kind of teaching and learning.

Leicester is an ideal place from which to write. It has become the focus for numerous enquiries, reports, newspaper articles, TV and radio programmes on interfaith issues. Within Europe it is felt to be the place that has gone furthest in enabling good interfaith and multi-cultural relations. Birmingham is also such a focus, and Europe often looks to Britain as a test case to see whether it is possible for her diverse citizens to live in harmony.

Leicestershire, which has a population of around 900,000, is a microcosm of England. It has a major city at its heart, expanding small- and medium-sized towns and large rural areas, some poor and declining, others rich commuter villages. The comparatively efficient Midland Mainline makes it possible for people to commute to London in an hour and a quarter. By the next census in 2011 Leicester, with a population of just under 300,000, is predicted to be the first British city in which those of minority ethnic origin will exceed those who have historically lived there. Most are of South Asian origin, the majority through East Africa. Already a high percentage of the children in its schools are Asian, a large proportion born in Britain. The special feature of Leicester's religious map is that it has a very large Hindu population, between 40,000 and 50,000 in the city, and many more within the county. It also has significant Sikh numbers, the most important Jain temple in Europe, and a fast-growing Muslim population, now at about 35,000, the majority of Indian Gujarati origin. There are small numbers of Jews, Buddhists and others. There are also around 10,000 Somalis, Muslims of recent arrival.

Though there is some poverty, especially amongst the considerable number of asylum seekers, on the whole these are resilient communities. There is much economic activity, and about one third of the wealth of the city is, it is estimated, generated within the Asian community. Many live in well-kept terraced houses and there is a strong sense of neighbourhood. Though clearly there are exceptions, educational achievement is generally high amongst the Asian community. A considerable number live in the affluent suburbs of Leicester or adjoining villages. There are some poor, largely white areas, such as Braunstone, in 2002 the seventh poorest local authority area out of several thousand across the whole country, while in 2004 the multi-cultural estate of St Matthew's had the second lowest per capita income in England.

This is the context in which this book is written. Every reader has his or her own. Some parts of Britain have tiny numbers of people of other faiths, for example Cumbria or Cornwall. A couple of London boroughs, such as Brent and Harrow, have even higher proportions than Leicester, with large numbers of Sikhs and Hindus, as well as Muslims. Most northern cities – Bradford as one example – have large numbers of Muslims, the majority from Pakistan. The eastern London boroughs have large numbers of Bangladeshi Muslims, as well as many Tamil Hindus. Birmingham and the West Midlands, where I worked for many years, have a vast Muslim population, mainly of Pakistani and Bangladeshi origin, many Sikhs, fewer Hindus.

This book is written with the conviction that the question of Christian response to people of other faiths is relevant everywhere, theologically, spiritually, pastorally and practically, as well as locally, nationally and internationally. It is also written with a sense of the privilege I have had over thirty years of learning from people of other faiths, of sharing my Christian faith with them, and enabling Christians, lay and ordained, of all major denominations to develop confidence in this area. To give the reader a feel for the kind of issues that will be addressed in this book, and how they arise not from theory but out of engagement in life, I will outline some of the areas or incidents I have been part of in the recent past.

1. In Birmingham and in Leicester I have for many years been involved in initiating and sustaining dialogue groups between different faiths, and before that was part of a Religious Friends Circle in India. In a recent editorial entitled 'Dialogue is for all' in the journal *Interreligious Insight* Alan Race begins with these words:

   > During the last 50 years the idea that the religions should be in dialogue has come of age. The significance of this truly evolutionary transition may yet have to unfold more fully before us, but the energy within the dialogical movement is gaining momentum every day. Truly, it feels as though we are living through a period of momentous transition.

   How can a dialogue group be initiated and its life and challenge sustained? What is dialogue and how can it be for all?

2. A university chaplain sought my advice. He had built up a close relationship with Muslims, both staff and students, on his campus. A Muslim from Iran started attending his Chaplaincy service and, after some time, asked to be baptised and become a Christian. He was aware this would cause much controversy, and might harm his friendship ministry. *How can the needs of community work and dialogue be balanced with the call to witness and respond to conversion requests?*

3. It can be with fellow Christians that difficulties arise. Friendships with Muslims can be seen as compromise with a demonic faith, as was asserted to me on one occasion when a Muslim was present. I asked the Muslim friend to comment. He quietly said he felt hurt that a religion followed by more than one million people should be seen as simply demonic, not least because it honoured Jesus as a prophet equal to Muhammad. I felt the same hurt when asked to address a branch of the Council of Christians and Jews. I dared to mention the Israel/Palestine conflict, being careful to be as even handed as possible. The Jewish response was polite and nuanced. The problem was with three Christians who denounced Palestine and everything Palestinian as contrary to the Bible and to the eternal covenant with David. This was a denial of the heart of the Council of Christians and Jews with its fine record of reconciliation. *How can we respond to those dogmatically certain within our own Christian community that they have the truth, the whole truth, and nothing but the truth?*

4. During Christian Aid week, my wife collected in our road. About 70 per cent of those who live there belong to faiths other than Christian.

Around 50 per cent gave. I collected for Amnesty three weeks later. All gave except one. At a meeting with representatives from Christian Aid, Islamic Relief and Khalsa (Sikh) Aid, I made the suggestion that, in certain areas like this one, perhaps there might be a combined collection for the common cause of human need in the developing world. In Leicester, when Muslims and Christians held a common collection recently, the example was given of Muslims, in the time of the Prophet, being enjoined to unite with other leaders in caring for the poor, orphans and widows in Mecca and Medina. *Where are the places we can join in common service to the wider humanity of different faiths?*

5. Our church is opposite the mosque. On one occasion its windows were smashed – clearly an act of vandalism carried out by youth, most of whom in the area are Muslims. The mosque president was very upset about the incident and sent a message of condolence. He said that, if it was Muslim youth who had caused the damage, they were no more true Muslims than if they had attacked the mosque. The church itself has about forty-five on the electoral role: there are up to 700 in this mosque on a Friday. *What is the place of the church in an area where Christians only now constitute 16 per cent of the population and are apparently declining?*

6. Asian Christians, who live happily alongside their Hindu or Muslim neighbours, are often confused about interfaith dialogue. Their conversion stories, or those of their parents or grandparents, often reveal the suffering they have had to go through to become Christians and to live as Christians in their country of origin. Has it all been a waste of time, if other faiths are equally good and can equally be seen as vehicles of salvation? Why are they so often ignored by those who follow the path of dialogue? They sometimes feel that those very ready to celebrate difference with other faiths, are not always so ready to celebrate difference within the Christian Church. They can be assumed, rather hurtfully, to be Hindus or Sikhs or Muslims by those who do not know better – and yet hardly recognised for their faithfulness by their fellow Christians. We will now write much of them in this book, but should always have in mind, *how do minority Christians of Asian origin fit into interfaith dialogue, and other questions discussed in the following pages?*

7. I have been involved recently in offering advice in a divorce case, in which one party is of British Christian background and the other is a Muslim from Pakistan. Knowledge of Islam and Pakistani culture was vital in my role as a mediator when the normal legal agents had failed.

A young Muslim woman shared with me the immense difficulties of her marriage to a Sikh, which have resulted in separation. A Christian mother is scared because her daughter is going out with a Muslim at university and wonders what she can do. Multi-faith issues often arise through family concerns. *What issues do interfaith marriages raise? Where is our pastoral role?*

8. I addressed an Anglican deanery synod in a beautiful rural area, half an hour away from Leicester. When I asked members what they wanted to be thankful for, they answered that they were thankful that they did not have the problems of Leicester. By this they meant, as they agreed when pressed, that they did not have all those religions and cultures (though many make their money there!). I was relieved when a woman priest said that not facing these realities also deprived them of opportunity. My reflection was on what 1 Corinthians 12 might mean in a diocese. Do all rejoice when one rejoices? Do all weep when one weeps? On a more positive note, we recently held a four-day course which was designed to be an induction to ministry with those of other faiths. Participants came from Lincolnshire, Cornwall, St Albans, Brighton, as well as more obvious areas. They came because they were interested; for none had it been a concern that the course had not arisen in their part of the country, and all went away excited at the possibilities they had seen for where they were, and not just in Birmingham and Bradford and Brent. *How can we involve those who live in areas in which multi-faith concerns are not their 'problem'?*

9. In Leicester there is an Ecumenical Committee for Relationships with People of Other Faiths. On the Committee there are people who are 'experts' but there are also representatives from areas which are not multi-faith. We seek a mixture of theological positions. Committee members include university, hospital and prison chaplains and someone who works in religious education. *How can we develop an ecumenical strategy for the Church in ministry and mission with people of other faiths, which covers the whole of a district/diocese, and not just a part of it?*

10. A group visiting a Hindu temple were shown round by a lay Hindu. When asked about the image of Krishna, he said that, for him, this has the same meaning as the passages in John's Gospel, 'Whoever has seen me has seen the Father', and 'I am the way, and the truth and the life. No one comes to the Father except through me' (John 14:9, 6). The image of Krishna is an image of God revealed, as the person of Jesus is. There is no way to come to the God beyond without going through

God with us. For Christians this is through Jesus, for Hindus it may
be through Krishna or Rama, or indeed Jesus. John 14:6 is a key text
emphasised by Christians who believe it excludes all except committed Christians from salvation. Here a Hindu was finding inspiration
in Christian scripture in a most unlikely place! *How do we use the
scriptures in interfaith dialogue? Whose possession are they?*

11. A white neighbour, one of a minority in the road, talked to me over
the garden fence one day. We heard the Call to Prayer from the new
local mosque. I asked her what she felt. She said, 'I do not mind it on
Fridays, their holy day. But I do object to it on Sundays, our holy day.
I do not go to church, but it is still my day!' She laughed and said that
there had been a local petition against the call to prayer, but they had
not asked me to sign it! Another local church has a small congregation in a vast building. A local Muslim community organisation
would like to buy the building for community use. *How are we to
respond to such issues related to buildings and religious practices in our
local areas?*

12. I was invited by Hindu friends to attend a lavish Hindu *Diwali* (festival of light) celebration. I was asked to take the sacred flame and wave
it before the deity, to do *arati*. I refused politely, though asked by three
different people. My clergy colleague had no such scruples and joined
in. Who was right? *What ceremonies and prayers of other faiths can we
participate in, and how do we decide?*

13. Conflict between Muslims and Hindus in Gujarat, and between
Muslims and Jews in Palestine was in danger of splitting local communities in Great Britain. Christians were able to facilitate meetings
to air the differences and agree common statements. *What can we do
as Christians to facilitate local understanding and appropriate action on
international interfaith issues?*

14. Christians were invited to attend a meeting which was to be
addressed by a learned Muslim theologian and jurist from Pakistan
on the theme 'Muslims and Interfaith Dialogue'. I found myself the
only Christian present amongst forty Muslims. Generally it was a very
positive talk for a Christian to hear and encouraged much more
Muslim participation. There were points, however, where I felt words
said about Christians, with good intentions, were not quite accurate.
He spoke, for example, of the way the religions of the book, Jews,
Christians and Muslims, had a similar ethical framework, affirming
'an eye for an eye'. An example he gave was of how the stoning of
women taken in adultery was inherited from the Torah and also
reflected upon in the New Testament. Jesus' response, as we know, was

very different to both this ethical principle and to the woman taken in adultery. I responded at some length, affirming what I could affirm warmly, but stating politely some differences. On another occasion I was visiting a mosque with a group of theological students. We were received very well by the Pakistani leaders. A new Muslim, an African Caribbean, gave his testimony, and, as a former Christian, affirmed how the cross was not necessary for salvation, and how he had been liberated from such a thought. The other Muslims looked embarrassed about the style of this presentation, the Christian theological students remained silent. I responded with an explanation of a Christian understanding of the cross. After we left, I asked them why they had not spoken. They said they were guests and did not want to spoil the atmosphere. *How can we engage in an appropriate form of Christian apologetic in a multifaith situation?*

Archbishop Trevor Huddleston gave his whole ministry to the struggle against colonialism and racism. Before he died in the 1990s, he told me that if he could begin again, he would dedicate himself to interfaith work. Inspired by his time as Archbishop of the Indian Ocean, he said that fighting the evils of colonialism had been the key task of the second half of the twentieth century, while developing understanding between religions would be the central challenge of the first half of the twenty-first century. We are now well into that century, and this book is written with that same conviction and with the desire to encourage readers to become immersed in that exciting journey. The style will encourage participation, addressing the kinds of questions that I have already indicated. There will be case studies, suggestions for group discussion, and prayer and meditation material. The aim is not to create a new religion, as some people wrongly assume when they hear the terms 'multi-faith' or 'interfaith'. Rather it is to enable all Christians who are willing, of whatever persuasion, to engage with sensitivity with these realities.   The call is to remain faithful to the gospel of Jesus Christ, which includes loving our neighbour, who is Hindu, Muslim, Sikh, Buddhist, Jewish, learning from them, and sharing our faith with them in word and action. Hence the book's title, *Celebrating Difference, Staying Faithful.*

QUESTION FOR REFLECTION
What for you or your group are the key questions that come to mind as you consider the issues that arise between Christians and people of other faiths? As you begin this book, what experiences have you had that have made you want to consider these questions?

1. DIALOGUE: EXPERIENCES, REFLECTIONS AND STRUCTURES

Dialogue begins when people meet people. This may happen by chance, or by intention. All kinds of interfaith dialogues happen in an entirely informal context, between neighbours, friends, work colleagues, fellow students, and so on. These are the most natural of experiences, and are to be much valued. They are possible for all, and can transform attitudes. An elderly Christian told me that it was through talking to her Muslim neighbour, Mrs Ahmed, that she had come to the conclusion that religious persons from different faiths have much more in common than do a Christian and a person of no faith, even if they share the same culture. An 83-year-old Christian woman relates her experience of going to a 'Keep Fit' class for the elderly. Among the fourteen participants the Hindu, Sikh, Muslim and Christian faiths are all represented. Fellowship has grown close, particularly through an exercise in which, as a ball is thrown, the recipient's first name is called out! For ten minutes at the end of the class, they relax together and share a poem, reading, prayer, or incident from life with its meaning, and through this the elderly English woman has learnt the beauty of Sanskrit chants, translated into English. They then just chat over a cup of tea. One day they shared Turkish delight from Mecca! This experience has taught her that the things that bring people together with their Asian neighbours are greater than those that divide.

Standing in a bus queue on a cold night, a Christian addressed a man next to him with the words '*Asalaam Alaikkam*'. The man almost dropped his cigarette with surprise, 'I have taken this bus for months and no one has ever spoken to me … I am not afraid, just surprised.' They sat on the bus together. He talked in an animated way, in broken English. He told of his family in Iraq and of all his troubles, and commented, 'Strangers here talk to animals, but no one acknowledges a fellow human being. It was a lovely thing you did, speaking to me.' The Christian pointed out the cathedral as they passed it, 'You can sit and be quiet there, no need to be a Christian to go in.' They got off together, and he waved goodbye. They never spoke again, but a person of faith had encountered another person of faith.

A young Hindu woman faced a lot of pressure at home. She was only allowed out to go to work. The cathedral was on her route home. Finding it open, she went in one day for some peace. The building spoke to her of holiness, and she sat and looked in awe at the beautiful stained glass windows before her. She began to go in regularly for a few minutes each day. A woman priest noticed her, and eventually engaged her in conversation which developed onto answering her questions about the Jesus she saw in front of her in the windows. The end-result, after two years, was her baptism. The beginning was this simple encounter.

A Muslim family invited a Christian family to their son's wedding. They said that they would love to come, but one of them would have to stay behind to look after a German guest. Immediately he was invited as well. They reflected on the open-endedness of such Muslim hospitality.

These simple meetings enable transformations – some large, some small – in the same way that Jesus' meeting with the Samaritan woman in John 4 was life-changing. By going to a place with which she was familiar (the well of Jacob), and by asking something of her (water), Jesus opened up a dialogue across faith, as well as across gender and caste. She gained living water, and he found a new truth, that God is Spirit, and those who worship should worship in Spirit and in truth. The location, whether Mount Gerizim or the temple in Jerusalem, does not matter. This story is an outstanding biblical example of dialogue in practice, with respect, directness and expectation from both sides.

However, there are contexts in which sustained interfaith dialogue can best be initiated by some kind of group encounter. At the local level, a group nearly always comes out of a prior friendship between at least two persons from different faiths. Such a friendship will have taken time to develop, and trust will already have been established. Clarity will also be needed about intentions, that neither party is attempting to convert the other. This question may be best confronted directly. My Muslim Imam dialogue partner was very happy to clarify this issue. He wrote an article for the diocesan magazine on how from a Muslim perspective he saw dialogue. In it he included this statement, 'I would like Andrew to become a Muslim, and I am clear that he would like me to become a Christian. Both such changes are highly unlikely. Acknowledging this, we engage happily in dialogue together.'

We may wish to avoid the word 'dialogue' altogether. For some, it is off-putting, representing confrontation, formality, or academic exercise. Formal dialogues used to take place between CMS missionaries and

Muslims in British India, and between missionaries and Buddhists in British Ceylon. They have also taken place at the National Exhibition Centre in recent years, between profiled Muslim protagonists and Christian respondents. Such meetings easily become centred on point scoring and attempts to show that one religion is superior to the other. We will see later that the word 'dialogue' does not have to have these connotations, but it can do. If this is a danger, then other words can be utilised, such as 'friendship group', 'meeting', 'forum', 'encounter', 'council' or simply 'group'. The UK Directory of Inter Faith Organisations, listing over 200 organisations, gives an idea of the range of formal and informal names[1] used for such groups.

When starting a group, it may be helpful for the leaders to set down a statement of intentions to reassure those who will attend. Probably it is better to leave these implicit, provided the leaders are clearly seen to be acting within the spirit of friendship. Any attempt to use the group for proselytising will soon become evident and should be politely confronted. If the group is to include Hindus, special care needs to be given to this issue. Hindus are easy to relate to at the level of friendship, but they have a deep suspicion of Christian mission. Not being missionary themselves, they feel vulnerable and often a target. They will need special reassurance that this is not 'the same old Christian thing'.

There is often pressure to establish aims and objectives before the group starts. What is the group for? What will it achieve? Such an exercise should probably be resisted. The group will work it out for itself, implicitly or explicitly, as it progresses. There needs to be a degree of flexibility. As people grow together, they will themselves decide whether something useful is being achieved. If they do not feel it is, after some time the group may well die. This should not be seen as a failure. If people from two faiths have met for a time and learnt from each other, then that is an achievement in itself. There may be a ripple effect, the extent of which is never known. Aims too may change as time passes. We should hope that there will be elements of surprise; the Spirit blows where the Spirit wills, as we are led into all truth. What is essential is persistence. Understanding takes time to build up. Frustrations will come, and probably misunderstandings. But if there is an underlying commitment, then transformation may come in unexpected ways.

If some kind of rationale is asked for, from Christians, something simple can be offered, such as this:

• All human beings are created equal by God, and that creation is good.
• Christ died for all, not just for Christians, and therefore the person I

meet from another faith is someone for whom Christ died, in the same way that he died for me.

- All are loved by God and I can show my love for God by loving my neighbour. The question 'Who is my neighbour?' is answered most sharply in the parable of the Good Samaritan. In this parable it is a person of another faith who exemplifies neighbourly love. Indeed, Jesus says that by his example he shows me what I must do to enter eternal life – I must be like the good person of another faith. A dialogue group leading to friendship is a way of loving my neighbour.
- In a world that is increasingly polarised by religion, showing that division is not inevitable can be a tangible gain.
- Faith is strengthened by sharing it with others. At the same time we can learn so much. Being rooted in Christian faith should go hand in hand with openness to others. We can hear the advice of Gandhi to missionaries to India, 'If you have come to give rich treasures of experience, and open your hearts to receive the treasures of this land, you will not be disappointed, neither will you have misread the message of the Bible.'
- It can lead to a journey of discovery. A Hindu scholar from South India was asked why he attended Christian worship daily when in England. He replied, 'The God whom I worship leaves a space outside my religion, which he fills from here every day.' The God whom we worship may be saying the same thing to us.
- Dialogue is not divorced from action. We may find ourselves working together to meet a local need or responding to a wider challenge. Alternatively, working together on a project may be the beginning of our talking together about faith.
- This may be a critical time in our history. In the face of so much polarisation in international politics, much of it around religion, can we show that religions and cultures can co-exist in peace and harmony? Dialogue groups can be an outward and visible sign that religious people can grow together and not apart. Are we to work together or are we to work separately, even against each other? We have a duty to do what we can to counter those who are pulling us apart. We may not be able to do much as individuals, but we should not 'despise the day of small things' (cf. Zech. 4:10).
- Britain is a place of opportunity. Within Europe, we are the only country in which such a wide range of faiths each have significant representation. This may be an accident of empire, but it can provide a God-given opportunity. The fact that those from the Asian sub-continent and elsewhere have full citizenship rights here, has given them a sense of relative security. Although there is still a long way to go, different cultures and

faiths have been increasingly valued and treated on an equal footing. Dialogue groups can make a further contribution. While travelling by train in India last year, I found myself in dialogue with a fellow passenger. We introduced ourselves to each other and, to my surprise, I discovered that he was not only a Christian doctor but the son of a bishop from North India! Before we put up for the night, he said he wanted to say one last thing to me. He said that, in the face of the exacerbating difficulties between India and Sri Lanka, Britain had a vital role to play in showing that people of different faiths could live together in a constructive way. It is an important message for all in Europe but especially in Britain, and he urged me to encourage others to work at this task.

All dialogue is contextual, and the reader is encouraged to consider what may be possible in his or her own context. Overall, what is possible in Britain is unlikely to be possible in any Muslim country, and increasingly difficult in a country like India where religion is much more politicised than it used to be. Within Britain's larger cities, these kinds of friendship programmes may seem easier to achieve. But cities vary greatly, in their demography, their social history, as well as their political realities. There is a significant difference in 'feel' between London and the cities of the Midlands and the North. More tangibly, a city's size makes an enormous difference. It is difficult to think of London or even Birmingham or Manchester as a whole, but much easier in the case of cities of around 300,000 people, such as Leicester, Wolverhampton or Bradford. Patterns of immigration are important, and immigrants' social class, background and education will be decisive factors. It is one thing to meet with professionals or business people with an East African background, well used to moving confidently as a minority even in East Africa and now prospering in this country, or with wealthy Arabs or Egyptians in London. It is another to encounter those who have come from a village background in Pakistan or Bangladesh, for whom the primary realities have centred upon their experience of fear or racism or discrimination, and who are now the target of vitriolic propaganda from the British National Party, or other similar groups. It is one thing to meet with groups long established in this country, fluent in English and confident about where they are going; it is another to meet with asylum seekers or recent arrivals from Europe or elsewhere, whose primary need will be support in establishing their identity in this country.

Significant centres of faiths other than Christianity are not always located in the places we might first think of. Hindu and Buddhist communities, which may well welcome contact and dialogue, often exist in rural or suburban areas. Examples are the large Tibetan Buddhist community, Samye Ling, near Lockerbie in the Scottish Lowlands, and a Hindu community in Carmarthenshire, South Wales, which has two names, the Shri Subramaaniyam Temple or the Community of the Many Names of God! There are fourteen different Buddhist communities located around Birmingham, and there are two small groups near Leicester. Numbers do not need to be large for there to be a meeting. A few committed people can start a useful conversation – even two or three, as modelled by Jesus on the road to Emmaus, when he entered into dialogue with two travellers with truly amazing results (Luke 24). Many can testify to what one deep friendship with a family of another faith has meant in terms of their mutual transformation. Perhaps such relationships can develop most easily where people are not living within vast communities but in more isolated situations: in such cases support from a local Christian family or group can be very welcome and lead to much sharing and rejoicing together.

A recent national report, *Local Inter Faith Activity in the UK* (Inter Faith Network of the UK, 2003), highlighted the importance of dialogue/friendship groups in helping to maintain and deepen interfaith relations, trust and community activity. Drawing on my experience in Leicester and Birmingham, where I have been involved in long-standing dialogue groups, as well as at a national and international level, I want now to look at groups established to enable Christians and people of specific faiths to relate together. Later in the chapter I look at principles of dialogue that can be used as guidelines for the various contexts in which readers find themselves.

Muslim–Christian groups

I have been involved in Muslim–Christian groups in a sustained way in both Birmingham and Leicester.[2] The group in Birmingham lasted about five years, and the Leicester group is now in its fifth year. There is also a Leicester Muslim–Christian Women's Group which is in its third year. The UK Directory referred to above lists other such local groups meeting in St Albans, Finsbury Park and Sparkbrook (Birmingham). The Finsbury Park group was very important at the time of the closure of the Finsbury Park mosque by the police because of the extremist preaching there; the Sparkbrook group, which has been meeting for twenty years, is the most long-standing of the recorded groups. Some others, such as the Wakefield Interfaith Group, mention only Christian and Muslim participation, and so fall into this category de facto, and there are no doubt many other groups meeting quietly around the country. There are also national groups, such as that composed of Shia Muslims and Anglicans which has been meeting in London since 2003.

My encounters with Muslim groups have led to the following reflections:

- It is vital that the group is based on at least one core friendship, and that both friends are equally committed to the ongoing life of the group as well as its initiation. This relationship (or relationships) can be infectious and can draw others in.
- Depth of friendship and commitment to attend with regularity are vital. This does not mean that others may not come in and out of the group. But these kinds of journeys take time and require a readiness to walk together.
- It does not really matter who does the administration – it depends on who has the resources and time. If it is one of the Christian members, so be it. We often feel we have few resources, but in practice, particularly if we are Anglicans, we have more than others can dream of.
- We should try to avoid an over-bureaucratic structure. Committees are not always helpful and often a small core group, even just two people, is enough. Where possible it is best to find volunteers to take on tasks as they arise.
- It is good to meet in different venues, Muslim and Christian, but this is not essential. If the group agrees that they prefer one particular venue meet there. The important thing is for everyone to feel at home in that venue.
- Whether or not there is prayer, depends on the nature of the group. If the Muslim partners have a Sufi background, this will come naturally. Prayers can be said before or after the meeting, and can be extempore as well as formal. The right time will become clear as the group develops. Leadership in prayer should be shared round, and it is important that both Muslim and Christian prayers are offered at any one meeting. If the Muslims are from a more conservative *deobandi* tradition, it may take a significant period of time before they are able to enter into prayer. They may prefer a period of silence, which can be prefaced by some intentions around the topic of the meeting, or the world or local situations. Sensitivity is required, and guidance on this can be found in the chapter on prayer (see esp. pp. 94–108).
- Scriptures can always be read. Be patient in hearing the Qur'an read in Arabic first. Hear its beauty, and recall that it has been recited by memory for fourteen hundred years. Then you will normally be given a translation. If you are not, ask for one. How the Bible is read becomes

important too: it should be read with conviction and inner meaning.

• Muslims may well want to take a break within the meeting to make their formal prayers. This does not take long, but can seem an interruption. Be patient, and indeed challenged, for this is the essence of the faith with which we are in dialogue. If the meeting is on church premises provide a place where they can pray. Either ask to witness the prayers or, as Christians, have your own time of prayer, perhaps using a short liturgy. It is sad if Muslims get the impression that they are the people of prayer, while Christians are people of talk and action only. We can sometimes give that impression. Monastic orders, whether monks or sisters, can make a big impact on Muslims, particularly when wearing their traditional habits. If they get the chance to explain their obligation to pray at least five times a day, they bear powerful testimony to the place of prayer within Christian life, As non-monastic Christians, we should use every opportunity we are given to explain that we also pray, and that it is also an obligation for us to develop a rule of prayer, and to demonstrate this. On the occasion of the vast demonstration against war in Iraq in February 2003 in London, it was a moving and challenging experience to see the Muslims with whom we travelled to London from Leicester, dropping out of the vast procession to pray in a mosque en route. Even more powerful was the sight of Muslim men and women using abandoned placards bearing such slogans as 'Not in my name' as prayer mats. They prayed in the gloom in a very muddy, cold and dark Hyde Park after the speeches had taken place, before getting back onto the warm coach. We Christians had no such plans, but fortunately a group from Leeds invited us to join them, in the middle of the crush, as they recited a liturgy before we went on our way.

• Topics for discussion will vary, and will depend on the group. In the early stages we may wish to discuss easier, inclusive topics such as the place of prayer, of family life, of fasting and of scripture. In Muslim terms, Islam and Christianity are both religions of the book, as is Judaism. It is important therefore that we study scripture together. We can select passages around a chosen topic. Here we should not try to mould the passages to say the same thing, but allow them to speak for themselves. We can balance exegesis, drawing out the meaning of the text in its original setting, with hermeneutic, its application in life. It is helpful to have an evening discussing the place of scripture in each faith, before going on to specific subjects. As Christians we need to explain the nature of the Gospels, in particular that they are not the dictate of Jesus, but witnesses to him, who is the Word of God. He is the equivalent of the Qur'an, not the New Testament. We will also need to explain how St

Paul fits in since he is often viewed with suspicion by Muslims because he is not a prophet. We can share why we use the Hebrew Bible, the Old Testament, and there will be much commonality of understanding here with regard to the patriarchs and prophets. We will also need to hear the difference between the status of the Qur'an, the *Hadith* and the *Sunna*. The *Hadith* is a body of laws, legends and stories about Muhammad's words and deeds. They give material for the Qur'anic injunction to follow the prophet as 'a fine example'. There are many collections, some more recognised than others, and they provide, along with the Qur'an, the bases for legislation. The word *sunna* means 'custom', and the *Sunnis* are those who follow the *sunna* of the prophet, and the *Hadith* is part of this. *Shia* Muslims differ in some aspects of the *sunna* they follow, as well as the different line of Caliphs, theocratic rulers, that they venerate.

- Following on from this a good subject is the place of the law. Within Islam this is known as *sharia*, though the science of application is called *fiqr*. It is very useful to spend one meeting hearing from an expert on the place of law in Islam and comparing it with Christianity. The discussion can also be broadened out to compare the place of the *Torah* in Judaic tradition and the New Testament understanding of law. Our knowledge of the *sharia* may be limited to the harshness of certain punishments, but through really listening to Muslims we can learn of its mystical significance for the faith and reach a comprehensive understanding.

- Another fruitful topic is the companions of the prophet and the disciples of Jesus, which can involve narrative as well as teaching. In the Sufi tradition, there is a practice of becoming a *murith* of a *pir*, disciple of a saint or spiritual guide. In Pakistan such figures are venerated around their tombs, but there are also living people who have taken on their mantle. An example is the *pir* in Small Heath, Birmingham, who have enormous followings and are believed to practise miracles in answer to prayer. Comparisons can be made with the Christian healing ministry.

- Standard theological topics include our concepts of God, what we mean by the Trinity, the Holy Spirit, the place of Jesus in the two faiths (he is prominent in the Qur'an and, as we often hear, it is not possible to be a Muslim and not honour Jesus as a prophet), Mary (there are more verses on her in the Qur'an than in the Gospels), the nature of prophethood, Muhammad and the question of whether Christians can accept him as prophet.

- Learning about each other's histories is also helpful. What are the origins and current realities of divisions within Christianity and within Islam? Here we need to be open and honest. Christians cannot celebrate the heart of our religious practice, the eucharist, together. Muslims will say they can always pray together, and this is largely so. But there are subtle differences between *Shia* and *Sunni* ways of praying. There are also the *Ismaelis* (a wealthy community, of whom the Aga Khan is the most prominent), who are related to the *Shias*, but clearly distinct: they have seven pillars rather than five and different disciplines of prayer. The *Ahmidiyyas* consider themselves Muslims, but are not considered to be so by other Muslims, since they hold to a later prophet than Muhammad. They have a major temple in South London, which, when it was opened, was described as Muslim in all the British press.

- Alongside these kinds of discussion it is important that groups tackle pressing issues as they arise in the community or between the faiths. One of these is the question of mission and conversion. Since both faiths are missionary faiths, this agenda poses no particular difficulty. However, there is a radical difference in understanding about the convert. The conversion of Christians to Islam is a reality, albeit one we probably find painful, particularly if they were practising actively. But it is something we live with, and normally family relationships can be sustained. When a Muslim converts to Christianity, it is not just a sad experience: he or she has done something that is forbidden. It clearly happens, but the convert cannot expect understanding and may even face persecution and, in extreme cases in some parts of the world, death. An enlightened view will be that any punishment will be up to *Allah* at the final judgement. Dialogue on this difficult topic is important. In our Leicester group, we reached a point of trust where converts from each faith were able to come and address the group, sharing their journey. This is unusual.
- Related to this is discussion about interfaith marriage and families, which is dealt with in the chapter on pastoral issues (see pp. 127–35).
- Of daily importance are matters related to education. Concerns will vary, but they will usually include faith schools and religious education (see the section within the chapter on community issues). It is good to arrange visits to both Christian and Muslim schools, to experience first hand ways of doing things that may often be contentious. The atmosphere in an Islamic school can often be challenging, since the atmosphere of learning found there is not always achieved in other schools.
- The place of women in the two faiths is a topic regularly raised. This is highlighted on any visit to a mosque, particularly one which admits only men, but will allow Christian women visitors. Linked with this is the use of *hijab* (scarf) and *burkha* (full covering).

- Important in recent years have been issues related to the enforcement of secular law. These include the anti-terrorism acts, the possibilities of anti-religious discrimination laws (as outlined in the Queen's speech, November 2004) and blasphemy laws.
- Another wide range of subjects relate to ongoing community life, including the important subject of racism. How have members of the group suffered from this? How far do they acknowledge their own tendencies to racism? In Leicester, we discussed this topic in relationship to the growing power of the British National Party in the north of England. We also considered the level of racism locally and further afield. It was a Muslim who said to us all, 'Let us not leave here without all acknowledging we have an element of racism in each of us.' An Imam added, 'A word to the Muslim brothers and sisters here; we should think why we welcomed actively the coming of Bosnian refugees, who were Muslims, but have not done the same for the large number of Somalis coming, who are also Muslims.' This was a significant statement to make in front of a group of Christians.
- Such is the nature of the world in the twenty-first century that international issues will often come to the fore. These will be concentrated on the areas where our two faith communities seemingly come into conflict, mainly but not exclusively in the Middle East, and centred on Israel/Palestine. Particularly sharp will be our discussion of those disputes in which British troops are involved directly. Demonstrating cross-faith solidarity through statements and actions becomes important, where possible using the media to highlight such collaboration.

Talking can flow into actions, and here are some suggestions, again based on experience:

- A good place to start is attending each other's places of worship, if possible while worship is happening. The way of prayer can show so much. The visiting of mosques during prayer is quite common, but it is important this is reciprocated with visits to churches. The witnessing of a eucharist can raise all kinds of questions, and talking through the experience together afterwards can be equally important. There will always be ambiguities about the situation of Christian women in attending mosques, and this can open up another opportunity for honest discussion around the position of women (see p. 170).
- Sharing food together, both the minimal hospitality at a meeting and full meals on occasions, is to be welcomed, particularly when it flows naturally. This can include members visiting each other's homes, especially at festival times. The question of *halal* requirements can be

difficult, but fruit, most biscuits and vegetarian food will normally be acceptable.

- In our divided society joint fundraising can be a powerful symbol. This can be for a common fund, such as Save the Children, at time of war or famine, or for two projects, one Muslim and one Christian, where money raised is given to both, without discrimination. Two examples I have been involved in have raised funds for a Muslim project in Kosovo and a Christian hospital in Gaza, and for the rebuilding of a mosque in Bosnia and for a Christian-run trauma centre in Gujarat. Publicity for these kinds of joint endeavours is important, not just in order to raise more money, but to show what can be done and how Muslims and Christians can work together. A higher profile can be given to the co-operative venture by putting on a joint fundraising dinner, with a charity auction at the same time. This is particularly effective when people are invited from areas where Muslims are not living.
- Work for asylum seekers can be undertaken together, as can other social projects, depending on local need.
- Taking part in demonstrations together can make a powerful impact, as the experience I related earlier in the chapter in connection with the anti-war demonstration showed. On that occasion three Christian clergy travelled by coach with fifty Muslims and the sense of solidarity we felt would not have been established if we had gone separately. The food they shared with us on the return journey was very special, almost sacramental in its way.
- Examples of public prayer together are given in a later chapter (see chapter 4).

A Muslim–Christian women's group may well have a more relaxed feel than a mixed group, and I end this section with a comment from a Muslim woman, a young mother from an Iraqi background, who has been part of such a group in Leicester for more than two years. The group has included a number of Christian women who come from an area where Muslims do not live, and stereotypes have rapidly been broken down through direct encounter, with a ripple effect on the places where they come from, whether suburban or rural.

> I wanted to be part of something that helped create better understanding between the two faith communities. I had been involved in Muslim Christian dialogue before and had assumed that the meetings would be the usual highly intellectual, highly theological speak. I found that this group offered an entirely different experience. While we do discuss theological issues and sometimes delve into

controversy, it is personal friendships, which sustain this group, and enable honest discussion and sharing of personal stories, with ease, comfort and fun. We laugh together and pray together. Our initiatives may not save the world, but they do a great deal for us as individuals and we take that back to our families and our communities. When we first started the group, many of us viewed the other only as a Muslim or a Christian but now we see the human in each other, the mother, the wife, the teacher and the nurse.

As a Muslim I know we still face many struggles in society particularly overcoming the negative stereotypes which fan flames of prejudice and hatred but what the women's group shows me (contrary to the doomsayers' expectations) is that we can and should coexist in a state of mutual understanding and friendship. If we are to understand Britain as it is today, it is vital that we look around us and learn more about diverse faiths and cultures, ethnicities and creeds. It is only then that we will learn to respect and appreciate each other ... and live together in true peace and harmony. As God says, 'O Mankind, We created you from a single (pair) of a male and female and made you into nations and tribes, *that you may know each other*' (Qur'an 49:13).

Hindu-Christian groups

Christians should remember here that they are engaged with a diaspora community whose first priority has been to establish themselves professionally and economically in Britain. As they have done this very successfully, they have also built up structures for their religious life, which mirror those they have brought from 'home', but also have needed considerable adaption within their new context. What is an immensely diverse religion within India, has taken on a more monolithic feel, perhaps of necessity, within a minority situation. A priority has not been to develop a leadership articulate in the kind of areas that religious dialogue has tended to focus on. Nor will an inclusive and all-embracing faith ever find it easy to talk at this level with any of the Abrahamic faiths, with their particularity, central scriptural bases, and tendencies towards exclusivism.

Nevertheless, dialogue between Hindus and Christians starts with a significant underpinning of goodwill. Hindus are seen as law abiding, hospitable, successful in education and business, and committed to Britain. Their religion is full of festivals, most notably the ever more popular Diwali, known to all school children, and now promoted by a number of city councils and celebrated on the streets, as we do in

Leicester. Inner workings of the religion are hard to understand, but it seems a good enough faith to live by.

Some Christians may find the thought of idol worship, many gods, and the caste system distinctly unattractive, to say the least. But Indians accept caste as the status quo, and there is a sense of the oneness of God behind the images that are seen. In the interests of harmony, many choose to put their doubts aside; however, not all can do this, particularly those for whom idol worship is a major stumbling block.

In the UK there is now a Hindu-Christian Forum which meets alternately in London and Leicester, the two most important centres for Hinduism in the country. Membership is restricted and there are normally two representatives from each Christian denomination and from each section within Hinduism, a total of about two dozen people. Though the Forum is still in its early days, it is important in signalling that Hindus as well as Muslims are important to Christians. This was also demonstrated by the visit of Rowan Williams, as Archbishop of Canterbury, to Leicester in 2003, on the occasion of a group meeting in the most important temple in the city. Here he was honoured as a 'saint', gifts were exchanged, the Archbishop giving a favourite Ikon, and a magnificent meal was shared.

The national group has encouraged the formation of local groups. The Leicester one is now in its third year, and steps are beginning to be made to establish groups in Scotland, Birmingham and London. The following reflections arise out of my experience of Hindu-Christian dialogue:

- Hindus do not divide life into segments: their faith is truly a way of life. Adjusting to life in Britain, so far from the homeland with which it is umbilically connected, has caused a certain amount of strain. However, gradually as they work out what it is to be British and Hindu, their faith community is gaining in confidence, and those who have experienced it in both India and Britain will notice both difference and similarity.
- Young people often live in two worlds – that of their families and that of their peer group. The elders are very concerned about this and seek to involve young people at all levels. They have instituted classes to encourage learning both about the faith and mother-tongues, and there have also been youth camps to foster a sense of identity. Hindus will therefore be very keen to involve young people in dialogue programmes. The difficulty can be to bring in practising Christian young people, who are often very suspicious of other faith adherents since they are likely to be involved with churches concerned primarily with evangelism.
- Most Hindus are very suspicious about becoming targets for Christian mission, a feeling stemming from experiences in India, as well as from encounters with particular groups in Britain. They do not wish to con-

vert others and fear losing their own youth, either through secularisa-
tion or conversion out of the faith. The fact that someone would wish to
do this is inexplicable to them, since there are many ways to God, and
they do not see any reason why anyone would need to leave their own
path, culture and family deities. This area can either be bypassed or confronted in a dialogue group. The first option is by far the easier one; the
second is hard work, but it may prove worth the effort. Our national
group spent a long time coming to an agreement on a statement of
goodwill in this area.

An exception in terms of mission is the Hare Krishna movement
(ISKON). This group, familiar to us from their presence in saffron in
our city precincts and their tracts and copies of the Gita, are an easy
community to engage in dialogue with. They are a strongly *bhakti*
(devotional) movement, centred on Krishna and on scripture; they are
highly disciplined and ethical in their way of life. Their centre near
Watford, *Bhakti Vedanta*, is a joy to visit. Here they rear sacred cows,
make excellent organic food and bake bread, and provide a ready welcome to all who come. They are also very committed to dialogue and
have produced an important statement concerning it, after prolonged
discussion with the Vatican.

• There are also other *bhakti* groups, such as the Sai Baba devotees, prominent in all our cities. Sai Baba is a familiar figure, with his bushy black
hair, and his image is found in many Hindu homes. He lives in South
India, and his followers are particularly prominent in the Gujarati community. His shrines will also normally include pictures of Jesus. The
groups hold Sai Baba meetings in halls and community centres, sometimes in church premises which they hire. I know an Indian doctor who
has made his garage into a Sai Baba shrine. They regard Sai Baba as a
living incarnation of God and believe that he has miraculous powers.
Such faith may seem alien to Christians, and certainly his style of life
cannot be compared to that of a Galilean peasant. But it is easy to see
how his devotees can also be devoted to Jesus.

There are many other groups: for example, the devotees of Sri Sri Ravi
Shankar hold weekly devotional meetings all over the world, following
the Weekly Knowledge which is e-mailed and faxed from the guru each
week, and the Yogeswar groups who follow the recently deceased guru
known affectionately as Dadaji. Non-Hindus are very welcome at these
groups. Another prominent movement in Britain is the Swaminarayan
Mission, also active in East Africa. This Gujarati-based group are the
builders of the amazing Neasden Temple in North London. Visitors are
always welcome in this outpost of North India, just off the North

Circular. They are very active in social and development work, as well as educational activity in the promotion of the Hindu faith. Their monks live extremely strict lives, literally giving up all, including family, with whom they are allowed no contact. I found it moving to meet two young men from Leicester in Ahmedabad, both of academic background, who had become monks. This is another group with which it is good to have dialogue, although the monks will only meet men directly. The meeting of the original Swaminarayan with Bishop Heber in North India in the late eighteenth century is recorded in their history as an important step on the path to dialogue.

- We were only able to agree the goodwill statement referred to earlier by accepting that it applied solely to Britain. We also agreed to discuss issues related to India only in so far as they affect life for Hindus and Christians here. Some sectors of Hinduism have become very politicised in India, and Christians have felt themselves victims of extremists at the local level, as well as facing anti-conversion bills in some states, which in effect prevent them being a missionary religion, and finding their social, medical and educational work the object of suspicion. However, Hindus here are mostly very sensitive in discussing such matters and usually say that they are not political in their thinking. This is very true of the majority, but much support goes to Hindutva (Hindu nationalist philosophy) inclined movements in India from groups scattered across the world. If we do raise such matters for discussion, it is also important to acknowledge the amount of mission funding from Christian organisations that has also gone to India. Most of this is beyond reproach, but some may also not have been used well.

- The same applies to discussion concerning the caste system. It is a subject that makes Hindus defensive, expecting, from experience, that they will come under heavy criticism. They may say that it no longer exists in Britain. It has certainly weakened, but most marriages still happen within castes, and the minority *dalit* ('untouchable') communities often worship in separate temples, dedicated to Guru Ravidas, who is venerated by both Sikh and Hindu lower castes. Another response is that it was never originally part of Hinduism, that it was imposed from outside, that it is rapidly weakening even in India, and that, anyway, it is no worse than the British class system. This was also said in Victorian India, where the colonial British presence revealed such class divisions. I have heard it claimed that any caste of person can become a priest in India these days. But for the most part it is Brahmins who are brought from India to preside as priests in British temples. It is tempting to challenge these claims, particularly when Indian Christians have faced so much difficulty in recent years. Indian Christians who visit wonder why we do not raise more questions. However, it is important to bear in mind that there are also many negatives that can be thrown at Christians, particularly the aggressive evangelistic methods used under the influence of groups from the American Right. It may be wiser to build up trust for a considerable time before raising such sensitive matters in a non-accusatory way.

- Having said this, there are real opportunities in dialogue groups with Hindus. Their hospitality makes their temples easy places to visit, and on any evening there are always tasty and varied refreshments on offer. It is not easy to reciprocate when most churches only rise to a cup of tea and a biscuit! In the group they will often sing devotional prayers, and occasionally bring a display of dance. They will find it easy to join in whatever prayer we offer, and we need not be afraid of singing either. They will also respond to church buildings and will express their feeling of being at home in places of holiness and prayer. This is a community that is easy to relate to at all kinds of levels, and we should rejoice at their generosity of spirit and readiness to share the best of their faith and culture, in a way that often puts us to shame.

- Topics of dialogue can include: the understanding of God; karma, free will and grace; the nature of salvation; the place of images and ikons; idol/image worship; the nature and practice of prayer and spirituality; non-violence and other ethical issues; the nature and meaning of key festivals, saints and gurus, and their unique qualities; the family cycle, questions of birth, death, reincarnation and resurrection; the nature and purpose of suffering; the person of Jesus and the meaning of incarnation and the cross; the person and writings of Gandhi; approaches to meditation. It can also be useful to look at questions related to living in Britain today and our task as religious people. People can be encouraged to tell their personal faith stories and reflect upon them. There can also be serious study of the scriptures: this can either be around themes, or group members of one faith can help those of the other to learn about a text, for example the Gita, or the Sermon on the Mount, or St John's Gospel. This is best done in small groups, but can be very rewarding.

- As with dialogue with Muslims, it may be possible, and very helpful, to do things together. This can include engaging with a local community issue, raising money for a common cause, engaging in advocacy for an issue of concern to one or other or both communities. Causes chosen will, of course, usually be multi-faith in concern and probably multi-faith in action.

- Visiting temples has become a common occurrence, but this should be reciprocated by invitations to come to church, to see the building but also to witness worship. Colourful times like Christingle, Harvest and Christmas are great opportunities. A visit together to a meditation centre such as a retreat house, or Hindu place of meditation will be powerful in its effect. Even better, but hard to organise, is a joint pilgrimage to India, which should include visiting Christian as well as Hindu shrines.

Even in areas where Hindus live in considerable numbers, Hindu-Christian dialogue in Britain has a long way to go. The theological challenge is greater than with Islam, since the two faiths have very different world views. Hinduism can either seem very exotic or very culturally based. But a faith that sustains at least 800 million people throughout the world, has withstood the impact of the Mughals and the Christian colonial invasions and is followed by around 80 per cent of Indians should be taken very seriously indeed. It has nearly 600,000 adherents in Britain and has a strong cultural identity, but, as with all faiths, is struggling to retain its young people who have to contend with all the secular pressures inherent in education and work life. We can give it every encouragement so that it can continue to provide a strong spiritual framework for future generations. This does not mean that some will not choose to become Christians, nor that we should not rejoice if they do, as long as it is freely chosen as part of their spiritual pilgrimage. But we must never make this community, which is still facing the insecurities of becoming rooted in Britain, feel they are being especially targeted.

Jewish-Christian dialogue

In one sense, Jewish-Christian dialogue goes back to New Testament times as the new Christian movement struggled to discover how to relate to its parent faith, within a context where it was rapidly becoming dominated by Gentile adherents. Attempts to remain within Judaism were doomed once it spread throughout the ancient world. John 9 gives evidence of the growing demarcation between synagogue and church. The relationship between these two faiths through history has been very difficult, as we all know, and although this reached its zenith in the Holocaust (or *Shoah*) in Europe, it was only the culmination of centuries of antisemitic attitudes and actual pogroms. Within Britain itself the story is ambiguous: the expulsion of all Jews at the time of the Black Death; the welcoming of them back by Oliver Cromwell who believed that Christians needed Jews alongside them; the stereotype of a Shylock revealing the kind of entrenched attitudes prevalent at the time of Shakespeare; and then, in more recent centuries, the growing stability of British Jewish communities, particularly in London, Leeds and Manchester, which were joined by refugees fleeing from persecution in mainland Europe. My mother's family was typical: arriving from northern Germany around 1890 to seek more security, they settled in Leeds, where they developed a high-quality cloth business, spurning the opportunity to join Mr Marks (before Mr Spencer) at the cheaper end of the trade! Religiously, they assimilated and became Unitarian, further cementing these ties through marriage. By the third generation in this country, the children were told not to affirm their Jewish identity within the school context, and they had adopted an anglicised version of their Jewish name.

The formation of the Council of Christians and Jews (CCJ) in 1942 was a milestone in interfaith relations and dialogue. The date is very significant and was a great act of faith at the time. It has over fifty-three branches in the UK today and 3,800 individual members. The task of confronting the antisemitism that had led to the Holocaust in so-called Christian countries was a strong motivating factor in the early years. The Council has worked tirelessly to build up local respect and engagement, at the same time having to come to terms with the dominance now of issues related to Israel/Palestine. It has made an invaluable contribution to facilitating opportunities for leaders, young people and branch members from both religions to travel to the Holy Land together, but this has become much more difficult now. Other vital components of its work have been the development of study programmes, the maintenance of the quarterly journal *Common Ground*, the organisation of visits to Eastern Europe and the employment of staff who can provide support for local groups. The International CCJ, which was founded in more recent times, provides opportunities for wider involvement, particularly across Europe.

The theological journey between these two faiths has centred upon a number of themes which have evolved over time. Post-holocaust theology and questions of repentance and forgiveness have been central for both sides. The question of Christian mission in relationship to Jews remains highly controversial. Is the Old Covenant abrogated by the New Covenant, or are God's promises eternal, in which case Jews remain with the original Covenant? Other important themes are: the place of the Messiah, and of Jesus, including the Jewishness of Jesus and of Paul, which had been largely suppressed for a long time; Israel and the land as a theological concept, as well as a practical reality; the place of prayer and spirituality, and whether we can pray together; the study of scripture, and recognition that what Christians call the Old Testament is in fact the Hebrew Bible.

Here too dialogue can lead to practical outcomes, an important one of which is the visiting of synagogues by Christians. This is easier within the Reformed/Liberal/Progressive tradition, where the service is predominantly in English. Liberals can attend Christian worship, but this would not be expected of those of orthodox faith. Work together has happened from time to time, one example being work camps in Israel. Holocaust Memorial day – 27 January – is an important symbol of memory and reconciliation, and efforts can be made to celebrate this publicly at a local level.

Three faiths groups

In three faiths groups Christians are involved with Muslims and Jews, as common people of the book. Local groups may vary in name. The one in Leicester is called, at the suggestion of an Imam, The Leicester Family of Abraham Group. Nationally, the Three Faiths Forum was founded in 1997. This is a high profile organisation, based in London, but part of its aim is the establishment and development of local groups. They also encourage the setting up of groups within various professions, such as medicine or the law.

It has been my experience that at the local level holding these three faiths together is not easy – not at the relational level, but when it comes to dealing with issues. The very similarity of the Jewish and Muslim faiths theologically and in terms of law and spirituality stands against the deep divisions over Israel/Palestine. Within the three faiths themselves there is a diversity of opinion over this issue. The Jewish community, for example, has groups such as Just Peace, which are strongly opposed to deepening Israeli government entrenchment and are working to bring peace with justice. Our group nearly broke up because of divisions in this area, and it was only possible to proceed following Christian facilitation of reconciliation around misunderstandings, and a moratorium on discussion of the Middle East for some time. The group was able to stabilise and move forward by concentrating on learning more about each other, our traditions and personal faith, and working to discover how best to contribute together to the good of the local communities.

Both Oxford and Liverpool have three faiths groups which meet at the invitation of the bishops of those cities. The Oxford group is the older of the two, having met since 1992, and is comprised of scholars who together work on publications.

Sikh-Christian groups

These are few and far between. In the UK Handbook, only one such group is recorded: it meets in Hitchen. There have long been initiatives in Southall, in Birmingham and in Smethwick. Roger Hooker was very involved in the West Midlands until his death a few years ago, and his successor as Interfaith Adviser, Chris Hewer, has been continuing to make sustained contacts. But groups of the kind envisaged in this chapter are not frequent. Since Sikhism is the fourth largest religion in the country, and one that is easy for Christians to relate to, this is a pity, and initiatives should be encouraged in areas where it is represented. It is encouraging that there is a lecturer in Sikhism at Birmingham University.

A further Christian role

From time to time, Christians may be called upon to advise on the establishment of groups not involving themselves. I found myself being asked to do this in Leicester, when there were thoughts of establishing a Hindu-Muslim Forum, in the wake of the violence in Gujarat in 2002. The resulting group met for some time and helped reduce tensions amongst the leaderships, though it has been difficult to sustain beyond the crisis period. But, having been established once, its re-establishment in the future, if there are further problems, will be much easier.

Such groups are significant also when the British National Party tries to target Muslims with vicious propaganda and to suborn Hindus and Sikhs to their side. Last year a tape was sent to clergy in Leicester, claiming to be prepared jointly with Hindus and Sikhs and including a Sikh voice. Its message was, 'Islam, a threat to us all'. On the cover of the tape were two sentences selectively quoted from the Qur'an: 'And Allah bequeathed to you their [the Unbelievers'] lands, their homes and their possessions, together with land you have never trodden' (33.27), and 'Fight those of the Unbelievers who are near to you, and let them see how harsh you can be' (9.123).

When asked to take on this role, Christians must be wary about doing more than facilitation. We cannot be arbiters in the affairs of two separate communities. As facilitators, we need to listen and understand the issues. We have also to tread a narrow tightrope in being even handed with both communities.

There are also Muslim-Jewish Groups, notably the Maimonides Foundation in London which employs two staff and has a great commitment to lessening tensions between these two faiths and building up their commonalities. There is also a small group in Hackney.

Christians Aware

Christians Aware is an organisation of long standing, which has a section dedicated to enabling Christians to be more aware of other faiths. They do this through overseas visits and through local initiatives, mainly in Southall and Leicester.

Ground rules/principles of dialogue

There have been several attempts to suggest such guidelines over the last twenty years, the most useful of which I have found to be the four principles of dialogue included in the document *Towards a Theology for Inter Faith Dialogue*, passed by the General Synod of the Church of England in 1984 and affirmed by the British Council of Churches and other member churches around that time. Their strength is their simplicity and their usability. Most interfaith work falls into these four interdependent categories. If there is a balance between the four areas, then it is unlikely that groups will go far wrong. They are as follows:

- *Dialogue begins when people meet people* (not when religions, philosophies, systems, institutions meet). This takes away the mystique of dialogue and opens it to all.
- *Dialogue depends upon mutual understanding and mutual trust.* The above accounts of dialogue in practice confirm that this is central. We need to reach the point when we can be honest with each other.
- *Dialogue makes it possible to share in service to the community.* Dialogue which leads to action is likely to be sustained, either as a group together or by inspiring individuals within the group.
- *Dialogue becomes the medium of authentic witness.* This principle is vital, since it removes the false dichotomy between *dialogue* and *evangelism.* Sharing good news happens naturally within a dialogue context. We are all called to witness to the faith that is within us. As Christians, we are called to witness to our faith in Christ – Christ crucified and risen. There need be no compromise here. If there is, then principle two has not been fulfilled.

During Advent 2003 I was involved in a conference in Oslo, which drew up another set of guidelines, offered to the churches of the Porvoo Communion (Anglican churches of the British Isles, and the Lutheran Churches of the Nordic and Baltic area). They included *Twelve issues for Christians in interfaith encounter*, listed here along with a précis of the commentary on them:

- *Building long-term trust.*
- *Speaking truthfully about the other.*
- *Sharing our faith.* Provided no one tries to exploit anyone else, we need

to respect those who hold differing positions on the balance between dialogue and evangelism.

- *Coming together before God.* Interfaith prayer and worship are explored.
- *Responding to changing societies.* We need to maintain a dynamic Christian presence in areas that are now minority Christian.
- *Nurturing faith through education.* Interfaith realities should be part of Christian education, particularly with children and young people who live in a pluralist society.
- *Supporting family life.* This includes questions related to interfaith marriage, and the education of children from such contexts.
- *Working for the common good.* This is a common goal, though there may be real differences when principle becomes practice.
- *Involving women and men.* The question of who participates is a delicate matter. We can only raise questions about the level of women's participation and show a Christian example.
- *Engaging with international issues.* Our agendas in Europe are inevitably linked with those of the wider world, where the communities with which we are in contact have connections. We need to show solidarity with those who are suffering, including Christian communities suffering persecution. But our local faith communities should not be held to account for everything that happens in the wider world.
- *Safeguarding the freedom to believe.* This affirms the statement in the European Convention on Human Rights (1950) that, 'Everyone has the right to freedom of thought, conscience and religion.' This includes the right to change faith, and to teach and practise the faith.
- *Changing religious commitment.* This highlights the possibilities for conversion across all faiths and the care of converts, an issue discussed earlier in the chapter. It also affirms that, 'where the Spirit is at work, we rejoice that conversions of people to the way of Christ may happen.' Not all will accept this with rejoicing.

Guidelines from the Inter Faith Network of the UK, which links many groups across the country within its umbrella, constitute another useful resource (available from the office individually or in bulk). They differ because they alone are written through the collaboration of all the participating faiths. They include this crucial paragraph about evangelism:

> All of us want others to understand and respect our views. Some people will also want to persuade others to join their faith. In a multi faith society where this is permitted, the attempt should always be characterised by self-restraint and a concern for other's freedom and

dignity. (There follows important guidance about respecting the wish of a person to be left alone, or to disagree with us. Also the need for sensitivity and courtesy, and the avoidance in appropriate means, or the exploiting of the vulnerable.)

My own guidelines for Christians who wish to establish and sustain a dialogue group are listed here. Each point is drawn from the accounts of faith groups given earlier in the chapter.

1. Two people from two faiths are enough to begin a group. Such a friendship provides a good basis for a dialogue group, and ensures that it can be sustained.
2. The essential basis of the group is our common humanity. If there is a feeling for this, then we can be honest about differences and share commonalities.
3. Flexibility is very important in terms of the timing and direction of the group. Agendas will not always be followed as expected; people may come and go; and what takes place after meetings may be as important as what happens during them.
4. Perseverance and stability are vital. We should not give up easily, and there may need to be considerable work between meetings, with networking between key persons. This can be by telephone, but telephone conversations should always be undergirded by meeting in person.
5. We need to be very clear about which faiths are involved, what can be expected from each, and where the sensitivities are likely to be.
6. Questions of hospitality are important, and will vary. Hindus and Sikhs assume that this is part of any occasion, and indeed it is their religious duty to offer hospitality. If we are entertaining Muslims or Jews, we need to consider the issue of what is *kosher* or *halal*. It is better to stick to Bombay mix or biscuits, checking they are *halal*, or to fruit or vegetarian food of some kind. The minimum is tea/coffee and biscuits.
7. We must expect to do things which we find uncomfortable. This may include sitting on the floor, drinking very sweet tea or receiving sweet meats in a temple (even if we do not eat them for conscience sake – see p. 108).
8. We must be sensitive to Christian women and their perceptions, without being unrealistic about what other faiths will allow, or what in practice happens.
9. Group dynamics are very important and become more complicated when we meet across faiths. Can we enable those who are lay people,

for example, to speak in the presence of an Imam, or juniors in front of seniors?

10. The quality of *empathy* is fundamental. Can we enter into the other person's world and understand his or her feelings, even if we cannot share them? Only in this way can we learn what it means for a Hindu to celebrate the birth of Krishna, or a Muslim to go on Hajj. Only in this way can we expect others to share our experience of what Easter means.

11. Listening needs to be much more than waiting till we can speak: it needs to be total. And that listening needs to cover whatever topics the other members of the group present.

12. In time we should not be reticent about challenging – telling the truth in love – rather than allowing misconceptions to continue. 'Caring confrontation' shows there is a maturity in the dialogue. However, we do need to judge carefully when the right time is for such a step. At the same time, we should not try to defend the indefensible within the practice of our faith or our faith communities. Dialogue is about conflict as well as about harmony. It may end in conflict resolution, it may not, but hopefully the personal relationships will be maintained and we can agree to differ.

13. We should remember that we meet as persons of faith and prayer: this means that we need to show respect by listening to people talk about their areas of experience, and share when we can. At the same time we meet as common citizens of our city or country. A group needs to be ready to range widely in its concerns, but it must be prepared to give a chance to people to express their personal faith, as well as the issues within society.

14. We should not be too concerned about results. The very fact that we are meeting regularly is an effective demonstration within our easily divided society and polarised religions. But we should be prepared to be surprised at where we end up, under the guidance of the Holy Spirit, in Christian terms. And we may never know the ripple effect of those who are touched in a group and then touch others.

15. Our groups should normally be open. Numbers do not matter in themselves, and we should remember what the twelve who followed Jesus achieved. How a group operates, will depend upon its size. One of the best ways to increase a group is through regular members inviting a friend. This ensures that those who come fall within the ethos of the group.

16. Where we sit is important. It may be easier to sit with a Christian friend, but we can do that every Sunday. A real breakthrough comes

in a group when we find ourselves agreeing on a particular point with someone from another faith more than with someone from our own.

Conclusion

As long ago as 1977 the Reformed Jewish prayer book gave special recognition to interfaith dialogue with its inclusion of a special prayer, which can stand as a meditation for this whole chapter:

> We are children of many traditions, inheritors of shared wisdom and tragic misunderstandings. In that which we share, let us see the common prayer of humanity; in that which we differ, let us wonder at the freedom of man; in our unity and our differences, let us know the uniqueness that is God.

I end this chapter with some thoughts on dialogue from a Jewish Rabbi, a Muslim and a Christian. The challenge in all dialogue is to move from attitudes such as fear, suspicion, rivalry, confrontation, indifference and separate worlds, to dialogue, encounter, friendship, transformation and mutual witness. This kind of journey may not always be comfortable as the majority of our co-religionists may not follow us, and sometimes we will become closer to people of other faiths than we are to our colleagues of the same faith. Rabbi Jonathan Magonet, writes, 'There is nothing so painful as returning to your own community and encountering the prejudices that you yourself have left behind, and often the task of re-educating your own people is harder than that of the initial dialogue in the first place.'[3] He goes on to explain that we may no longer be at ease in our own country: 'Those who have experienced interfaith dialogue know that from now on there is an invisible partner forever present who acts as a kind of superego watching over our more inflated claims and dubious comparisons.' Transformation is not always comfortable, as the Samaritan woman found out!

Asghar Engineer, an eminent Indian Muslim, commends Guru Nanak for his attempt to work out a creative synthesis between Islam and Hinduism, and then writes of a series of Sufi saints, ending with the eleventh-century saint from Spain, Muhiyuddin Ibn Arab.[4] He emphasises that love is at the centre of God's heart and that the entire creation is the manifestation of God, and therefore of love. This means that all barriers between human beings and their faiths need to be demolished, with a new emphasis on spirituality rather than ritual, in the search for the under-lying unity between faiths. Such a dream, coming to us over ten centuries, may be idealistic and may not even desirable, as we rejoice in the indi-viduality of each faith. But the sentiment behind it – that God is love and religions should reveal that love in their dealings with each other – is the foundation for all our human attempts at dialogue and encounter.

This all represents a great change in the discourse about the relations between faiths since the nineteenth century. The Lutheran theologian and interfaith activist Kasja Ahlstrand has written a paper on the changes she feels have taken place between 'hard' and 'soft' Christian attitudes.[5] A 'hard' approach emphasises boundaries, uniqueness, conversion, unity, hierarchical authority, philosophical truth, the necessity of either/or, truth and science, the total depravity of man, the need of sinners for forgiveness, ultimate values and God's laws, commandments and obedience, hierarchical relations, God beyond, the narrow gate, salvation and heaven, God/Jesus as Lord and King, proclamation of the word, faith as truth. A 'soft' approach focuses upon openness, connectedness and reconciliation, diversity, experiential authority, psychological truth, the possibility of both/and, wisdom and art, God's image, woundedness and the need for healing, provisional values and human rights, empowering and creating, mutual relations, the God within, the wide embrace, healing and this earth, God/Jesus as Friend and Life, listening/mystery/experience, faith as trust. Soft Christianity focuses easily upon the healing of communities, less so on biblical dialogue and truth claims. In the Questions at the end of this chapter, the reader is challenged to consider whether he or she is 'hard' or 'soft'. Most of us are probably a mixture, and the same applies to our dialogue partners. We need to recognise implicitly where each person is coming from, respect one other and act accordingly.

I end with some inspiring thoughts from Chiara Lubich, the 84-year-old founder of the Focolare ecumenical movement, which is on the 'soft' side of the above analysis! At the centre of this spirituality is a kind of asceticism of the heart, which comes from meditating on Christ forsaken and leads to individuals emptying themselves for the sake of the other. Chiara has recently linked this with interfaith dialogue:

> you can understand another's religion by getting under the other person's skin, really becoming one with the other, but to become one with the other, we must first become nothing ... As the other feels understood and heard, so mutual love comes to life, and true dialogue can take place.[6]

The obstacles to this happening lie in ourselves:

> not knowing how to really love, to make yourself one with the other, suffering if they are suffering, rejoicing if they are rejoicing.

She calls us to 'imagine a world enriched by diversity'. Although she describes London as 'the most cynical of cities', she says it could become the most spiritual if it could but develop its interfaith dimension. This is a challenge to all the readers of this book.

QUESTIONS

1. Would you describe your own particular brand of Christianity as 'hard' or 'soft'? Consider the implications of each for interfaith dialogue with Hindus, Muslims and Jews.
2. How would you explain the place of Jesus in your faith, and why you hold that belief, to a Hindu, a Muslim and a Jew?
3. Do you consider evangelism and dialogue incompatible with each other? If so, which do you see as a priority? If not, how do you see the two relating?
4. 'Dialogue begins when people meet people': reflect on your first encounter(s) with a person (or persons) of another faith. What did you learn and what did you share? How were you changed?
5. What stereotypes do Christians have of Hindus, Muslims and Jews? What stereotypes do they have of Christians? What steps can we take to break these down?

2. PRESENCE AND ENGAGEMENT: STRUCTURES FOR CHRISTIAN RESPONSE

Alongside the dialogical response to the multi-religious society, as discussed in the previous chapter, there are other structures operating at various levels, which I will outline in this chapter. It is noteworthy that they have increased considerably since 9/11, or at least become more focused and less controversial. It no longer seems necessary to ask *whether* we need to get together to tackle interfaith issues, but *how* we should do it. We will consider first formal structures in which Christians are participating, and then look at the different contexts for churches and how they respond.

Councils of Faiths

Councils of Faiths exist in many cities and towns, the majority having been formed only since 9/11. The membership of some of the longer-established groups, such as those in Birmingham and Leicester, may be restricted by constitution. The Leicester Council of Faiths was established in the late 1980s through a Christian initiative. It has honorary presidents from three faiths, Christian, Hindu and Muslim, who help to give it legitimacy. There is an elected chair, at present a Sikh, an executive with representatives from the nine recognised faiths, and a council. The recognised faiths are those that participate in the national Inter Faith Network. The local council has named representatives from each faith – between two and four according to size – and a limited co-opted membership. There is an office and centre, provided by the Methodist Church at a low rent, which is paid by Leicester City Council, who also make a grant to pay the salary of a half-time administrator. This Council has a strongly establishment feel, and its purpose is to fulfil a role between the faiths and the city. It is a body to which the City Council can turn for advice, as can other groups within the city, whether educational bodies, the service sector, the police, the media and so on, and educational presentations are often made. There is a regular newsletter and publications on the faiths of the city and their places of worship. These would be much missed if they did not exist. Councils of Faiths of this type are not dynamic in nature but tend to respond to what comes before them, but their role seems to be expanding as faiths become more important within the local and national context.

Another example is the Loughborough Council of Faiths. In this smaller town, membership is open to whomever wishes to participate, after a trial period of a year. It includes the Church of Jesus Christ of Latter-Day Saints and Pagans, as well as the mainline faiths. Regardless of size, each faith has three representatives on the Council. The meetings have a more informal feel, with people sitting round in a circle. The current mayor is the Council's President. The Council concentrates on doing things together at a local level. Christian representatives are chosen by Churches Together in Loughborough, while in Leicester each denomination has representatives.

Both are effective within their limits. In most places, however, the inclusion of Pagans would be seen as very difficult by some major faiths, in particular by Muslims, Jews and Christians. Their inclusion in Loughborough alienates certain groups of Christians and comes at a cost. The Council of Faiths can become a symbol of inclusiveness at the cost of effectiveness.

A third example is the much larger city of Birmingham where the Council has a lower profile. It has not received council funding. Its chair changes annually, in alphabetical order of faiths – Bahai, Buddhist, etc. – which is very egalitarian, but, in my experience, makes continuity of leadership difficult. The Council of Faiths in Birmingham, with its vast Muslim population, faces a common dilemma: namely, whether it is better to go for maximum inclusiveness and equality, or for representation according to the number of each faith's adherents. Most have opted for breadth of representation, which clearly over-represents small minority faiths such as Bahais, Jains or Buddhists, who are often very committed in the interfaith field. As a result, large groups such as Muslims and Christians may not have the influence their numbers would imply. Consequently, their leadership may not feel that the Council of Faiths is an area into which they wish to invest their energy. This problem comes to the fore on public occasions, such as a prayer gathering around a crisis, for example, the war in Iraq. If a public meeting is held, each faith takes part, with, say, a reading and a prayer. All faiths take an equal part, and so a community of 100,000 makes the same contribution as a community of 500 or less. Major Christian Churches such as the Roman Catholic Church may be completely unrepresented on the platform, since there is only one Christian spokesperson, usually the Anglican bishop. So also with large sectors of the Muslim community. A spontaneous occasion will allow greater participation, as happened in Birmingham in relationship to prayer for Iraq, but not everyone finds such informality easy.

The Inter Faith Network of the UK

This is a national body, which includes representatives of nine faiths and of local interfaith councils. It has an important representative function and is often consulted by outside bodies, government, etc. It is not within its remit to deal with international issues, unless they are causing problems in the UK. It has an annual meeting, which brings together large numbers of practitioners around a theme, as well as regular meetings of its executive committee. It also produces useful publications and commissions particular pieces of research.

World Congress of Faiths, and International Association for Religious Freedom

These two organisations, which have their headquarters in Oxford, have a long history of commitment to dialogue, peace and justice. There is also an International Interfaith Centre in Oxford. The World Congress of Faiths and International Association for Religious Freedom give strong support to the Parliament of the World's Religions, which met originally in Chicago in 1893, when the modern interfaith movement was born, and next in Chicago in 1993, in Capetown in 2000, and in Barcelona in 2004. Especially commended is the journal *Interreligious Encounter* (see Bibliography). A recent addition to such international groups is the United Religions Initiative, founded in 2000, whose UK Charter was signed in the Millennium Dome.

Faith Leaders' Meetings

This is an alternative structure which has arisen in certain cities, particularly since 9/11, or since the disturbances in northern cities earlier the same year. They have generally been formed at a time of crisis when it has been important to act quickly and decisively. Usually it has been the Anglican bishop who has convened such meetings, enabled by his Interfaith Adviser. The bishop is normally respected across faiths and has the moral authority to invite people. He may well be known as 'our Bishop' by people of other faiths. It is important too that he involves other Christian denominations, if possible not only those on Councils of Churches but also black-led churches and others who will co-operate.

Having been set up to respond to an emergency, meetings have continued on, say, a bimonthly basis and have been able to respond to issues as they have come along. They do not duplicate the work of the Council of Faiths, since they are more about engaging in a conversation and direct speaking, without formal structures and with no limitations on discussing political or sensitive issues. Locally, we have one guiding principle, which is that if an issue arises between two faiths it should normally be referred to the dialogue group concerned or be considered outside the meeting. Among the matters we have considered have been: faith issues for a general election, Afghanistan, Iraq, Gujarat, Kashmir, Israel-Palestine, the *hijab* controversy in France, regeneration, policing issues and terrorism. In Birmingham, such a group was called for the purpose of reassuring Muslims at the time of the Bosnian crisis, and they have played an important role when there have been inter-religious or community tensions.

Committees for Relations with People of Other Faiths

These are bodies of Christians and can have various names. There are national groups such as the ecumenical Churches Commission for Inter Faith Relations (CCIFR) and the Inter Faith Concerns Group of the Church of England, as well as United Reformed, Methodist and Roman Catholic groups. They act as a support group, receive and write reports, focus interfaith activity and raise the interfaith profile within their churches. In the Anglican group, we have recently considered such areas as theological education, conversion, interfaith marriage, faith schools, Christians in minority Christian areas and interfaith dialogue initiatives. Work is commissioned, leading, for example, to a report on the use of church buildings or on interfaith prayer and, from time to time, debates at the General Synod.

There may also be a local group. This can be quite a lonely sphere, and mutual encouragement is important. There may be local work to be initiated, for example, concerning how Christians are to respond to their interfaith context, which is a different agenda from that of a Council of Faiths, which involves all faiths. Such a group, whether or not it has formal committee, should ideally be ecumenical, though often is not.

Most Anglican dioceses have an Interfaith Adviser. This person's role includes, amongst other things, advising the bishop, co-ordinating work, building up networks of trust, taking appropriate initiatives and enabling the education of Christians. The Adviser may be paid on a full-time or part-time basis, or may work in a voluntary capacity, depending on the population in his or her area and the commitment of church leadership to address the issues involved. Such Advisers usually also make their ex-pertise available to other denominations. In Lancashire only, the Adviser is an ecumenical and full-time appointment. There is also a National

Adviser, currently working for both Anglican and ecumenical structures.

Education for Christians

This is a priority. It is much easier in areas where people of other faiths are numerically strong. A balance should always be maintained between listening to people of other faiths as a resource and visiting their places of worship for purposes of exposure, and the facilitation of Christian reflection on the kind of areas discussed in this book. For churches which are within or near cities, it is quite easy to facilitate visits to places of worship. These should be well prepared for and should be followed by sufficient time for reflection. Members of a course should be encouraged to ask questions, as Jesus did in the Jerusalem temple! I distribute a simple reflection sheet, to be filled in after and not during the visit. It includes simple, open-ended questions, such as: What did you feel before you went? What did you feel after you had been? What did you see, hear, experience? What do you know about the community that uses this building? What questions did the visit raise about God, faith and practice? What did you learn about your own faith? How did the visit affect your understanding of Christian mission? Feelings are as important as head responses and often lead to surprising comments. For example, some Christians of evangelical persuasion and conservative theology find themselves enjoying a visit to a Hindu temple, with its charismatic feel, and put the 'idols' in brackets. They respond to the informality and the coming and going of an all-age community. Those of the Catholic tradition tend not to worry about the images/idols, but find the informality a little off-putting. Going to a mosque produces a range of responses, depending on gender and how far austerity of prayer, worship and building appeal. Often how people respond within the Christian tradition to their own Christian experiences is a guide to how they are likely to respond across faiths.

I have developed a number of local courses. *Unfamiliar Journey* is a six-week course for those who live in areas where there are not many people of other faiths; *Deepening the Journey* is aimed at those who live in cities. Each course is usually attended by between twenty and twenty-five people from a range of backgrounds, some having little or no experience of other faiths while others have long experience, either through their working life or through marriage or family connections. Such courses are normally ecumenical and are put on to respond to a felt need, with a member of the clergy usually, but not always, a key enthuser. After introductions it is useful to begin by asking people to share in buzz groups any relevant encounters they have had and to articulate their key questions. The programme can then be tailored around the priorities of those attending the course, but it should normally include a balance between different faiths, between the theological, the pastoral and the practical, as well as between increasing knowledge and being challenged as Christians, in the way that this book proposes. A suggested course programme is given below, but it should be emphasised that this is just a starting-point:

Week 1: Introductions. What is dialogue and why dialogue? What are our issues? What are the issues internationally, nationally, locally? Preparation for mosque visit.
Week 2: Visit a mosque. Dialogue with an Imam and members.
Week 3: Reflections on the mosque visit. Questions that arise theologically, practically, spiritually, in terms of mission. Aspects of the Christian encounter with Islam. Preparation for visit to Hindu temple.
Week 4: Visit a Hindu temple and hear some passages from the Gita being explained.
Week 5: Reflections on the temple visit. Questions that arise, as for mosque visit. Christian theology of religions and biblical questions, in the light of what has been experienced.
Week 6: Questions of mission and conversion. Other questions outstanding from our issues of the first week. Ways forward.

It is also possible to run courses focused around particular religions, with titles such as *Understanding Islam* (or Hinduism, Sikhism, Judaism, etc.). Here I feel the ideal balance is a Christian facilitator and a teacher from the faith being studied, though two excellent courses about Islam have not followed this pattern: one developed successfully by Colin Chapman named *Cross and Crescent*, and the other led by Chris Hewer, which a large number of churches have followed in Birmingham.

Christian response to other faiths should be included in all levels of theological training – from adult education, lay ministry training, and clergy training, both initial and continuing ministerial education (see also chapter 6). This has been difficult to achieve because of a lack of vision, lack of resource personnel and pressures upon syllabuses. Since 9/11 the will may have improved, but there is far to go in the other areas. But even two evenings within a preachers' course of two years or a week within ordination training can signal the importance of this subject. Ideally, teaching on other faiths should appear right across a syllabus – in pastoral studies, certainly, but also within theology, biblical studies, missiology, spirituality and elsewhere. Few can become experts, but all can address the kinds of concerns outlined in this book. Moreover, by considering Christian theology within a multi-faith framework, students sharpen understanding of their own faith. Having a thought-through theology of religions is also important.

At a higher level, advantage can be taken of local universities where there is a religions or theology faculty, and other possibilities for specialist learning. This can enable training of future specialists in this field.

Presence and engagement: The response of churches

The 2001 census revealed that there are 550 Anglican parishes in which more than 25 per cent of the population belong to other faiths, or 10 per cent to any one faith other than Christianity; there are 950 Anglican parishes in which over 10 per cent belong to other faiths. Thirty-six out of forty-three dioceses have at least one such parish, and some obviously have many: for example over 70 per cent of parishes in London and 34 per cent in Birmingham.[1] Some parishes will have as much as 80 per cent of the population belonging to other faiths.

It can be difficult, particularly for the elderly members, to accept that the demography has now changed dramatically. The challenge is to discover a vision for the church as it can be in the modern environment, not as it has been. I outline here some examples known to me, which are representative of situations up and down the country.

St Philip's, Leicester

In the parish in which I live and minister, St Philip's, Leicester, those naming themselves as Christian in 2001 were 16 per cent of the population. A recently produced photographic history of the church shows vividly that in the 1960s it was home to a vast choir, large Sunday School, many uniformed organisations, and both morning and evening congregations numbering in the hundreds. It was the seat of the Archdeacon, as parish priest, with a couple of curates. A photograph now would show a congregation of thirty, with an average age of over sixty-five. The choir can only function when at least three are well enough to come. Great efforts are made to lower the age profile, and there are now several younger families, with a Sunday School a couple of times a month. But that remains fragile. Meanwhile, of the thirty- to forty-strong congregation perhaps three a year die, move into residential care, or relocate to be nearer children.

There are two free churches in the vicinity which both face a similar situation. None of the three has any major problems with their building, the problem is lack of people. A regular United Service is held, since there is a local covenant of unity. On that occasion, the host church will have a larger congregation.

The church is not in a poor area, and its members are largely retired professionals. But 72 per cent of the population is now made up of people of other faiths. Opposite the church is a fine new mosque, attended by a Friday congregation of about 500, with double that number in Ramadan. This has tipped what was a mixed Muslim/Hindu/Sikh area into becoming largely Muslim. Some white people have left the area because the price of houses has gone up significantly as a result of demand from Muslims. Others want to live nearer their children. White flight need not be a racist phenomenon, and many stayed a long time after Asians began to come to the area. But now, the white people who remain are largely the elderly who cannot afford or do not wish to move, some students, and a small number of people like ourselves who like to live in this kind of area. There are very few white families with children. The nearest school to the church has just one white child. Other children go out to neighbouring schools such as the nearest church school, which is in a mixed area and has children from various faiths.

Thanks to the good fortune of a major fire within the last decade, the church has recently been refurbished, reducing the worship area to half the original size and creating a very convenient hall and meeting rooms. The excellent facilities are in continuous use by community groups, Asian wedding parties, a nursery school meeting mornings and afternoons (all Asian), and for dialogue groups, Christian educational groups, and even the Gilbert and Sullivan Choir! This means that the church is seen as friendly and open to the communities around. The relationship with the mosque is cordial, with the occasional misunderstanding about, usually, car parking when there is a Muslim festival!

There is engagement with the Muslim community through the dialogue and friendship programmes centred on the church. But these groups consist of the clergy of the parish, and clergy and lay people from elsewhere. The congregation are on the whole glad to have them there, but they do not have the time and capacity to be involved. Their energies are naturally given to maintaining the church and its worship, and they have shown great loyalty and commitment. At their stage in life they need considerable pastoral care.

The problem, however, is, where is the future to be? Should we maintain a Christian presence in this kind of area? If so, why? What is our understanding of church and of mission? And how are we to fulfil this? In November 2004, the Church of St Philip's undertook a great venture of faith in voting support and a considerable amount of money to enable the establishment of a centre for the training of Christians for interfaith ministry (see Bibliography and Resources).

Parish of the Presentation, Leicester

Another group of churches lies deeper in the inner city, the Parish of the Presentation, Leicester. Four Anglican churches have been combined under one team leadership. The area used to be well known for its Afro-Caribbean community, and they still have a strong, though ageing, presence in two of the churches in the area, as well as in the Methodist church. There is an active Roman Catholic church, with a Catholic school, drawing mainly Catholic children from beyond the area, as well as locally. The congregation is multi-ethnic, with a strong contingent of Goan Catholics. They are friendly with but not actively involved with the Asians around them. There is a still strong evangelical church with a long history, which maintains its witness through prominent public posters, unambiguous in their affirmation of Jesus as the Way, the Truth and the Life and making clear that the wages of sin are death! The area is now densely Gujarati Muslim, with about twenty mosques in the area. There is a large, recently arrived Somali community. All schools are full to over-flowing, and nearly all the children go to *madrassas* (after-school classes, see p. 152). One of these is held in a church hall. The churches have social engagement projects and a good relationship with the Hindu temple on the edge of the area, which gives regularly to Christian Aid week and other causes. One of the churches is happy to hold Gujarati classes at the back of its building, which is much appreciated. The church traditions are mainly Anglo-Catholic, with daily mass. One has a very small congregation within a vast building. The decision has been taken to declare this redundant, and the question now arises of whether it might be sold to a Muslim community for social use. The often unheralded ministry of Christian teachers within the schools is a vital part of engagement in the area (see chapter 6).

St Paul and St Silas, Lozells, Birmingham

Another church, St Paul and St Silas, Lozells, Birmingham, is set within a mixed faith area, largely Bangladeshi or Kashmiri Muslim. It has been an area of considerable social tension, with a history of disturbance involving Afro-Caribbeans, many from outside, and Asians. Money poured in after two Asians were burnt to death in their shop, following a drugs raid by the police on a Caribbean public house, which was subsequently closed down. The Anglican church here has an open evangelical tradition with a largely Caribbean congregation. It has an Indian woman priest, and she has initiated a number of responses to the context. Every Saturday a small group – made up of Hindus, Sikhs, Caribbean Christians and one white

Christian, one Algerian Muslim asylum seeker and the priest – picks up litter to improve the environment, about twenty-five bags each time. 'God expects us to behave in a responsible way and to give an example to children who are ashamed of their area.' There is no waiting for financial backing, they just get on with it. A summer outreach programme to enable children to be off the streets has similarly involved a range of faiths: it has a multi-faith team leadership, including Rastafarians, and Vietnamese Buddhists have been among the parents helping on outings. Discussions have also been held about the fears of each group living in the area, including the white British population, easily forgotten. They talk together about what they can do to counter common problems such as drugs, violence and vandalism, problems across generations, education and family life; in doing so trust has been built up and challenges raised about how their respective faiths focus upon responsibilities and not just privileges in society.

Opening the doors of the church has been another key decision, so that it can be experienced as a safe haven for mothers and children of all faiths with activities being organised both during school holidays and throughout the year, which are open to all. These include providing activities for mothers of pre-school children. Courses as diverse as social care, nursery nursing and driving build trust across faiths! Here there is an attempt to create a 'new way of being church'. 'We can live in beleaguerement and fear, and appear to be condemning everything, or we can share a new and inclusive vision of salvation,' the priest said to her Parochial Church Council. 'We can make our walls stronger, and praise God within those walls. Or we can work to set people free, and share the life of Christ with them, as we open wide our creaking doors.' The PCC itself has gone through a process of education. They agreed the following principles: 'We will celebrate God as creator with people of all faiths in the parish. We will respect each other's differences, and handle them sensitively. And we will promote harmony and goodwill by working together.'

This has also involved a new attitude to asylum seekers, seeing those of all faiths as neighbours. There is need to make room at the inn – even for those they do not know and even when their priest is not present. The priest has even enabled eighty-year-olds from her congregation to enter a Kurdish house, with an old and dirty carpet, to drink tea without milk and listen to endless stories. The meetings have to take place late at night, because the refugees are being exploited for labour and required to work long hours. The priest is known there as 'Mamma Imam'! She also urges congregation members to smile at refugees they see. It takes only a little to please – saying *Asalaam Alaikkam* creates an amazed response, or *Nabed galio'*, 'God be with you' in Somali. They reply, 'Thank you, thank you.' Giving gifts at Christmas is another way forward, which can be a multi-faith activity. The Sai Baba group unexpectedly brought two car loads of food in response to the priest's sharing of the message of Advent and Christmas with their members. It was for 'people in need', and the priest was trusted fully to distribute it, as she would know who was in need. At their request she has also enabled groups of teenagers from the Sai Baba group to visit the places of worship of other faiths. The church has become a link. She has taken the Sikh priest to the Hindu temple, and in response he has donated tea and sugar for the pre-school children, an example of Christian mission being done by a Sikh. She asks the Hindu priest directly for sugar, butter, tea and spices, which are given generously.

The Martyrs, Leicester

A fourth parish, the Martyrs, Leicester, has an open evangelical tradition. The population of the inner-city area is much more mixed, with Hindus, Muslims and Christians – perhaps 25 per cent from Asian and 75 per cent from European backgrounds – and with about 1000 students living in the area. The church is lively and a centre for all kinds of activities. It has a strong core congregation, with 200 plus members of all ages, the majority from the parish, and it also has cell groups. Its clergy and a limited number from the congregation are involved with the Asian community. Two courses have been held, including one by an Imam on understanding Islam. In the 1990s there was a project for Asian outreach, which employed two people, but funding then dried up, and priorities changed. The present vicar has developed good links with mosque and temple and has been invited to speak to Muslims in crisis times. There is much work with asylum seekers, Muslim and Christian, which is largely clergy led. The vicar comments over all:

> The main difficulties lie in taking these positive relationships at leadership level to the worshipper on the street. It seems that neither church, temple, nor mosque can easily bridge that gap. The challenge is how to move beyond living peaceably with parallel lives, to seek conceptual spaces for constructive engagement.

The Parish of Oadby

Thirty years ago, the suburban parish of Oadby, just outside Leicester, had a population of 3000, now it is 25,000. In the St Paul's area of the parish, house prices have risen 130 per cent in the years 2001–4. Christians are now a minority in this affluent area, constituting 49 per cent of the population, with Hindus 15 per cent, Muslims 18 per cent and Sikhs 12 per cent. These figures are taken from the 2001 census but the proportion of people from other faiths continues to rise. A local school made a visit to the church recently: out of the seventy-five children in the party only one was white. The church has been considering what being engaged positively with this changing population would mean. The church building and centre is a vital element in this engagement, enabling relationships to be made with the organisations that are ever eager to use it. Examples are: an Asian elders' group, a Karate group, a Muslim women's group, an Asian dance class. A users' consultation group has been started to enable the different groups and representatives of the church to meet each other. The head of the *madrassa* has helped the church to get access to the school where it meets. In an area where people normally lead very private lives and can live alongside their white neighbours, yet alone their Asian ones, for many years without speaking, the congregation are having to renegotiate what they as a church are here for. In an area of suburban politeness it is often the Asians who break the ice. There has been discussion about replacing the screens in the church with glass windows to allow people to see in to the Christian heart of the buildings. The church has an evangelical background but church members are not quite sure how to express their faith in the changed circumstances in which they find themselves. They need help building up their confidence. These were some of the issues discussed on a lay training course held in the parish.

Market Harborough

Another type of context is that of a market town outside a multi-faith area. An example is Market Harborough about fifteen miles from Leicester, which has a population of 18,500, with a district population of 78,000. In 2001 only 1.2 per cent of the population claimed to have a faith other than Christianity. Many in the town will be surprised at this low figure, since the impression is that there are more Asians than there used to be. Many of the small shopkeepers are Asian; they have been there for a long time and are trusted and well accepted in society. Leicester is regarded as being far enough away not to have a major impact, though attitudes may change if there is a greater influx of people of other faiths. The churches remain predominantly white. There has recently been an increased interest in learning about other faiths among Christians over the age of fifty, who did not have the advantage of learning about them in school. In a recent course held there, members were impressed with the friendliness and openness of Hindus encountered on visits organised to Leicester. They were even more impressed with the Muslims they met who went against their stereotypes and, at a time when Muslims are seen with such ambiguity within wider society, welcomed them warmly to their mosque.

The rural church

A final context is the rural church. It should be remembered that unless the villages are very remote, their members will often commute to work in nearby cities, or will have lived in multi-cultural areas in the past. They will also encounter people of other faiths on holidays, as well as through their television screens. Three churches in rural settings in Leicestershire have recently indicated a wish for structured contact with people of other faiths. The village of Claybrooke, near Lutterworth, has established a link with a Hindu temple in Leicester. The parish of Swithland requested me to bring a Muslim to a special service, during which he and I had a dialogue; following on from this I invited members of the congregation to visit a mosque and neighbouring church in the city. When I preached in the Avon Swift group of parishes near Lutterworth, the one reference I made to Muslims was taken up in discussion after the service: this prompted me to offer to bring an Imam to a meeting, and it will be interesting to see where this leads. At the same service, a woman met me to discuss her concerns about the relationship developing between her daughter and a person of another faith. These all fully white villages are demonstrating an openness to the issues discussed in this book.

Much of the Church's response is seen outside the parish structures: in chapter 6 I will look at engagement within community and secular structures. The challenge at the congregation level is clearly contextual. For those who live within multi-faith areas in cities where Christians are a decreasing minority, the most pressing questions centre around what the church is here for. Is it to enable trust and understanding to develop between communities of faith and others living in the area? Is it to sustain a Christian worshipping presence and witness? Is it to work with others for the common good? Or is it to engage in mission/evangelism, however that is defined? A recent survey of Anglican parishes in these kinds of areas has shown that the clergy at least place the order of priority of those four possibilities in the descending order, i.e. building trust is first, mission is last. This is a matter worthy of reflection. Perhaps understanding of mission is narrow, and the other purposes can be included within mission. It may be that the area of evangelism has been left to churches outside the mainstream and to organisations dedicated to evangelism amongst Asians and others. Certainly such efforts are evident in many places.

The much-discussed Anglican synodical report *On building a mission-shaped church*[2] does not engage much with multi-faith parishes or areas. There is a need for much more consideration of the rationale for the large sums of money needed to sustain the church and its witness here. Courses such as those I outline above are urgently needed to enable those who finance such parishes from suburban and county areas to appreciate the task that is being engaged in by their colleagues within the cities and to be helped to understand that they are doing this on behalf of the wider Church. It is an exciting venture, and those from the wider area can be encouraged to engage in it also, through support of churches which are unlikely to be sustainable without outside help, through direct participation where opportunities can be offered, and by recognition that we are all part of one world and one Church, not segmented into separate areas of concern. St Paul's exhortation in the Epistle to the Romans is usually applied to individuals: 'Rejoice with those who rejoice, weep with those who weep' (12:15). But it can also be applied to churches in various situations. And it is not always weeping in the interfaith areas. I hope that this book will show how much rejoicing there can be in living and worshipping in areas like the 550 parishes referred to above.

QUESTIONS

1. Find out, if you do not know already, about interfaith structures in your area and Christian participation in them. Who are the resource persons? Are there any ways in which you or your group could take things further, beyond reading this book?

2. How would your congregation see mission in terms of people of other faiths? Where would you see the priorities in Christian engagement?

3. THE MOST FREQUENTLY ASKED THEOLOGICAL QUESTIONS

While other chapters focus primarily on how people approach dialogue from a practical perspective, in this chapter I address theological questions directly. There are eleven questions which are consistently raised by course participants. I answer eight in this chapter and tackle others elsewhere in the book.

1. What is the place of Jesus in other faiths? How is Jesus unique?

There is often an assumption that Jesus is the possession of Christians, that he was born, lived, died and rose for them. But, of course, he lived and died a Jew. And if his life and death mean anything, that meaning is universal. He is the second Adam: 'as all die in Adam, so all will be made alive in Christ' (1 Cor. 15:22).

Jesus has fascinated people of all faiths, and indeed those of no religious faith. People from all cultures as well as faiths have responded to him. Hence the plethora of artistic images of Jesus throughout the ages right up to the contemporary world. Most of these paintings are by Christians, but not all: there are examples of works by Hindus and by Muslims, for example a nativity scene painted by a Muslim artist.

It is vital to listen to people of other faiths and to ask what, if anything, they make of him. In explaining Christian belief, it is good to affirm commonalities before going on to clarify where Christians have a different understanding. That is why Christians are Christians.

Islam

Islam is the only religion which has references to Jesus, *Isa*, deeply embedded in its scripture. The Qur'an has ninety-three verses referring to the prophet *Isa*, and there are more verses about *Maryam* (Mary) than there are in the Gospels. Jesus was born of the virgin Mary by Allah's command. He was a prophet for three years, from age thirty to thirty-three. But he had even more miracle powers than the Jesus portrayed in the New Testament. He could talk as a baby, make birds out of clay, heal lepers, give sight to the blind and raise the dead. He will return as a sign of the final judgement.

As well as these similarities, there are great differences. No teaching of Jesus is recorded; that is all in the *injil*, the lost gospel. But his teaching, if we had it, would be confirmed in the Qur'an, which holds all the revelation necessary. He is a prophet, as indeed were those who came before him, and Muhammad, the last prophet, who came afterwards. But he is not more than a prophet. Allah can have no son or daughter, Allah is one and in-divisible. Moreover, *Isa* was not crucified, he was taken up by Allah. It was mistaken followers who insisted on worshipping him (and indeed Mary).

Muslims will affirm that it is not possible to be a Muslim without believing in Jesus. This assertion should be respected, and not devalued because it is not Christian belief. Nor need Christians be reticent in explaining why differences are important to them. In return we must expect Muslims to ask how we view Muhammad. Do we see him as a prophet? This is a tough question to respond to. In his ethical teaching and way of acting, he has considerable likeness to the Old Testament prophets or John the Baptist. But can we call someone who denied explicitly the divinity of Jesus a prophet in the same sense as those who pointed forward to the coming of Jesus as Messiah? We may well then want to give the answer that he is and he is not.

Hinduism

It is a frequent experience for Christians to hear Hindus say how much they love Jesus. They easily absorb Jesus as one of many gods, as exempli-fied by a temple in Leicester which has a painting of Jesus on its ceiling, with the Buddha and Hindu gurus. Jesus can be seen amongst the images of Hindu gods in all Sai Baba groups, along with Sai Baba himself. A Hindu may take Jesus as his/her *ishtadeva*, preferred deity, or way of seeing God. What they do not find acceptable, however, is the idea that allegiance to Jesus should be exclusive and that the only way of salvation is through him. He easily becomes one of the *avataras*, incarnations normally of the God Vishnu. According to Geoffrey Parrinder, the characteristics of *avataras* such as Rama or Krishna are as follow:

- The avatar is real, bodily and visible.
- They are born of human parents.
- Their lives mingle human and divine qualities, including miracles.
- They die, since incarnations of God are limited in time, as well as bodily form.

- Some at least are historical. For example, the Buddha is now included. Krishna and Rama are mythical figures. Modern saints such as Ramakrishna or Mahatma are often also named among them.
- They reappear: The Gita affirms, 'from age to age, I come into being.'
- They reveal a personal God and a God of grace.[1]

Ovey N. Mohammed has outlined some real similarities between the notion of salvation offered by Krishna and that offered by Jesus in the New Testament. In both cases, it is God who takes the initiative, by becoming incarnate and offering salvation through grace, repentance and forgiveness. Knowledge of God comes through detachment from self and action for the welfare of humanity. Our ultimate salvation is eternal communion with God beyond this world.[2]

Clearly, the fundamental difference is that the incarnation of Jesus is unrepeatable, as the hymn puts it, 'Once, only once, and once for all, his precious life he gave'.[3] Christianity appears, to the Hindu, to require an exclusive commitment to Jesus. This they can accept, but not for all people, including Hindus, for all time. They feel that it devalues their deepest beliefs. By virtue of the doctrine of reincarnation Krishna may be reborn again and again, 'Many births have passed for me' (Gita). Undoubtedly, resurrection, which is fundamental to the Christian world view and which is based upon the experience of Jesus, is radically different from reincarnation.

Unlike Jesus, the avatars do not die a victim of evil forces. They live and work on earth, but heaven is their home. They are much more like the Jesus of the Fourth Gospel than the Jesus of the Synoptic Gospels. But even in John, the flesh is very real and the death very concrete in its awful reality. The avatars walk this earth, but their feet hardly leave footprints on the ground; they may or may not be historical, and indeed some are animals, but that makes little difference to their coming as appearances of God (a kind of theophany).

Many Hindus have responded to Jesus while remaining Hindus. Some are highlighted in *The Acknowledged Christ of the Hindu Renaissance* by the orthodox theologian M.M. Thomas.[4] I quote from four of them (the reader may like to consider how striking a resemblance these views bear to those of many contemporary Europeans!).

Rammohan Roy (1772–1833) was a Bengali reformer, who entered into frequent dialogues and disputes with the first Baptist missionaries to Bengal, led by William Carey. He responded above all to the moral teaching of Jesus. He fought a personal campaign against the caste system and a successful one against *sati*, ritual widow burning.

The consequence of my long and uninterrupted researches into religious truth has been that I have found the doctrine of Christ more conducive to moral principles and better adapted for the use of rational beings than any other which came to my knowledge.

I regret only that the followers of Jesus, in general, should have paid much greater attention to enquiries after his nature than to observance of his commandments, when we are well aware that no human requirements can ever discover the nature of even the most common and visible things, and moreover that such enquiries are not enjoined by the divine revelation.

Keshab Chandra Sen (1838–84) founded the Hindu reform movement, Brahmo Samaj, and had personal mystical experience of Jesus, resulting in a passionate search for an Asian Jesus. These passages raise the question for today, what kind of Jesus do we portray?

My Christ, my sweet Christ, the brightest jewel of my heart, the necklace of my soul ... for 20 years I have cherished him in my heart ... the mighty artillery of his love he levelled against me, and I was vanquished, and I fell at his feet saying, 'Blessed child of God, when shall others see the light that is in thee?'

When we hear of the lily and the sparrow and the well, and a hundred things of Eastern countries, do we not feel that we are quite at home in the Holy land? ... Jesus comes to us in his loose flowing garment, his dress and features altogether oriental, a perfect Asiatic in everything. Surely Jesus is our Jesus.

I and the Father are one ... Surely the idea of absorption and immersion in the deity is one of those ideas of Vedantic Hinduism. The most illiterate man is heard to say that he and the Lord are one! The doctrine of absorption in the Deity is India's creed, and it is through this idea, I believe, that India will reach Christ. Will he not fulfil the Indian scriptures? I am reminded of the passage in the Gospel which says, 'I am not come to destroy, but to fulfil.'

Mahatma Gandhi (1869–1948) needs no introduction. He was deeply inspired by the teaching and example of Jesus and read the Sermon on the Mount each day, along with the Gita and Qur'an. Like Jesus he died giving his life for others. These quotations again raise all kinds of contemporary questions: about what makes a Christian, about whether the historical Jesus is important, about the relationship of the historical Jesus and the

Christ of faith, about those who are Christlike in their actions and are not his followers, and about the necessity or otherwise of conversion to Christianity.

> The message of Jesus Christ, as I understand it, is contained in the Sermon on the Mount. The spirit of the Sermon competes, almost on equal terms, with the Bhagavadgita, for the domination of my heart ... the gentle figure of Christ, so patient, so kind, so loving, so full of forgiveness that he taught his followers not to retaliate when abused or struck, but to turn the other cheek – it was a beautiful example, I thought, of the perfect man.

> God did not bear the cross only 1900 years ago, but he bears it today, and he dies and is resurrected from day to day. It would be poor comfort to the world if it had to depend upon a historical God who died 2000 years ago. Do not then preach the God of history, but show him as he lives today through you.

> I do not need the prophecies or miracles to establish Jesus' greatness as a teacher. Nothing can be more miraculous than the three years of his ministry.

> It is not he who says Lord, Lord, that is a Christian, but he that doeth the will of the Lord, that is a true Christian. And cannot he who has not heard the name of Christ, do the will of the Lord?

Pandita Ramabai (1858–1922) was a remarkable high caste convert to Christianity. A woman ahead of her time, she was called Pandita, the learned one, by Hindus. She was the first woman member of the Congress Party, which brought India to independence, and through advocacy and educational projects fought for the education of women in British India, less than 1 per cent of whom could read. She became a Christian in England when teaching at Cheltenham Ladies' College! Like many converts, she hated denominationalism, since her conversion was to Christ.

> After a visit to a Christian home for 'fallen women' in Fulham, she observed, 'I had never heard or seen anything of the kind done for this class of women in my own country ... I asked the Sisters to tell what it was that made the Christians care for and reclaim fallen women ... I realised after reading the fourth chapter of St John, that Christ was truly the Divine saviour he claimed to be, and none but he could transform and lift up the downtrodden womanhood of India, and of every land.

No-one can have any idea of what my feelings were at finding such a Babel of religions in Christian countries ... I did not adhere to any particular sect, nor do I do so now. It was enough for me to be called a Christian, on the grounds of my belief in Christ as saviour of mankind.

Sikhism

Sikhs do not accept the avatar concept. God is manifest through his name, through truth, through righteousness. No human form is needed. However, Sikhs can easily relate to Jesus as the Word of God found in St John's Gospel. Guru Nanak said, 'One word and the universe throbbed into being, hundreds of thousands of rivers began to flow' (*Adi Granth* 3), and, 'O disciples of the True Guru, know that the word of the Guru is perfectly true; God, the Creator, causes it to be uttered' (*Adi Granth* 308).

Sikhs also appreciate greatly the concept of Jesus as the innocent martyr, who lived an enlightened life, but like many Sikh Gurus and ordinary Sikhs, suffered death at the hands of wicked men. They also take suffering very seriously. However, they would not accept that Jesus suffered vicariously for the sins of others. They also can relate well to Jesus as teacher and to the scriptural account of that teaching, since theirs is very much a religion of the book.

Buddhism

Buddhists rely on the teaching of the Buddha, while Christians ultimately respond to the person of Jesus. For Christians Jesus is God as well as man, he is 'God with us'. Moreover, his death on the cross is not just a moral example of selfless love, but is the decisive moment of God's encounter with humanity, with an objective as well as a subjective reality. It avails for all humanity at all times, indeed for the whole universe. It is not just an example of non-violent behaviour nor a symbol of ultimate detachment. It is the moment when Jesus dies vicariously for the sins of humanity. For Buddhism, each of us must take responsibility for our own life.

The teachings of the two founders are different in style, with the teaching of Jesus being more in story form, but in terms of content, there are great parallels as well as differences. These are illustrated in the writings of the Sri Lankan theologian Aloysius Pieris.[5] In his work *agape* (divine love) and *gnosis* (knowledge) meet in the figures of Jesus and the Buddha. As can be expected, neither faith has a monopoly on either value; it is in the meeting of opposites that the most fruitful dialogue often comes.

Judaism

Clearly the Jews have never recognised Jesus as the Messiah. This rejection by Jesus' own nation is felt painfully by many Christians. Dangerous assumptions can be made which have led and can lead to antisemitism. For example, outside the cathedral in Strasbourg there is a statue of two women. One wears a crown and holds a sceptre, and looks forward with vision and hope; the other has a broken sceptre and is blindfolded, unable to see! Hans Ucko sees in this statue a representation of church and synagogue. With this kind of image around, it is not surprising that it is difficult for Jews to think anything positive about Jesus.

Of course, Christians believe that Jesus, as the Messiah, inaugurated the kingdom of God, a kingdom of justice, righteousness and peace. But this is not what Christians have lived up to; neither is it what Jews have experienced. In many ways, the messianic age has hardly started.

Having acknowledged this, there is a readiness amongst some Jews at least to recognise Jesus as a great moral teacher, who drew, as their rabbis do, on the traditional wisdom of his people and had a vivid way of explaining things. He also had something of the biblical prophet about him, in his denunciation of injustice and self-righteousness. Christians and Jews differ in their answers to the question, 'Whom do you say that I am?' (Mark 8:29). But, provided that the Christian does not insist that the second covenant annuls the first, there can be dialogue even here about the person of Jesus. Will Herberg, a Jewish Professor at Drew University (1901–77), wrote of the Jews having a covenant of faithfulness and Christians a covenant of mission, to bring people of all cultures into the new covenant people.

Conclusion

The often asked question about the uniqueness of Christ is, in a way, an unreal question. Every reader of this book is unique. In the same way, the Buddha, Moses, Muhammad, Guru Nanak, Krishna and Jesus are all unique. They each have a distinctive personality, teaching, life story and impact on the world. The above accounts of how other faiths see Jesus illustrate perhaps the distinctiveness of each of their responses, but also the particularity of the Christian understanding of Jesus. We are Christians because we hold that belief, and not another. The exercise of engaging with people of other faiths is not about devaluing their belief, but of valuing it, learning from it and also clarifying why we hold the particular belief about Jesus that we do. If we did not hold this belief, we would be Muslims or Hindus or the kind of people in western society who hold that they live under the world view and moral framework that he laid out, who admire him greatly, enjoy his festivals and may be prepared to believe that he was a prophet – but no more than that. The essential difference relates not so much to his teaching and ministry as to his death and resurrection. This leads us on to questions of salvation.

2. Can people of other faiths be saved and, if so, how?

In certain ways this repeatedly asked question is a particularly Christian obsession, which causes people great anxiety. Some ask it because they wish to be reassured that they as Christians have something special: that being a Christian is worth the effort. This can also be associated with an equal certainty that those of other faiths are not saved, which gives an imperative to the mission task: to bring them into the fold, to enable them to be baptised, or to be 'born again', to 'know Christ as their Lord and Saviour' (depending on the church background of the person asking the question).

Other Christians consider that this is an illegitimate question. Each faith has its own understanding of the aim of life and of the truth of where ultimate destiny lies. Therefore, it is wrong to impose the views of one faith on another, and each should judge from within its own parameters. For example, the Hindu view of salvation is around the definition of the two words *moksha* or *mukti*. According to one philosophy, salvation is achieved when the individual realises his or her oneness with the divine and becomes absorbed, like salt in the sea or a river entering the ocean. In another interpretation it is not a question of ultimate absorption, but of the personal will remaining in relationship with God, which can be achieved through *bhakti* (devotion), through *yoga* (disciplined medita- tion) or through *karma* (good works done without seeking reward). *Reincarnation* is part of the process, and it may take countless lives before a person reaches the point of salvation.[6]

Buddhists aim for *nirvana*, which is achieved when a person has been able to eliminate desire and the clinging to self. It centres on liberation from attachment, from aversion and from ignorance about our true nature. Suffering is not the problem, but its mastery over us, from which we need to be released. We are responsible too for the salvation of all creation. Hence, the centrality of compassion in Buddhist practice. Such a way is open to all of any faith who follow the path.

In Sikhism, salvation depends on the grace of God and is about union with God. Guru Nanak wrote:

> Good actions may procure a good life, but liberation comes only from his grace.

If a man goes one step towards him, the Lord comes a thousand steps towards him.

In Islamic understanding, all depends on the will of Allah, who saves whom he wills and condemns whom he wills. People will be judged by their deeds, their religious piety and their concern for the poor. Heaven is the reward, which includes being in the closer presence of God. Punishment is being cut off from him. As for those who are not Muslims, the Qur'an is not very clear, but there seems to be hope, at least for Jews and Christians: 'Believers, Jews, Christians and Sabaeans – whoever believes in Allah and the Last Day and does what is right – shall be rewarded by their Lord; they have nothing to fear or regret' (2.62).

Judaism uses the word 'redemption'. This may be individual or corporate, in this world or beyond, materially related to the land of Israel or spiritual. Although Judaism is concerned primarily with Jewish people, it usually extends generosity to people of other faiths based on God's covenant with Noah, which is for all people and is limited in its demands.

Looking at this survey, it is clear that it is Christianity that is the most ready to rule out salvation for those who are not its adherents. But there are other possibilities, and we will now examine a variety of options that have been proposed in answer to this question.

Christian perspectives on salvation

Before we can ask, 'Who can be saved?', we need to ask, 'What is salvation?' Although it is an impossible question, I will make an attempt at answering it. Salvation has two dimensions, the first in the here and now and the second in eternity. Salvation in the here and now relates to how one lives one's life within the human community. It relates to wholeness of life and liberation from fear, oppression and want. It is about being accepted for who we are – by ourselves, by our family and community and by the wider world. It is about realising our human potential and our feeling at one with the divine reality, however that reality is conceived. It is about having a sense of hope, faith and love and knowing a quality of life, 'eternal life', now. Salvation in the beyond means that quality of life being affirmed and infinitely transcended within the bounds of eternity. This second dimension of salvation means being in a relationship with the divine that is immediate and is experienced within a communion of saints that is intensely personal in terms of those we love. It is the realisation of the promise contained in 1 Corinthians 13:12, 'For now we see in a mirror, dimly, but then we will see face to face. Now I know only in part; then I will know fully, even as I have been fully known.'

Is this salvation, as I have defined it, open exclusively to Christians? Or is it available to all through their own faiths? Or is it open to all, but anchored in Christ as the way for all? These three positions have become known in recent decades as *exclusivism, pluralism* and *inclusivism.* They are inadequate and increasingly being questioned, but they are useful here to help us reflect on this issue.

The *exclusivist* holds that, at least in terms of ultimate salvation, only those who acknowledge Jesus Christ as Lord and Saviour, or undergo baptism into the visible Church can be saved. The former position is held within more evangelical Protestant circles, and the latter was held in the Roman Catholic Church from the time of Cyprian until the Second Vatican Council in the 1960s. The view is argued largely from the Christian Scriptures which seem to require such a faith commitment. It also rests on the cross and resurrection of Jesus being held as central to the faith. They are *the* saving events, and they avail only for those who believe. There may be many good people following other faiths, and indeed those faiths may sustain people in this life, providing salvation now. But ultimately there are choices to be made, which will determine whether or not a person will go to heaven. Those who maintain this position hold varying views on whether those who have never had a chance to know Christ will be excluded from the possibility of eternal life. But those who have heard clearly the message of Christ, must take responsibility for the consequences of their decision. This approach obviously gives strong motivation for Christian mission.

Challenging questions for exclusivists are: Does God create people as good (cf. Genesis 1–3), and then ultimately damn the majority of them? What of those who came before Christ? What of the Jews?

The *pluralist* holds that people are saved within the tradition that they follow, through appropriate commitment and practice. Salvation can be envisaged as a mountain top, with many paths leading up it. Or there are several mountain tops, each with their own refuge at the summit. There is little biblical support for this approach, but much from experience. People seem to find wholeness within the various faiths. As John Hick, the most famous exponent of this view, points out, there are roughly a proportionate number of saints in each faith tradition. This approach fits with the modern educational understanding of Religious Education. Children can learn about the many faiths and benefit from them, without judging them. But there are a number of questions which this position raises. Can all religions be equally true? If not, what are the criteria by which it is possible to judge which is more true and which is less true? In practice, does not each religion judge by criteria from the depths of its own faith? And, if we consider the New Testament, is not the Christ event, his cross and resurrection, seen to be of universal effect and not just an event for one community? Does every path up the mountain lead to the top, or are some false trails leading over precipices?

The *inclusivist* believes that people are saved through Christ alone, but Christ is seen as including people of other religions. God alone saves, and God can only save through Christ. Christ is the human face of God, revealing above all that God is a God of love and forgiveness. When the question is asked as to whether people are saved in spite of their religion or through their religion, such a God will find many ways to include people, for he is as generous in salvation as he is in creation. The theological basis for this position is found in creation theology and also in the concept of Christ as the Word of God, the *logos*, without whom nothing is created which is created, and who is the source of life and light for all. It is also found in the understanding of the Spirit. The Spirit was moving over the waters at creation, she/he is also the Spirit of Christ, and the Spirit blows where she/he wills. The Spirit's activity is not confined within the Church. The fruit of the Spirit are found wherever there is love, joy, peace, patience, kindness, generosity, faithfulness, gentleness and self-control (Gal. 5:22–3). In the same way the characteristics of the kingdom of God are to be found within and without the Church.

Certain Bible passages can be read to point in this inclusive direction. One example is the Beatitudes, in which Jesus teaches that those who are 'blessed belong to the kingdom of heaven; they will be called children of God and they will receive mercy. There is no indication that it is only Christians who are blessed. The parable of the sheep and the goats appears to open the possibility of inclusion to those who do works of compassion without seeking reward, who do not necessarily know the name of the Lord (Matt. 25:31–46). The parable of the Pharisee and the Publican is a significant example of someone being 'justified', 'saved', by the simplicity of his prayer of dependence: 'God be merciful to me, a sinner' (Luke 18:9ff.). The devout of other faiths often pray such a prayer, and the Muslim *salat* (prayed five times a day) expresses such a sentiment each time the forehead touches the ground.

What are the difficulties for the inclusivist? It may appear that inclusivism requires universalism – that everyone in the end will be saved. For some, that is a heresy, for others a logical consequence of the almightiness and generosity of God. But this is not a necessary corollary of inclusivism. God wishes to include all, but people may exclude themselves, both in this life and beyond. That is part of free will. Others claim that this is a subtle form of Christian imperialism. They are included through Christ – Karl Rahner coined the term 'anonymous Christians' – though they do not know it. This objection is to some extent avoided if we make it clear that it is God who is including them, because of their Christlike way of life and commitment to their own faith. From the Christian perspective, the Word of God, or the Spirit of God, working through other faiths is of Christ. Moreover, every religion has its own criteria for judging what is good and true in their own and other faiths.

Exclusivists would probably say that only they have a motivation for mission. Certainly pluralists have every reason to call for the working together of people from all faiths for the common good. They have no reason to seek for conversions. Inclusivists can rejoice in those who convert. But this is not because they cannot be saved without such a conversion – that is a question for God. Rather they desire others to join the Christian community, because there they have 'life, and have it abundantly' (John 10:10). There they can know explicitly what they already knew implicitly.

3. How do we evaluate the scriptures of other faiths? Can the Qur'an or the Bhagavadgita, for example, be accepted as books that reveal God, at least in part?

For some, this possibility is ruled out completely. Revelation is through the Word of God which is the Bible, and that is the end of it. This approach is illustrated by the story of the meeting of two famous theologians, the Swiss giant of Reformed Theology Karl Barth and the Sri Lankan ecumenical statesman D.T. Niles. Niles asked Barth, 'Can a good Hindu be saved?' Barth replied without hesitation, 'Certainly not.' Niles asked, 'Have you ever met any Hindus?' Barth replied, 'No.' 'Then how can you rule this out?' Barth said emphatically, 'Easy, a priori.' Those who hold this position may not have looked at the scriptures of other faiths, or heard them explained by a devotee of the faith. For them, Christian revelation is contained only in the Bible.

Even those who are prepared to consider the scriptures of other faiths with an open mind, do not always find it easy. This is because the style of any scripture is culturally conditioned by its time and place of authorship. People who try reading the whole Qur'an in an English translation usually find it indigestible, lacking in stories and not logical in order. They also find particular sections off-putting and offensive, as they appear to have very dogmatic views of non-Muslims and clear denials of the incarnation and crucifixion. But it should be remembered that it is also not easy to read the Bible without an interpreter. It also has much that is unsavoury or mysterious.

It is helpful to listen to scripture being explained by a person of the faith whose holy text it is. For example, in dialogue groups Muslims can interpret the Qur'an for Christians, and vice versa. *Exegesis*, drawing out from the text its original meaning, needs to be combined with *hermeneutics*, applying the text to our daily life. It is worth going even just once with a group to a mosque or temple and, after the visit, asking the guide not just to tell you about the building or doctrines, but to read a passage of scripture and explain it. This may help you to find your own answer to the question with which this section began.

By way of example, here are some extracts from the scriptures of other faiths. First, the Gita:

> I [Krishna] am the goal, the upholder, the Lord, the witness, the abode, the refuge and the friend. I am the origin and the dissolution, the ground, the resting place and the imperishable seed. (9.18)

> Whosoever offers Me with devotion a leaf, a flower, a fruit or water, that offering of love, of the pure heart, I accept. (9.26)

> I am alike to all beings. None is hateful, nor dear to Me. But those who worship Me with devotion, they are in Me, and I also in them. (9.29)

The Qur'an:

> Allah [God] is the one who causeth the grain and the date-stone to burst, producing the living from the dead, and who produceth the dead from the living; who causeth the dawning to burst forth, and who hath appointed the night as a rest, the sun and the moon as a reckoning; who hath appointed for you the stars that you may guide yourselves thereby in the darknesses of land and sea. (Surah 6)

The Sikh scriptures:

> One man by shaving his head hopes to become a holy monk, another sets up as a Yogi, or some other kind of ascetic. Some call themselves Hindus; others call themselves Musulmans, among these there are the Shiahs, there are the Sunnis also, and yet man is of one race in all the world; God as creator and God as good, God in his bounty and God in his mercy, is all one God. (Guru Gobind Singh)

The Buddhist scripture:

> There are three kinds of persons existing in the world: one who is like a drought, one who rains locally, and one who pours down everywhere.
> How is a person like a drought? He gives nothing to all alike, not

giving food and drink, clothing and vehicle, flowers, scents and unguents, bed, lodging and light, neither to recluses and Brahmins nor to wretched and needy beggars. How is a person like a local rainfall? He is a giver to some, but to others he gives not. How does a person rain down everywhere? He gives to all, be they recluses and Brahmins, or wretches, needy beggars. *Itivuttaka* 65

Looking at such texts may well lead us to conclude that God's revelation can indeed be found in various scriptures. This is already inbuilt within the Christian faith, since the Hebrew Bible is included within the Bible. The Old Testament contains the remarkable book Job, for which there is no evidence that it was written by a Jew. It also contains books like Jonah, in which the pagan people of Nineveh, to which Jonah is sent, reveal more openness to God than the prophet himself. In the New Testament, we find Paul affirming that God has not left himself without a witness in any culture or community, since the natural world displays his nature (Rom. 1:19–20). In Acts 17:28, Paul quotes from the scriptures of the Greeks with approval: "'In him we live and move and have our being"; as even some of your own poets have said, "For we too are his offspring.'"

It is the Spirit who gives knowledge and discernment and 'will guide you into all the truth' (John 16:13). Naturally we will look for what is compatible with the New Testament, and we will find much that is. But we need to hear these scriptures in their own right and not immediately impose our judgements, which will prevent us really 'listening'. We may find ourselves guided by great Christians who have gone to the heart of such scriptures. Prominent among them is Kenneth Cragg, the former Bishop in Egypt, now over ninety, who has written forty-one books in the area of Muslim-Christian dialogue, the most ground-breaking of which is *The Call of the Minaret*.[7] We can also read Bede Griffiths' Commentary on the Gita, Aloysius Pieris' writings on the Buddhist scriptures (referred to above) and Owain Cole on the Sikh scriptures (see Bibliography).

To end this section, I would also add that revelation of God is not confined to scriptures. Revelation is found in the natural world; it is found in prayer and mysticism; it is experienced in relationships. Moreover, great theologians such as Thomas Aquinas found the imprint of God in philosophers such as Aristotle, and the early Christian apologists Justin Martyr and Clement of Alexandria speculated on the salvation of Plato and others. During the Middle Ages much of the wisdom of the Greeks came to theologians through the medium of Islamic scholars.

4. How do we account for great commonalities between religions in the ethical field? And why do religions nevertheless fight each other?

At their heart, the various religions seem to be able to agree on basic values, for themselves and the world. However, in practice, major clashes arise wherever religions act in an aggressively missionary way, and wherever religion is combined with nationalism or fanaticism. Even Buddhism and Hinduism can become violent, though non-violence is at the heart of their faiths, for example, in Gujarat or Sri Lanka. But Islam and Christianity tend to be the religions most sure that they are right. They are both universal religions, with a self-understanding that they are to evangelise the world. There are few countries in the world where they are not both major forces.

It is salutary, therefore, to look at commonalities. The Golden Rule, for example, is found within the scriptures of all the major faiths:[8]

> In everything do to others as you would have them do to you; for this is the law and the prophets. (Jesus, Matt. 7:12)

> Treat not others in ways that you yourselves would find hurtful. (The Buddha, Udarna-varga, 5.18)

> This is the sum of duty: do not do to others what would cause pain if done to you. (Mahabharata, 5:1517)

> Not one of you truly believes until you wish for others what you wish for yourself. (The prophet Muhammad, Hadith)

> What is hateful to you, do not do to your neighbour. This is the whole Torah, the rest is commentary. (Hillel, Talmud, Shabbath 31a)

> I am a stranger to no-one; and no-one is a stranger to me. Indeed I am a friend to all. (Guru Granth Sahib, 1299)

Granted this general agreement, how is it to be worked out in practice? It is hard enough at a personal level, but what about beyond that – at a community, national and international level? Here there is a search for a 'global ethic'. One of the prime movers in this search, Hans Küng poses the question, 'What is good for human beings?'[9] He clarifies:

> By a *global ethic*, we do not mean a global ideology or a *single unified religion* beyond all existing religions, and certainly not the domination of one religion over all others. By a global ethic we mean a

fundamental consensus on binding values, irrevocable standards, and personal attitudes.

The report of the third Parliament of the World Religions (1999) rightly said, 'the greatest single scandal in which Earth's faith traditions are now involved is their failure to practise their highest ethical ideals in their relations with one another.'[10] Any particular religion may be the right one for a particular person or community. Most of its adherents will naturally regard it as the religion which satisfies and hold that it is nearer to the truth than the alternatives. That is why they adhere to it. But beyond that there needs to be respect, tolerance and, more than that, mutual engagement for the common good. In a now celebrated sentence, Hans Küng has said, 'No human survival without world peace, no peace without peace between the religions, and no peace between the religions without dialogue.' We might also add, 'and without peace within religions'! We looked at how such dialogue can happen in chapter 2. But the question still needs to be asked: when religions work together, what are they working for?

The kind of list that most religions could agree upon – and indeed have done in the past – might include:

- care for the excluded, the marginalised, the poor, the hungry, refugees, the sick, the lost, the disadvantaged, children and women: practical care, works of compassion, but also advocacy for their rights
- recognition of equality before God, and before the world community, of people of all cultures, races, castes, classes and faiths
- advocacy of human rights, including freedom of expression, freedom from torture, freedom of political association
- terms of trade which do not penalise those who are already at the poor end of the world, freedom from crippling international debt
- rights to universal education and health care, which is comparable wherever a person lives, particularly in the face of diseases such as HIV/AIDS and malaria
- a common concern for the environment, with mutual responsibility accepted for its preservation for future generations
- a responsible attitude towards the arms trade; increasing controls on weapons of mass destruction, in the powerful as well as in developing countries
- support of international institutions such as the United Nations, the European Union, the Commonwealth, for the benefit of all and not just the powerful
- commitment to universal human law, involving support of international courts and tribunals

- universal condemnation of the use of international or local terrorism, and co-operation on means to combat it, combined with a universal commitment to eliminate the causes, which feed such extremism
- condemnation of all forms of religious extremism, of whatever faith, which lead to violent confrontations.

Most of these would also be shared by many secular people. Of course, the philosophical basis for why each faith thinks as it does will differ, but the practical outworking will be similar. Moreover, such a list gives no place for privatised or purely personal religion, which is a particularly Christian tendency. '"My religion" satisfies my personal needs, but need not interfere with how I think about other things.'

Any consensus on a global ethic must include not only an emphasis on human rights, but also on human responsibilities. This is a strong theme in all religions: 'I am my brother's/my sister's keeper.' The founder of the Iona Community, George MacLeod, used to say that to choose to dig one's garden rather than read the newspaper is a political act. He also said that a sermon needs to be prepared with a Bible in one hand and a newspaper in the other. The search for a global ethic has a long way to go. It needs the kind of co-operation discovered in the fight against apartheid in South Africa, which produced a remarkable consensus, across religion and ideology, and transformed the most divided communities in the world into a rainbow people. We all need to be challenged to ask ourselves: what does such an ethic mean for my life? How can I co-operate with others locally to bring transformation to my community, my city, my village? It has been said that any nation should be judged by how it treats the marginalised within its borders. How do we treat asylum seekers and refugees, the homeless, single mothers, the elderly and so on? A further ethical challenge is how we can care for such people across our faiths.

5. Other religions exist and appear to thrive. Is this against God's will? Is it a temporary phase, until all are gathered in? Or is this part of God's provision?

6. How do we account for the evident goodness, love and sense of spirituality found in people of other faiths? Is this the activity of the Spirit within them?

Anyone who has spent time in multi-faith contexts, whether in Britain or elsewhere, will affirm that they have met remarkable people who hold a faith other than Christianity. This does not mean that these people are any better than those special Christians whom we all know. They reveal the same kind of qualities, such as: a sense of faith, of stillness and of prayer; compassion, kindness and a concern for justice for others, which is expressed in practical action; a willingness to give of their resources and time when there is a need, and a deep sense of self-sacrifice.

This question usually arises within a Christian group when someone shares an example of such a person and wonders how this can be squared with teaching that seems to ring-fence such goodness within seemingly narrow Christian boundaries. There are three possible options. The first is that the goodness is not real goodness but has ulterior motives – yes, I have heard this being imputed! The second is that it has nothing to do with their religion: they are just naturally good. The third is that narrow Christian boundaries have to go, and the fact has to be accepted that good-ness can flow from the outworking of other faiths. This can then either be attributed to the faiths themselves, or to the hidden Christ, the Logos, or the Spirit working within them and within those faiths.

An elderly Christian expresses surprise that at Diwali and Eid the Hindu and Muslim neighbours living either side of her send her a pro-portion of the food they are sharing with their families. Their gesture encourages her to send some of her Christmas fare back to them. The young daughter of a Christian family falls seriously ill and is hospitalised for three months. The most consistent visitor, outside her family, is a Hindu, who spends time with her very regularly, thus making an important contribution to the rehabilitation process. A Hindu temple community is stirred by the call for funds during Christian Aid Week. Its president telephones the local Christian priest completely unexpectedly and asks him to come the following Sunday to receive a cheque for £501. During the annual street collection for Amnesty International it is a Muslim who goes beyond giving change or a £5 note and takes out a cheque-book to make the largest donation. A whole row of Muslim neighbours attend the funeral of a 94-year-old Christian woman, who throughout her life made racist comments.

These are small, everyday examples. If the persons concerned were asked why they did the things they did, they would respond that it was because of the need in front of them and because of their religious faith, which teaches them to help others. We each need to reflect on these issues and come to our own conclusion.

7. How do we use the Bible in the encounter between faiths? Do we look at particular verses or the overall picture? For example, how do we interpret John 14:6: 'I am the way, and the truth, and the life. No one comes to the Father except through me'?

The Bible, both Old and New Testaments, is written out of particular contexts. The Qur'an comes from one context: Arabia in the early seventh century AD. It consists of revelations to one person, dating over a period of perhaps twenty years, from around 610 AD. The Qur'an itself does not change, but much depends on the place and time into which it is being interpreted.

The Bible consists of sixty-six books, covering a millennium of time and a vast range of social and cultural backgrounds. There is always an inter-religious context, whether the people of Israel find themselves in Egypt, in the wilderness, in Palestine or in Babylon. They are surrounded by other gods: the gods of Egypt, Assyria, Canaan, Babylon, of Greece and of Rome. There is the very crude idol worship of the Baalim, with its animal and even human sacrifice; there is also emperor worship, mystery religions, high Greek philosophies. The Bible contains no explicit reference to, or even hidden acknowledgement of, the existence of the Indian faiths of Hinduism or Buddhism. Islam and Sikhism were, of course, later in origin. By far the majority of the writers of the Bible's sixty-six books were Jews.

The contexts in which the Bible is being interpreted are also constantly changing, which leads to significant variations of emphasis. For example, the growth of awareness of international debt has led to greatly increased application of the Jubilee text in Leviticus, taken up by Jesus in Luke 4. When the question of the ordination of women to the priesthood was being debated, on one side of the argument certain texts related to male and female equality in Christ gained significance, while on the other texts related to how women are to behave in church were emphasised. Recent discussion of the gay issue has led to people reading the book of Leviticus with a new zeal!

The same has happened as interfaith issues have come to the fore. Certain texts have been highlighted as providing critical insight about how we are to think theologically, or behave practically. The challenge is whether individual texts can be considered binding, or whether we need to look overall to the general thrust of scripture: seeking to discover what kind of approach to people of other faiths such a God would encourage, rather than what this or that text says about such a relationship. The ensuing picture is, of course, not divorced from particular texts, but emerges from them, without any one or other becoming decisive.

The central Christian understanding of God is of a God of love, forgiveness, generosity, freedom, faithfulness and justice. The opening chapters of Genesis present us with a vision of everything being created good, but as the story unfolds, things begin to go wrong, as a result of human beings' misuse of the freedom they have been given. A number of Jesus' parables, such as the Prodigal Son, the Labourers in the Vineyard, the Lost Sheep, reveal the longing of God for transformation and a returning to him. This is also echoed in many of his stories which have the theme of reaching out to the lost and inviting them to a great feast. It is shown above all in the whole life story of Jesus – his birth, ministry, death and resurrection: these are the lengths to which God will go to reveal his love and to bring reconciliation both within humanity and between human beings and God. The understanding of God which is created has love at its centre; the message is: 'perfect love casts out fear', 'God is love', 'faith, hope, and love abide, these three, and the greatest of these is love.'[11]

What are the relevant texts? Here are some examples, with a short comment on each:

- Exodus 20:1–6: the first four commandments, with the affirmation of the oneness of God, the honouring of his name and firm condemnation of idolatry. This raises the question, what is idolatry?
- 2 Kings 5:1–19a: the healing of Naaman. In this story a mighty Syrian, a non-Jew, seeks healing from leprosy from Elisha, the unconventional prophet of Israel. When healing happens, Naaman recognises the universality of the God of Israel. He receives forgiveness in advance for still having to enter the temple of Rimmon and bow down before an idol. This story is very relevant for 'secret Christians' (those many who are Christian believers but keep their conversion secret. See pp. 119–26 for wider discussion related to issues of conversion to Christianity.). There are no boundaries to God's healing love. It is taken up very significantly in Luke 4:27, Jesus' sermon at Nazareth.
- Proverbs 8: the picture of Wisdom, a vision of the immense breadth and depth of its activity, which knows no bounds in terms of time or space. Wisdom is the master worker, the delight of God, the one created before all. It is the source of knowledge, discernment, prudence, intelligence, nobility, righteousness, peace and life. Wisdom 7 and Ecclesiasticus 24 are similar 'wisdom' passages. Comparisons can be made with John 1, and, above all, Colossians 1, where this kind of language is applied to Christ.
- Isaiah 45:1–17: the universality of God's salvific presence. There is nothing outside God's sphere, even Cyrus, the Persian king. Though he does not know it, he is God's instrument, his anointed, and is called by name. God is the Lord of all, of light and darkness, of good and evil. The God of Israel is the universal God.
- Jonah 3:7–4:1–11: the forgiving and gracious God, who reaches out to the people of Nineveh. The prophet Jonah has received God's special

care, but resents the extension of that care to a notoriously heathen city.

- Matthew 28:16–20: the challenge to evangelism. It is a foundational missionary text, which needs to be addressed by those who see their main calling as being one towards dialogue.

- Matthew 25:31–46: one of several texts in which the criterion for judgement seems to be how people live their lives, whether they do works of mercy without expectation of gaining entry to heaven. The concept of doing good without reward is easily understood by a reader of the Gita (cf. *nishkarma marga*). It is a case of 'You will know them by their fruit' (Matt. 7:16), and 'Not everyone who says to me, "Lord, Lord", will enter the kingdom of heaven, but only one who does the will of my Father in heaven' (Matt. 7:21). Some ask, is Christianity a religion of grace, while other religions are religions of works? This is a false dualism, as the text shows. All religions are religions both of faith and of works. The key question is the motivation for the works.

- Matthew 5:1–11: blessedness is attributed to various groups – the poor in spirit (in Luke, the poor, cf. Luke 6:20), those who mourn, the meek, those who hunger and thirst for righteousness, the merciful, the pure in heart, the peacemakers, the persecuted. There is no indication that they must be Christians. It is about their dependency on God and their concern for justice. Can this be seen as an inclusive text? It is certainly a beautiful text to read on interfaith occasions, as it communicates across all faiths (see p. 112).

- Luke 18:9–14: in this parable, the Pharisee, who considers himself much better than others, is convinced that he is right with God. The Publican does not even enter the temple, but says the simple prayer, 'God, be merciful to me, a sinner.' It is he, the Jew of doubtful credentials, who goes away justified, saved. What of people of other faiths who make a prayer like this? Are they commended, justified, saved? Here we have a text where the emphasis is on faith, rather than works: an illustration of justification by faith, through grace.

- Luke 10:25–37: who is my neighbour? How do I inherit eternal life? By being like my neighbour of another faith. The commands to love God and love our neighbour are at the heart of all religions. In this parable a Samaritan, a despised outsider, does what the priest does not do. Is he just an example of how to enter eternal life, or can he himself enter eternal life?

- John 4:1–42: Jesus' encounter with the Samaritan woman. It demonstrates Jesus' willingness to receive from a person of another faith, an untouchable, a woman, a sinner. New truths come from dialogue. 'God is Spirit, and those who worship him must worship him in spirit and in truth' (v. 42).

- Acts 10: through the Spirit the conversion of Cornelius, a God-fearer. Peter is converted to the realisation that God has no favourites. This text deals with many issues related to conversion.

- Acts 17:16–34: a practical example of dialogue. Paul goes to where the Greek philosophers are. He observes and listens. He listens to what is good in their scriptures and builds on what he can affirm. He also affirms the centrality of Christ, without using the name, and his resurrection. He does this at the end, not the beginning. He demonstrates his readiness to face controversy, failure and contradiction.

- 1 Corinthians 8: practical advice on interfaith encounter in connection to the question of food sacrificed to idols. Whilst the principle of acknowledging the sensitivities of those with less experience is established, at the same time there is the affirmation, in verse 6, that there is only one God and one Lord Jesus Christ, and so there is no real problem about eating food offered to non-existent idols.

- 2 Corinthians 4:1–18; 5:4–21: the mission imperative of reconciliation between God and human beings, and between persons. This is a central focus for Christian ministry with people of other faiths: we are impelled by the love of Christ (5:14). 'In Christ God was reconciling the world to himself' (5:19). Does 'the world' include Muslims, Hindus and Sikhs?

Two passages which are continually quoted in connection with this question are John 14:6 and Acts 4:12, neither of which was originally concerned with this issue, but are seen by some as foreclosing the whole issue of salvation and people of other faiths.

- Acts 4:12: 'There is salvation in no one else, for there is no other name under heaven given among mortals, by which we must be saved.' This seems clear enough. But it comes at the climax of a healing miracle when Peter is answering the question, 'By what power or by what name did you do this?' True, in Luke the word for 'healing' and the word for 'eternal salvation' are the same, and the statement can be taken more broadly. But it remains primarily about the healing power of Jesus, rather than being a universal theological statement. If Jesus is God, the text is saying that all healing is through God. The power of the name of Jesus is, of course, recognised across faiths in the healing context.

John 14:6: 'I am the way, and the truth, and the life. No one comes to the Father except through me.' This statement, which comes within the farewell discourse of Jesus in the Fourth Gospel, is taken out of context even more often. It does not, of course, say that no one comes to God. Clearly the Jewish people had done that. This text should not be used to exclude the possibility of a relationship with God within Muslim, Sikh and other communities. Jesus speaks about relationship with the 'Father'. This is the particular way of relating to the universal God that he offers, as emphasised in the Lord's Prayer, with its permission to address God daily as 'Abba'.

Two further points. 'The way' is not simply declaring faith in Jesus. It comes just after the story of Jesus' washing of his disciples' feet and his commandment that they likewise should wash one another's feet. This is the way of self-sacrifice that few follow. Jesus will soon go to the cross. Taking up the cross and following him is too much for almost all the disciples including Peter, despite the fact that at the end of chapter 13 he affirms that he is ready to give up his life. The way is narrow: how are we to follow? We can leave others to God's mercy.

We should also note the text, 'In my Father's house there are many dwelling-places' (14:2). This is a text often forgotten by those who only quote John 14:6. It can also be linked with John 10:16, 'I have other sheep that do not belong to this fold.'

Overarching all these verses is the question who does the 'me' refer to in the phrase 'except through me'. Is this Jesus of Nazareth, the incarnate one? Or is this also the Christ, the eternal Logos? If the latter, then John 14:6 can be seen as a universal statement – whenever people come into a deep relationship with God, they come through the eternal Logos. That Word has been made flesh in Jesus, but it is not confined to his person; it is found wherever people follow the way of self-sacrifice implied here. If Jesus is the Logos, 'without him was not any thing made that was made' (John 1:3 KJV), and in him is life. His statement can then be seen as inclusive, not exclusive.

I would now like to include two personal responses to this text. A Sikh convert to Christianity regards this as his conversion text. Through it he discovered that the God he knew in Sikhism was the same God he met in Jesus who, as the servant of others, gave his life for humankind. It was the same God that he knew, and indeed still knows, through his Sikh upbringing and the teaching of his mother. His discovery of Jesus in no way invalidates his past journey. He now knows more of the personal in God through encountering Jesus, the way, the truth and the life.

The other is from a Hindu. He too loves this verse. He says that God, in Hinduism, is both impersonal and personal, beyond thought and turned towards us. The God revealed comes in many forms, such as Rama or Krishna. The Jesus of John 14 is God revealed. This is the God of love, giving himself for others. It is a beautiful picture, an indication of the way, the truth and the life. The only way to the God beyond, is through the human face of God – 'no one comes to the Father except through me'. He would be quite shocked if we told him that this text actually does not include him but in fact excludes him.

8. How do the various faiths respond to the key question of suffering as part of the human condition?

When preparing a new lay training course, I was encouraged to include a five-week module on the theme 'Evil, Suffering and a God of Love'. The questions of suffering and evil pose different challenges depending on the world view of each faith. The fact of suffering is universal, as illustrated strikingly in the story of the Buddha. When, as a young man, he left his father's palace and set out on a journey to discover the real world from which he had been shielded, he was confronted by someone who was very sick, someone who was very old, and a funeral procession. He had to face the question: why suffering, why evil? It is one which all humanity must face, whether of religious faith or not. Even in a Marxist classless society, people will still grow ill, will age and will die. How then do the main faiths respond?

Hinduism

In classical Hinduism, the two concepts of *karma* and of *samsara* hold the keys to the understanding of suffering. *Karma* is the fruits we inherit either from our former life or from the consequences of our actions in this life. Suffering is the result of evil actions. A person can rescue him or herself by developing a right attitude to those sufferings through detachment. They are real, at one level, but they are not ultimate. We live in a world of *maya*. This has been called 'illusion', but 'contingent' (temporary, and not eternal) is a better description. Suffering is caused by regarding what is temporary as eternal, by clinging to things which are passing, such as possessions, health and relationships; to do so is a sign of our ignorance, *avidya*.

Samsara is the cycle of birth and rebirth. It will always involve suffering, through the process of life and death. *Moksha* – salvation – is to go beyond that cycle by realising our oneness with the eternal.

Views vary on whether anyone can realise such release, or only those in the so-called twice-born castes, or only men and Brahmins. It is as a result of *karma* that someone is born 'untouchable' (modern term *dalit*), with the suffering that it entails. Some Hindus believe that anyone who is devout in prayer and meditation, and is involved in good works without desiring praise, can be treated as 'brahmins', and in this way find release.

Gandhi developed the ideal of non-violence (*ahimsa*) and aligned himself with the sufferings of Jesus in the way he consciously took suffering upon himself. He was influenced in this by Jain and Buddhist ideals. He said, 'Non-violence in its dynamic condition means conscious suffering. It does not mean meek submission to the will of the evil-doers, but it means pitting one's soul against the will of the tyrant.'

In the *Upanishads* it is written,

> Through the ripening of the fruits of past actions, a person does not attain any rest, like a worm caught in a whirlpool. The desire for liberation arises in human beings at the end of many births through the ripening of their past virtuous conduct.

> A person sorrows not who is not connected with the sources of sorrow.

Sikhism

Sikhism has a similar world view to Hinduism. Suffering is a fact of life, as are pain and pleasure. It is one's attitude to them that determine one's fate:

> It is absurd to ask for the gift of joy and the withdrawal of sorrow. Pleasure and pain are the two garments given to man from the divine court. Where one is bound to lose by speech, it is best to keep silent. (*Adi Granth* 149)

What counts is attitude to the divine and to fellow human beings, not solving the mystery of suffering. Of course, martyrdom has a special place in Sikh tradition, and many gurus have given their life for the community.

Buddhism

Buddhism focuses upon suffering (*dukkha*) as central to the human condition. It is caused by the fact that humans are conscious beings, aware of the gap between what they long for and what they have, and of the transitory nature of all life. The teaching of the Buddha centres on the Four Noble Truths and the Eightfold Path, which enables human beings not to avoid suffering but to rise above it. The term *nirvana* is very difficult to define, but when a person realises *nirvana* he or she is no longer reborn to further suffering. A person does not have to die to reach *nirvana*: it is attainable now through following the teachings of the Buddha. It is a condition of *anatta*, realising 'not self'. It is the end of craving, but not 'annihilation' as is sometimes thought.

The Four Noble Truths state:

> The Noble Truth of suffering is this: birth is suffering; ageing is suffering; sickness is suffering; death is suffering; sorrow and lamentation, pain, grief and despair are suffering; association with the unpleasant is suffering; disassociation from the pleasant is suffering; not to get what one wants is suffering.

> The Noble Truth of the origin of suffering is this: It is this thirst (craving), which produces re-existence and re-becoming, bound up with passionate greed.

> The Noble Truth of the cessation of suffering is this: It is the complete cessation of that very thirst, giving it up, renouncing it, emancipating oneself from it, detaching oneself from it.

> The Noble Truth of the Path leading to the Cessation of suffering is this: It is simply the Noble Eightfold Path, namely right view; right thought; right speech; right action; right livelihood; right effort; right mindfulness; right concentration.

The central picture of the Buddha is of infinite compassion and loving-kindness within this world of suffering and sorrow. That compassion spreads to all human beings –whether they are connected to us, whether they are our enemies or whether we are indifferent to them – and also to all of creation.

The following story, known as the Parable of the Mustard Seed, illustrates the Buddhist view of suffering. Gotami has one young son who dies. Distraught, she seeks medicine to revive him and is guided to the Buddha. He asks her to bring him a handful of mustard seeds, collected from every house where no one has lost a child, husband, parent or friend. She goes off with joy, but gets nowhere. Again and again she is told, 'Do not remind us of our deepest grief.' She grows weary. At nightfall, seeing the lights of the city going out one by one, she thinks to herself, 'How selfish am I in my grief! Death is common to all.' She buries her child and, returning to the Buddha, finds comfort in his way.

Later on in the history of Buddhism the idea of *bodhisattvas* developed. These are enlightened persons, who could rest in *nirvana*, having attained perfection, but who return to the world, because no one can reach *nirvana* unless all do, and give their lives for others.

Islam

God is all powerful; God is all merciful and compassionate. Yet still there is suffering. Since human beings cannot question God, two reasons are given for suffering: it is either punishment for what we have done consciously or unconsciously, or it is a test. Whatever happens, it is ultimately from God.

The following extracts illustrate the Qur'an's teaching on suffering:

> Every soul tastes of death, and we test you with evil and with good as a trial, and to us you will return. (xxi.36)

> If a wound bruises you, a similar wound has bruised people previously. Such days we deal out among men in turn that God may know those who believe. (iii.134)

> God does not burden a soul except according to its capacity. (xvii.16)

> To God belongs everything in the heavens and in the earth; he forgives whom he wills, he punishes whom he wills, and God is forgiving, compassionate. (iii.123)

Clearly there is commonality with the Hebrew Bible in terms of this theology.

Shia Islam has added a new dimension by teaching that those who suffer despite their innocence, particularly martyrs such as the three early martyrs, Ali, Hassan and Hussain, will be rewarded. Here we see the saving benefits of innocent suffering, which assures the victims of their place in heaven. Another voice is the mystic Rumi, who said that 'pain and suffering make one aware of God'.

Judaism

Pain, suffering and death are not part of the natural condition. The early chapters of Genesis record how they enter the world as a result of human sin. This approach, if seen as theological commentary, gives a high place to human responsibility. However, since the whole world belongs to God, he is ultimately supreme. As Isaiah 45:6–7 asserts, 'I am the Lord and there is no other, I form light and create darkness, I make weal and create woe.' Whether it comes through the natural world or through the evil actions of humanity, the fact of suffering is accepted. What is questioned is its distribution.

This is developed in two main directions. One view is that if an individual or community sins, then the suffering that results will last for generations. This is seen in Deuteronomy 5:9, where Moses warns the people that those who bow down to idols will be punished to the third and fourth generations, and in the books of Samuel and Kings where time after time the behaviour of the king leads to punishment for his whole people and future generations. The alternative view is articulated by the prophets Jeremiah and Ezekiel, who say that, when someone eats sour grapes, it is their teeth that are set on edge and not those of their children or grandchildren.

Of course, the book of Job centres on this theme of suffering, but there are no simple answers. Job is adamant that his suffering cannot be attributed to any sin on his part – neither conscious nor unconscious. His friends' advice is useless. In the end, all he can do is acknowledge the mystery of God. The book of Ecclesiastes takes a pragmatic view: there is a time for everything, and we should accept things as they are.

Neither of these books takes refuge in a belief that all will be set right in life after death. This is, however, the conclusion of the apocryphal literature. Examples are found in the Wisdom of Solomon 3:1–5, 9, which speaks of the souls of the virtuous being in the hands of God where no torment will ever touch them, and in 1 Enoch 103, which describes the goodness, joy and glory being prepared for those who have died in righteousness.

Mention should finally be made of the Suffering Servant passages, particularly Isaiah 52 and 53. These chapters give a beautiful picture of redemptive suffering, as the innocent suffering servant is led like a lamb to the slaughter. In Isaiah 53:11 we read, 'The righteous one, my servant, shall make many righteous, and he shall bear their iniquities.' By his wounds we are healed.

Christianity

There is only space to give a few glimpses. Because God is love, God is Almighty and human beings have free will, the question of suffering has a particular sharpness. If God could stop suffering, why does he not do so? If he does not want to interfere with free will, what of all the suffering not caused by human sin?

Any Christian response will centre on Jesus, the cross and resurrection. As Philippians 2 makes clear, God cared enough about the plight of the world to empty himself and take the form of a slave, becoming obedient unto death, even death on a cross. In so doing, 'in Christ God was reconciling the world to himself' (2 Corinthians 5:19).

How the cross is so effective remains a mystery of faith, and one hard to explain to people of other faiths. The cross gives no supernatural answer to the problem of suffering, but provides a way through it: as Luther said, 'We go through no darker door, than he has gone before.' We are assured that nothing in life or death, nothing in all creation, can separate us from the love of God in Christ Jesus (see, e.g., Romans 8:39). This faith led the great German theologian and martyr, Dietrich Bonhoeffer, to affirm from his prison cell, 'Only the suffering God can help.'

9. Do we all worship the same God? What is the place of the Trinity?

10. Can Christians pray/worship with people of other faiths?
See chapter 4.

11. Are dialogue and evangelism compatible, or must we choose one or the other? Do we seek conversions?
See chapter 2.

4. INTERFAITH PRAYER AND WORSHIP?

A Christian priest was visiting a hospital patient, who was awaiting serious surgery. The patients in adjacent beds were a Muslim and a Sikh. The priest was about to leave, when the son of the Muslim patient asked where he was going. 'I am going to church to pray for my friend.' He added as an afterthought, 'Would you like me to pray for your father?' 'Yes, please,' the son replied, without hesitation. 'For we all worship the same God,' replied the priest. 'Of course we do, because there is only one God. Can I pray for your friend at my mosque prayers?' With rather more hesitation the priest replied, 'I would be very pleased if you did that.' A few days afterwards, the Muslim patient heard that he was to have his operation. The son called the priest, 'I would like you to pray with my father now.' The priest offered a prayer for healing, beginning 'O God, O Allah'. Both patients came through their operations. If the prayers of only one person were to the true God, did they avail for both? Or were both praying to the one God?

This story illustrates vividly the challenge that lies behind the frequently asked question: *are we as Christians worshipping the same God as people of other faiths?* This question worries Christians more than it does people of other faiths. I was called to the deathbed of a close Muslim friend, requiring me to drive fifty miles. When I arrived, I found the friend in a coma. The Muslim family asked me to pray for him there and then. I said, rather feebly, that he would not understand. They said that did not matter. He would know; he loved my voice and my prayers. And anyway, God would hear! No hesitations.

An army chaplain told me how, while he was on duty in Basrah, Iraq, a seriously wounded Iraqi Muslim soldier was brought in suffering great pain. He gave his name as Sabah. The chaplain felt he should pray and murmured a prayer in English, not understandable by the prisoner, and then found himself praying spontaneously in tongues. He felt sure that God would use his words to comfort the man. He then decided to learn a little Muslim prayer in Arabic from his Kuwaiti colleagues. This prayer he used with another very agitated prisoner who was near to death, and he appeared to find peace. He comments that he remains a strong and orthodox Christian, but is convinced that God, as he experiences God, is broad enough to encompass the faith and prayers of another religion, and so bring healing and comfort through his words.

A Turkish Muslim woman suddenly appeared at church one Sunday when the eucharist was being celebrated. She came again the next week. The priest asked her why she had come. She said, 'I feel the presence of God here. I am not welcome to enter the mosque across the road, as a woman, and I want to be with people who are praying to God on my day of leisure.'

A Christian woman befriended two young Hindus on a work placement in Birmingham. She met them when queuing for a bus. They told her that she was the first person outside work who had spoken to them. She invited them for a meal. Gradually they became friends. One day, her house bell rang at 8 a.m. The two Hindus said they wanted a word. It was the birthday of one of them, and they wanted to present £101 (Hindus always give a round figure plus one!), for Christian work with orphans in India. Their tradition is to give, not receive, on their birthday. They trusted such work because it was in the name of Jesus. Could she say a special birthday prayer to Jesus? She asked why they were not going to the nearby Hindu temple. 'Where we go does not matter, you have been Lord Jesus for us, and God is everywhere.'

These stories are not necessarily consistent with doctrine. A personal God is not part of the world view of Theravada Buddhists. A Sri Lankan monk, who had been much involved in interfaith work, was hospitalised after a major car accident. After his discharge, he remarked that it was really good to be involved in such work. Not only had his fellow monks chanted for him, but he had received the prayers of a Muslim family, a Hindu priest, an Anglican bishop and a Roman Catholic monk. With a twinkle in his eye, he added that he had got better quicker than the doctors expected!

These real-life incidents throw light on the frequently asked questions: are we all praying to the same God? And is there only one God? The pastoral response is clear that where people are seeking the healing power of God, theological niceties tend to fall away. They are not acting out of desperation or 'hoping against hope'. While they will follow faithfully the rituals and prayers of their own faith tradition, they have little hesitation in transcending them also.

In 2003 the Islam in Europe Committee of the Conference of European Churches (CEC) and the Council of European Bishops' Conferences published a paper of reflections and texts.[1] The paper includes this quotation from a German Lutheran document:

> The perceptions of God (in other faiths) undeniably are different. However, we cannot force the Spirit of God to conform to our theological thinking! Therefore the possibility of praying together does not depend on theoretical agreement about a common perception of God. God's reality goes far beyond our human understanding. Prayer with the other – without glossing over real differences – may generate new insights. On the other hand, the Spirit of God binds us to God's Word. Because of this, prayer must not be instrumental, recruited for worldly purposes. In the end, it is to the grace and mercy of God that Christian and Muslim address their prayers.

Another ecumenical document makes this evocative statement:

> We see inter religious prayer as a sharing in the 'groaning of the whole creation', longing for fullness of salvation and liberation, partaking in the groaning of the Spirit, 'the Spirit who sustains us in our weakness since we do not know how to pray.'[2]

The Pontifical Council for Interreligious Dialogue has stated:

> Inter religious prayer is an expression of the coming together of all the 'scattered children of God.' It is a sharing in the common journey towards the fulfilment of the Kingdom of God ... Prayer together is an invitation to friendship, to share the reality of a loving God who is our Creator, redeemer and sustainer.[3]

The question of whether we worship the same God is usually formulated in doctrinal terms. Some want arguments to back their instinctive feeling that we do. Others are sure we do not, and want this proven. In terms of the Latin questioning words, for some it is a *Nonne* question, expecting the answer 'yes'; for others it is a *Num* question, expecting the answer 'no'. For a third group, it is a totally open question on which they seek guidance, a *-ne* question.

A Lausanne (evangelical) document exemplifies the *Num* approach:

> According to the Bible the one God revealing himself finally in Jesus Christ excludes different perceptions of God. Muslims who do not believe in Jesus Christ do not pray in a different way to the one God, but miss the only God and worship a human perception of God, pray to a none-God. Therefore, Christians and Muslims can neither pray side by side nor together to the one God, the Father of Jesus Christ.[4]

In this group's view, 'The common prayer to the "same" God is the first step in the direction of syncretism.'

The answer given by other faiths varies. In Islam the question is answered by the *shahada*. This is the short credal statement used constantly in their prayers, as one of the five pillars. It affirms 'there is no God but God'. There is only one God – not two, three or many Gods. God is beyond description, for we are humans and not God. Human beings must fall down in submission before him. God is not there to be questioned. He is the God of Ibrahim, Ishmael and David, of Moses and Elijah. He is the God of Mary and Jesus (the prophet *Isa*), and of Muhammad. He is the God of Jews and Christians, as well as Muslims, hence the special status of 'people of the book'. Christians are worshipping the one God, even if not in the ideal way; they are not guilty of *shirk*, of blasphemy.

Such a confidence is revealed in the enormous popularity of church schools for Muslim families. A Church of England school in Keighley, Bradford, has almost all Muslim children on its roll. Its OFSTED report in 2003 included a commendation for 'the very strong contribution made by RE, visits and links, extensive extra curricular provision to the spiritual, moral, social and cultural development of all pupils'. This is very similar to the experience of Christians in countries like Pakistan, where church educational institutions provide opportunities to reach out to Muslims. Behind this popularity is an understanding that the same God is worshipped in such Christian institutions.

We can comprehend what people believe by observing how they worship. In reverence and submission to God, religions may come close together. But when words are used, differences begin to arise. For Jews and Muslims these differences can appear minor, revolving around which books they use and, above all, about the status of Muhammad. The gap between Christians and Muslims is much wider. Muslims often say to Christians, 'We all worship the same God, we just differ about Jesus.' But to differ about Jesus is to differ about the heart of Christian faith. I invited some Muslims and Jews to witness Compline. They loved the ethos, but the Trinitarian ascriptions to the psalms and the references to Jesus as Saviour were clearly stumbling blocks for them.

If Christians are talking with Muslims about God, it is essential for them to begin by reassuring them of their belief in the oneness of God. Only within that belief should they explain Jesus. So also with the Holy Spirit. Christians are not tritheists, but monotheists. The underlying question is whether Christology – our understanding of Jesus – means that we see God so differently as to make the assertion that we believe in the same God merely vacuous. Or whether Jesus adds enormous depth to Christian understanding of God, but does not take it into a different realm. Christians will differ in their response to this question.

How Christians see the Holy Spirit is easier to explain. The Spirit is a way of describing the reality of the presence of God, within the individual, within the community of the church and within the wider world. Just as, in the Qur'an, Allah is described as being 'closer than our jugular vein', so the Holy Spirit is a way of describing God within whom 'we live and move and have our being' (cf. Acts 17:28). Just as, for a Muslim, true experience of God is not confined to the Muslim *ummah* (worldwide community), but is guaranteed there, so for a Christian the Holy Spirit knows no bounds and blows where he wills, but nevertheless is named within Christian experience.

In respect to the Muslim tradition, it is not that there is nothing more to be said about God than that God is God. There are ninety-nine beautiful names for God at the centre of the Muslim practice of *dhikr*, practising the remembrance of God. They describe something of the essence and activity of God. One example is the frequently used description *bismillah*: God is merciful in essence and practises mercy. For Christians who doubt whether Muslims worship the same God, it is a useful exercise to go through the ninety-nine names and see which ones they can own and which they find difficult or impossible to apply to God. The latter will invariably be a small minority. Many of them can be found within the Old Testament. Jesus may have transformed our understanding of God in certain ways, but, loyal Jew as he was, he never wished to negate what had come before him. This does not mean that the differences are insignificant. Nor does it mean that both traditions place the same meaning on words. But we may wish to err on the side of generosity rather than suspicion, not least because Christians themselves often differ greatly on their interpretation of vocabulary. The following extract is from the beginning of a litany based on the ninety-nine names, which can be used by Christians or in a Christian-Muslim gathering:

> You are the Merciful
> You are the Compassionate
> You are the King
> You are the Holy One
> You are the Fount of Peace
> You are the Protector of Faith
> You are the Guardian
> You are the Incomparable
> You are the Strongest

Response: Lord, hear us, have mercy upon us.[5]

Another way into this question is to consider the recorded prayers of each faith. Do they seem to be addressed to the same God, and do their sentiments echo a commonality of understanding? Kenneth Cragg's book *Common Prayer* gives numerous examples of such prayers.[6] Here are two of them:

> Praise be to God. O God, thou art the One to whom we give thanks. I pray to the Lord to forgive us for those things which we have done and those things which we shall do in the future. Lord God, drive away from us all sorrow and the envy of our enemies, and deliver us from the evil of this world and the next. *Abubakar Tafawa Balewa*

> My God and my Lord, eyes are at rest, stars are setting, hushed are the movements of birds in their nests, of monsters in the deep. And thou art the just who knows no change, the equity that swerveth not, the everlasting that passeth not away. The doors are locked, watched by their bodyguards. But thy door is open to him who calls on thee, my Lord, each lover is now alone with his beloved. Thou for me art the beloved One. *'Abd Al-'Aziz Al Dirini*

The *Oxford Book of Prayer*[7] also has an excellent section of prayers from all faiths:

> My soul, hearken unto me. Love thy Lord as a fish loves water. The more the water, the greater its joy, the greater the tranquillity of its body and mind. Without water it cannot live one watch of the day. Only god knows the anguish of its heart. *Harmindar Singh (Sikh)*

> When the heart is hard and parched up, come upon me with a shower of mercy. When grace is lost from life, come with a burst of song. When tumultuous work raises its din on all sides, shutting me out from beyond, come to me, my Lord of silence, with thy peace and rest. When my beggarly heart sits crouched, shut up in a corner, break open the door, my king, and come with the ceremony of a king. When desire blinds the mind with delusion and dust, O thou holy one, thou wakeful One, come with thy light and thy thunder.
> *Rabindranath Tagore (Hindu)*

> May I become a medicine for the sick and their physician, their support until sickness come not again. May I become an unfailing store for the wretched, and be the first to supply them with their needs. My own self and my pleasures, my righteousness, past, present and

future, may I sacrifice without regard, in order to achieve the welfare of all beings. *Santideva (Buddhist, AD 700)*

Of course, this does not mean that a Christian could say every prayer from another tradition, and vice versa. However, the fact that there is so much commonality must pose a question for those who hold that the God we worship is not the same. Perhaps the *sufi*, or mystical tradition of Islam, brings us closest to commonality. The experience of Sufi saints comes close to that of Christian mystics, as they try to describe the indescribable, the sense of being enveloped in God. An example is these words of Al-Ghazali's, the greatest of Sufi masters:

> Praise be to him who alone is to be praised. Praise him for his grace and favour. Praise him for his power and goodness. Praise him whose knowledge encompasses all things. O God, grant me light in my heart and light in my tomb. Light in my hearing and light in my seeing, light in my hair and light in my skin, light in my flesh and light in my blood and light in my bones. Light before me, light behind me, light to the right of me, light to the left of me, light above me, light beneath me. O god, increase my light and give me the greatest light of all. Of thy mercy grant me light, O thou most merciful. *Abu Hamid Al-Ghazali*

There are echoes here of the fifth verse of St Patrick's Breastplate: 'Christ be with me, Christ within me, Christ behind me, Christ before me ... ', and 1 John 1:5, 'God is light ... '.

For a Christian, the question of whether Jews worship the same God would seem to be a simple one. This is the God Jesus worshipped. Early Jewish understanding was of a tribal God, albeit a most powerful one, as is demonstrated in the clash between Yahweh and the local gods, the Baalim, in the time of Elijah. But gradually, God became universalised, notably in the creation stories in Genesis and in such psalms as Psalm 139, which declares that 'even the darkness is not dark to [God]', and affirms that God's Spirit is everywhere:

> Where can I go from your spirit?
> Or where can I flee from your presence?
> If I ascend to heaven, you are there;
> if I make my bed in Sheol, you are there.
> If I take the wings of the morning
> and settle at the farthest limits of the sea,
> even there your hand shall lead me,
> and your right hand shall hold me fast. (vv. 7–10)

We can note also Psalm 87:

> Among those who know me I mention Rahab and Babylon;
> Philistia too, and Tyre, with Ethiopia –
> 'This one was born there, they say.' (v. 4)

Most notable of all is Isaiah 45:5–7,

> I am the Lord, and there is no other;
> besides me there is no God.
> I arm you, though you do not know me,
> so that they may know, from the rising of the sun
> and from the west, that there is no one besides me;
> I am the Lord and there is no other.
> I form light and create darkness,
> I make weal and create woe;
> I the Lord do all these things.

God as the God of the whole earth is also seen in the prophets. In Amos 9:7, the writer affirms:

> Are you not like the Ethiopians to me,
> O people of Israel? says the Lord.
> Did I not bring Israel up from the land of Egypt,
> and the Philistines from Caphtor and the Arameans from Kir?

So also in Third Isaiah where we find this remarkable passage:

> On that day there will be a highway from Egypt to Assyria, and the Assyrian will come into Egypt, and the Egyptian into Assyria, and Egyptians will worship with the Assyrians. On that day, Israel will be the third with Egypt and Assyria, a blessing in the midst of the earth, whom the Lord of hosts has blessed, saying, 'Blessed be Egypt my people, and Assyria the work of my hands, and Israel my heritage.' (19:23–5)

A bold question arises by extension from this verse: can Jew, Christian and Muslim all be blessed as the work of God's hands? A similar and wider thought comes from Malachi 1:10–11:

> I will not accept an offering from your [Israel's] hands. For from the rising of the sun to its setting my name will be great among the nations, and in every place incense is offered to my name, and a pure offering; for my name is great among the nations, says the Lord of Hosts.

There are two challenges here. The first is against any Christian complacency that their worship is acceptable if their way of life belies their belief. The second raises the question of where true worship can be found. Is it within the three Abrahamic faiths – or can incense and pure offerings be found more widely?

This leads us onto the question of Hindus, Sikhs and others: do *they* worship the same God? And what of those Buddhists who claim not to worship God at all?

Sikhism

Sikhism is the simplest faith to relate to here. It is monotheist and focuses unambiguously on one scripture, one God, and the gift of God's grace. Anyone new to inter-religious experience would probably find a hospitable Sikh *Gurdwara* the easiest introduction. In the face of multifarious Hindu understandings of God, Guru Nanak defined God as follows:

> There is One supreme eternal reality; the true one; immanent in all things; sustainer of things; creator of all things; immanent in creation. Without fear or enmity; not subject to time; beyond birth and death; self-manifesting; known by the Guru's grace.

The monotheism is emphatic, and there are strong condemnations of idol worship: 'Apart from God there is no other. The Lord is both creator and cause' (AG 626[8]). The Gurus (mystical sages and teachers) saw God strongly in the natural world: 'The whole phenomenal world you see, O man, is the visible image of God. Yes, in it, I see the face of God' (AG 622).

The main way of revelation, however, is through God's word, *shabad*: 'The true creator is known by means of the *shabad*' (AG 688). 'The Guru's word is a shining jewel which reveals the divine by its light' (AG 1290). The main way of describing God, the indescribable, is through his *nam*, 'God revealed', similar to *shabad*. There are many hymns, and the phrase most often heard when visiting a *Gurdwara* is *Vahiguru*, which means 'Praise to the Guru' or, more succinctly, 'wonderful Lord'.

There are several phrases in the *Adi Granth*, the Sikh scripture, which remind Christians strongly of the Prologue to the Fourth Gospel: 'God is hidden in and enlightens every heart' (AG 597). 'God pervades all created beings; God creates all and assigns to all their tasks.' At the same time, immanence is balanced by transcendence: 'The one who permeates all hearts is transcendent too' (AG 294). God is the creator of all, and there is no sense of duality: 'Whatever God wills has happened; there is no other doer' (AG 154). God is also beyond gender: 'You are my father, you are my mother, you are my kinsman, you are my brother' (AG 103), words to warm a feminine Christian heart.

The main point of difference lies, as usual, in the place given to Jesus. He can be a great teacher, but not God, for 'God has no form or features' (AG 750). As so often, John's Prologue represents the stumbling block: 'the Word became flesh and lived among us' (1:14).

Hinduism

Hindus believe in countless Gods, often numbered in the millions, and so how can their belief or worship be likened to any of the monotheistic religions?

In order to answer this question we need to try to discover what lies behind the devotion (*bhakti*) to different gods, such as Vishnu, Rama, Sita, Krishna, Siva, Saraswati, Laksmi, Kali, and all the gods beyond number found in Indian villages, some with temples, some just stones under trees. By studying the scriptures, listening to the hymns of devotion and, above all, talking to Hindus educated in their faith, a different, if still complex picture emerges. God is seen in absolute and impersonal terms, as the ultimate reality (*Brahman*), the first cause of the universe, eternal, all pervading and all transcending. This *Brahman* is *neti, neti*, 'not this and not that'. In some forms of Hinduism, that is all that can be said, and the aim is to seek the union of the soul (*atman*) with *Brahman*. But other schools emphasise that God is also personal, and *Brahman* is 'truth, consciousness and bliss'. (Christians have likened this understanding to the Trinity.) As such, God can be worshipped as lord, king, judge, master, mother, father, husband, friend, beloved, creator, destroyer. These aspects can then be personified in the various deities, whose stories are recounted in the scriptures. Oneness is then manifest in multiplicity. These include the *avataras* – the gods such as Vishnu, in particular, but also Rama and Krishna – who at certain times in history, whenever evil was reigning supreme and righteousness needed to be reasserted, took various incarnate forms.

Oneness is emphasised in the *Rigveda*, which asserts, 'Truth is one but the sages call it by manifold names' (1.164.46). These names and forms can be male or female, and normally worship of the deity is balanced between the two. Aspects of God are enshrined in the image and in the stories around the image. For example, Saraswati is the goddess of wisdom; Lakshmi the goddess of wealth; Ganesha the remover of obstacles; Krishna the divine child, beloved, friend, teacher and liberator, and, in the *Bhagavadgita* (the most read Hindu scripture in recent times) both the immanent and transcendent God: 'I am the goal, the upholder, the lord, the witness, the abode, the refuge and the friend. I am the origin and the disillusion, the ground, the resting place and the perishable seed' (9.18).

This complexity means that there can be no easy answer to the question of whether Hinduism can be compared to a monotheistic religion. It partly depends on the particular Hindu. There is freedom in the complexity of Hindu faith to envisage God or the gods in many ways. But where God is seen as personal and transcendent, and is affirmed as one, though in many forms, then it is hard to say categorically that Hindus are not worshipping the same God. And, indeed, if there is only one God, then that must be the case, unless they are captured by illusory or demonic forces. Some early missionaries talked about the satanic darkness of Hinduism. But as time went by and they encountered their scriptures and the devout and often saintly lives of Hindu teachers and ordinary worshippers, they began to change their simplistic views. This applied too at the mystical level, where the yogic and meditative practices of Hindu sages seemed to lead them into the kind of oneness with the divine, which Christian mystics also affirmed. And certain Christians trod the path of integration, as they found at the centre a commonality between Hinduism and Christianity, such as the spiritual pioneers Abishiktananda, Bede Griffiths (see below), Sister Vandana and Sister Ishpriya.

This is some of the background information a Christian visiting a Hindu temple needs to have. Simply to write off what is seen as 'idol worship', only reveals ignorance, as well as being very hurtful to the always graceful Hindu host. The visitor is likely to be confused and needs to ask questions. But such questions should be asked with a real wish to learn and respect. The Hindu respondent may use the word 'idol'. It is likely he or she means 'image' or 'symbol'. We can remember that the New Testament sees Jesus as the 'image of the invisible God' (Col. 1:15). The opening chapter of Genesis reminds us that we are all made in the image of God. In 1 Corinthians 15:49 we read, 'Just as we have borne the image of the man of dust, we will also bear the image of the man of heaven.' Of course, an image can become an idol, so human beings can make themselves a God, as, for example, the Roman emperors and Hitler. In Christian tradition, Mary can be the greatest symbol of devotion, obedience and motherhood, but in popular tradition she can become deified. The bread and wine of the eucharist bear enormous meaning, as indicating Jesus' real presence amongst us. But, to the casual observer at least, some kinds of devotional practice would indicate that the elements are being worshipped as idols.

Buddhism

Here, at least, the answer appears clear: Buddhists do not worship the same God as Christians, because they do not believe in one God. All their devotion is centred on the Buddha and his teachings. Elizabeth Harris helpfully quotes from Ven. Bhikkhu Bodhi, a Theravada monk (Theravada Buddhism is the southern and oldest form of Buddhism and is found in Sri Lanka, Burma, Thailand, Cambodia, Laos):

> We do not regard the Buddha either as personal God or as an *avatar* ... For Theravada Buddhism, the Buddha always remains a human being, yet the supreme human being, 'the extraordinary man' ... his role, for Buddhism, always remains that of an exemplar and a teacher, the Supreme Teacher; he is never conceived either as world creator or as personal saviour. He 'saves' others only showing them the path by which they can save themselves.[9]

He is, of course, given theistic attributes, such as boundless loving kindness, compassion, joy and equanimity. But he remains a man, however much popular devotion may seem to deify him. Various other gods also appear in such popular devotion, but they are subordinate to the Buddha and appear to involve the absorption of local religions and of animistic forces. These can include the gods of Hinduism, images of which can be seen in Buddhist temples, indicating the way that Buddhism came out of Hinduism. These gods may be approached to ask for particular benefits or to avoid particular disasters.

Mayahana Buddhism, the northern form of Buddhism, is found in such countries as Nepal, China, Korea, Japan and Vietnam. Tibetan Buddhism is often included, though it is also called Vajrayana Buddhism. It has a more developed concept of the Buddha, in which the human and historical Buddha is supplemented and to a large extent transcended by the cosmic Buddha as eternal, ever-present and stretching across and beyond time and space.

Buddhists practise meditation rather than pray and should not be enveloped in a general concept of spiritual practice. However, in terms of ideals and the importance of wisdom, compassion, detachment and discipline, Christians have always had much to learn from Buddhists. The place of the Buddha as exemplar can be likened to that of Christ for Christians. However, the two faiths' view of God will always differ.

The question of praying or worshipping with a person of another faith is often confused with the question of salvation. An example is the famous

Open Letter to the Leadership of the Church of England signed by two thousand clergy which was published in *The Times* in 1992. They wrote that gatherings for interfaith prayer and worship conflict with the duty to proclaim the Christian gospel, and 'imply that salvation is offered by God not only through Jesus Christ but by other means, and thus deny his uniqueness and finality as the only Saviour.' Out of compassion, I might pray with someone whom I am convinced is on the way to eternal damnation: in such a situation my primary concern theologically should logically be to pray for their conversion and rescue from such a fate. But if I am prepared to leave that question to God, praying with someone of another faith is similar to praying with anyone else. When I am called to be with parents whose son has just been killed in a road accident, I respond not to speculation about their eternal destiny, but their need at the time.

Practicalities of interfaith prayer and worship

The more interfaith encounter there is, the more the possibilities and difficulties that may arise in this area. As with the story of Christian ecumenism, if we never meet in any significant way, questions of prayer and worship together will not arise. There may be much to learn from this precedent, radically different as it is in some ways. For example, issues related to sharing the eucharist between the Roman Catholic Church and other Churches arise more often because of the level and frequency of contact. It was only after the Second World War that Roman Catholics were first permitted to say the Lord's Prayer in public with their fellow Christians. Fifty years later anything is possible except the sharing of the sacrament of unity. It is the very success of the ecumenical movement that makes this more and more difficult for those who are not Roman Catholics to understand. But this does not mean that the sacrament is never shared. There are individuals who decide for themselves, and there are particular contexts such as ecumenical conferences where occasional sharing takes places. This has no sanction, but it happens. Moreover, these restrictions are one way. From the Anglican perspective there is no objection to an Anglican taking communion in a Roman Catholic mass. It is rather sensitivity to the ecumenical reality that will prevent someone doing this. We will see many of the ecumenical issues mirrored in what follows as we look at the practicalities of interfaith worship and prayer.

We turn now to look at official church reports and studies on interfaith prayer. Prayer together, or alongside each other – an important distinction – can arise through personal encounter, family occasions, group dialogue meetings, civic, national or international occasions, or through response to emergencies. Preparations can be meticulous for formal occasions, while requests for prayer in personal situations are often spontaneous and necessitate an immediate response.

It must be understood that being in favour of prayer or worship with people of other faiths in particular circumstances does not mean being in favour of it on all and every occasion. Nor does it mean that because one is prepared to be inclusive of people of some faiths, or some people of those faiths, that one is thereby saying anything goes. There will need to be criteria, expressed or implicit. However, particularly in this country, where, for all our often defeatist attitude, Christians remain in a large majority with much inherited power, these criteria should be generous. In another kind of country, where Christians are persecuted or beleaguered or a tiny minority, then it may well be necessary to have strict rules, for the sake of survival.

Writing about the eucharist in *The Open Church*, Jürgen Moltmann[10] says that in the light of Christ, who opened his arms wide on the cross, we should be expected to justify not every inclusion but every exclusion. Yet, so often the Church has acted in exactly the opposite way. In connection with interfaith prayer, then, I believe we should look to say yes, rather than no. This does not mean that on occasion we do not end up saying no. But we look first to include, which will mean at times taking risks. Risk is not in itself wrong, if we are clear it is for Christ's sake, and not for gimmick or for our glorification or to shock more conservative Christians. If we do make a mistake from time to time, can Christ not look after himself? A senior South African priest was asked at a local Church of England Deanery Synod what his key observation about this Church was. He replied quietly but firmly, 'You are a church which finds it so difficult to take risks.'

How then are we to establish our criteria? Boy George, in an interview published in *The Independent* on 9 September 1992, said, 'God to me is total, unconditional love. I have Sufi, Christian, Buddhist friends, and I respect what they believe in, and in their temples I bow down. I believe there is a force out there that matches us step by step. I am not explaining it brilliantly, but it is a feeling for me.' This would seem at first a very naïve view. But even here there are criteria: God is unconditional love; the force out there is personal, walking with us. There is also an owning of experience: 'It is a feeling for me.'

Talking with the Samaritan woman Jesus comes forward with a clear principle which springs directly from dialogue:

> The woman said to him, ' ... Our ancestors worshipped on this mountain [Mt Gerizim], but you say that the place where people

must worship is in Jerusalem.' Jesus said to her, 'Woman, believe me, the hour is coming when you will worship the Father neither on this mountain nor in Jerusalem ... God is spirit and those who worship him must worship in spirit and in truth.' (John 4:19–21, 24)

In other words, it is not place or words or ritual that are to be determining factors, but integrity, spiritual heart and direction to the creator God.

Private prayer

How we pray with another individual will depend on the relationship with the person concerned, and the feel of what is right. It may occur in the home, within a hospital ward, at times of bereavement and between neighbours. It may occur before a meal when grace is said, or before going on a journey. We may be asked to pray, or we may feel it right to offer to pray. Clergy would perhaps find this easier to do, but the witness of being ready to pray as a lay person is all the more profound. How the prayer is said will depend on a number of circumstances:

- the nature of the request
- the religion of the person concerned, and the appropriateness of particular concepts
- their own background within the religion they come from – within Islam, whether they are Sufi-influenced, for example, or within Hinduism, whether they come from a Bhakti tradition
- the trust that has been established with the person concerned
- our confidence in how to respond – if we are not used to praying with other Christians, then words may not come easily. But in the end, as with any prayer, it is not the eloquence of the vocabulary, but the sincerity of heart and intention that is central
- our determination to pray, and not preach, which is quite inappropriate. Whatever words we are using, we are holding the person up before God and surrounding them with his love, as shown in Jesus Christ
- whether or not we are being asked to pray as Christians. We do not need to make explicit what is implicit.

Our use of the name of Jesus will depend on the circumstances. But if it is a prayer for healing, we can use the name of Jesus – those asking for prayer probably recognise Jesus as a healer.

Another situation is when we are asked to pray for someone, but not in their presence. My travel agent, who is a Muslim, was awaiting a bypass operation. He was very worried about the operation and asked for my prayers. When he came through safely, he said my prayers were part of this, and he asked me to continue praying for him. As with all prayer, it is important, particularly for clergy, to remember to pray for someone when asked to do so and not just say yes and then forget. This is even more important when it is a person of another faith who is placing trust in us.

Hindus may ask us to join them as friends for a family function, which may be accompanied by certain rituals. On one occasion I was asked to breakfast in the home of a Brahmin. This was proceeded by daily *puja* (prayers). At the end of the rituals, we were offered blessed water and sandalwood paste, which I accepted. It did not mean that I was accepting the rituals, but the integrity of the welcome and the sincerity of this prayer, offered daily for thousands of years, as the foundation for the life of a family whom I knew well for their loving kindness. It would have been churlish to reject what was offered.

The same applied when I attended a Hindu funeral, which took place in a house in Birmingham. The sacred flame was waved over the four corners of the deceased body by a brother and then passed to all who were present. I held my hands over it, as others did, and commended the deceased to God. The Brahmin priests had chanted numerous words, which were clearly very meaningful. But I was there as a Christian and a privileged guest and friend. If I had been given the opportunity to offer a Christian prayer, I would have done so, but I offered it anyway in the heart.

People from other faiths may also offer to pray for us. On one occasion a Sufi Muslim friend came to see me when I had a bad and persistent headache. He showed sympathy and offered to pray for me. To my surprise he put his hand on my head, prayed freely and then blew over my forehead. I did not find it difficult to accept this. Here was a friend offering the best he could, and, whatever terms he might use, I could interpret this as the healing spirit of God.

Regular prayer between two people of different faiths may also develop. This used to happen with one of my Muslim friends. Each time we met we would have a discussion on a particular topic, be it religious, community, international or family affairs, and then talk about our scriptures together. Then, at the end of our meeting, we got in the habit of offering a prayer one after the other as kind of prayer partners. I cannot recall who began this process – I imagine it was the Muslim since we normally met at his house. At one point he faced an enormous family issue. He summoned me to his house, asked me to take certain practical actions, and then asked me to pray. If we are not sure how to pray for a matter of deep concern. we can suggest remaining quiet and offering an issue to God. To sum up, if trust is there, we cannot go far wrong. And if trust is not there, probably the question of prayer will not arise.

A remarkable Indian priest in Handsworth, Birmingham, Jemima Prasadam, has told me a number of deeply encouraging stories, which depend entirely on the hard-won trust she has built up since arriving in this 'toughest' of parishes in 1996. She began by visiting her church members, who are mostly of Caribbean origin, in their homes. Their neighbours, the majority of whom belong to other faiths, began to pass comment: 'Why is this Indian visiting a West Indian? You must be a social worker.' 'Yes, kind of!' When visiting a 91-year-old they remarked, 'You must be a health visitor?' 'Yes, you can call me that.' The children who came from the *madrassa*, began to say, 'Hello, hello'. She was then seen visiting a white woman on a Saturday. A bright Asian girl said, 'You must be a home help, coming on a Saturday!' 'Yes, I do help. I pray for people in their homes and in the church.' 'Ah, we understand, you are a woman of prayer, even though you are not a Muslim!' There followed a dialogue about prayer sitting on the pavement, after which she was invited to a Muslim house. From that day onwards she has been known as 'Auntie Vicar'! Her advice about building up trust, which anyone can put into practice, is to begin with attentive listening to *their* stories of God. They will then listen to our stories. No one has a monopoly on the creator God. It is essential that we remove the tag of 'arrogant', which so many Christians are accused of being.

It is because of such trust that she can take what some would see as risks – which are not risks – such as being invited to *Iftar*, the meal which breaks a fast in a Muslim household, and taking her Bible with her, and reading it openly when the family are saying their prayers. This can lead to discussion, often beginning with the children asking questions.

She was very moved one day when a leading local Sikh priest said she looked very tired. 'Yes, I need to recharge my spiritual batteries.' 'I want you to feel better, physically and spiritually. Why not come to our *Gurdwara*? It is a quiet place, and you can read our holy book, or you can bring your holy books, and read them. We can even give you a quiet room. For the same God is here. God is God!' Christians tend to agonise. Others just do!

She makes the sign of the cross when she enters a *Gurdwara* or temple. She is clear about her freedom in Christ. She feels it when she hears the Sikh call to worship, 'Long live the truth, long live the Lord's name'. The whole atmosphere takes her back to Old Testament monotheism and she affirms that for Sikhs the *Gurdwara* is, as it is translated, 'the door to God'.

Beyond this, there is what Roman Catholics call 'dialogue of depth'.

Through prayer and meditation, differences are transcended. Words then become superfluous. This place has been reached sometimes between Hindus and Christians in ashrams in India, between Buddhists and Roman Catholic monks in Japan or Europe, and between some Christians and Sufi Muslims. Such experiences may be rare, but they show that unity is realisable. It was described by Father Bede Griffiths before he died. He was the leader of *Shantivanam*, the well-known ashram in South India where Hindus were as at home as Christians, where the mass was celebrated daily in a deeply Indian way, and where yoga and contemplation were taught as part of a daily programme. He said that Hinduism and Christianity were miles apart at the level of doctrine, but that at the level of the spirit they could meet at the closest level 'at the heart of the lotus' (which Christians would call 'Christ within'). Sister Ishpriya, a Catholic nun, wears saffron to indicate that she is making a journey of cultural and religious disarmament, as she enters into the world of Hindu mystical experience.

I shared an experience of great depth with a Thai Buddhist called Fuengsin. She was married to a Roman Catholic and had one son. Only five feet tall, she gave her life to being a voluntary Buddhist chaplain and teaching Buddhism. She and I became dialogue partners and led numerous classes together. She once described her idea of heaven as being in such dialogue with friends. Her sentiment echoed that of an Indian dance group who portray Jesus meeting different faiths by him dancing with each one and eventually with them all together! Dialogue does not have to be heavy, but can be fun!

Fuengsin suddenly became very ill with cancer, and I was with her through her journey through death. She asked for my prayers while I was with her in her pain, and I prayed for her at the eucharist, which I told her I was doing. One evening, I was visiting when her son came. He said that he wanted to pray with his mother. He whispered to me that he did not know what to say. She heard this and understood his difficulty. She placed his hand on her diseased stomach and said, 'Pray to Jesus for me'. Theologically, Buddhists and Christians are far apart about the very notion of such prayer, but she gave him the confidence to pray.

One day, I received a message to come to the Roman Catholic hospice, since she was dying and her monks had been summoned from London to do the last rites. She was lying on her bed now wheeled into the chapel. There was a delay, and surrounded by her husband and others, I read Psalm 23 and offered a prayer of commendation. When the monks arrived, they brought a Buddha statue, flowers and holy water. Where were they to put these? I indicated they should put them on the altar, the only table there! There was a beautiful ceremony of words and chanting, encouraging her to let go and surrender herself to the *dhamma* (nirvana). That night she died. I noticed that above the altar and her now tiny body was a crucifix, Jesus with open arms. Those arms, I felt, were receiving her, as the arms of the God of love, while for her the surrender was to the age-long Buddhist traditions that had served her so well. Perhaps an example of mutual inclusivism!

I was asked to speak at her funeral. I emphasised what she had taught me and then read 1 Corinthians 13, which I felt summed up the qualities of love that I had seen in her. I also joined in a remarkable liturgy which involved each person touching the shoulder of the person in front, so that there was a human chain through the hundred or so people, and respond-ing to the instruction from the monk to let her go by forgiving her what she had done wrong to us – nothing! – and asking her to let go what we had done to her. This enables *karma* to be released. We were then asked to spread compassion from her, through each other, to all our absent family members, to the rest of the world and all of creation!

This story, which I have told at length, shows what can be learnt from one friendship, and how words of dialogue become a dialogue of the Spirit, a dialogue of depth.

Prayer in groups

I am concerned here with prayer that arises in ongoing dialogue groups (see also chapter 1). In a Hindu-Christian group prayer will probably arise quickly. Hindus will find no problem in praying with Christians because of the inclusiveness of their understanding of faith. They are likely to venerate Jesus, and prayer can be offered in the name of Jesus without hesitation. There may be more sensitivity from the Christian side, because Hindu prayers are likely to mention the names of Krishna, Rama, or other Hindu deities. There is also likely to be chanting in Sanskrit or some other Indian language.

In this semi-public context, we can bring in an important distinction *between prayer with each other, and prayer alongside each other.* Prayer *alongside* each other means that a person from a faith offers a prayer integral to that faith and members of the other faith are committed to respecting that prayer, but may not feel they can pray it. Prayer *with* each other means that people of the other faith enter into the prayer and own it as their own. The latter clearly requires more trust and experience of each other. It is important that people are given the space to take either position. This may depend to a large extent on how long each person has been in the group and where they are as Christians. Those who have an inclusive approach may not see a problem. But that does not make them superior to those who do have difficulties and with integrity are attempting to find their own way.

Groups can be encouraged to take steps towards prayer at the right time. The first step will perhaps be silence together; the second step will be to make prayer intentions followed by silence; the third step the actual use of prayers, either prepared and formal, or informal around the themes of a meeting. Prayer is the natural result of being together; if it is not, we end up doing everything together – speaking together, arguing together, eating together, taking action together – but not doing the distinctive thing that religious people do: praying.

We can be too careful with words. At the beginning of the first Gulf War, Christian members of a group went to a mosque. After offering solidarity, I was asked by the Muslim leader and co-leader of our group to pray. I prayed very carefully, not mentioning the name of Jesus. However, I was put to shame as my friend offered prayer as a Muslim: 'May those who are now dying in terrible ways in the deserts of the Middle East, whether Muslim or Christian or Jew, know a better life with God, in the name of Moses, peace be upon him, of Jesus, peace be upon him, and of Muhammad, peace be upon him.'

My final example is, sadly, a negative one. An eirenic Buddhist monk from Sri Lanka stayed for three months as Visiting Fellow in the United College of the Ascension. I was embarrassed when Christian mission students from around the world expounded understandings of Christian theology which would inevitably consign him, as a non believer, to outer darkness. He reassured me, 'Even if someone rejects the possibilities of interfaith dialogue, they are nearly always kind, or at least civil to me. If anyone appears unfriendly, I remember them in my meditation, spread kindness towards them, and they usually become friendlier. One person found me difficult, but I found he had had some major difficulties with people of other faiths, and I understood why he felt as he did.'

A colleague asked him to conduct a meditation in the weekly common prayer time held between Selly Oak Colleges. Those from the United College of the Ascension came in considerable numbers. Another Christian college decided officially to discourage their students from attending, although one staff member bravely still came. The monk led the meditation in a characteristically inclusive way, encouraging participants to focus on Jesus while he focused upon the Buddha. It was a loving kind-ness meditation, *Metta*, which he likened, for Christians, to God's love. We were asked to evoke compassion for ourselves, for our families, friends and neighbours, for those to whom we are indifferent, for our enemies, and finally for all living beings. He ended by saying, 'I know it is your custom to say the Grace. Could someone please lead the Grace?' I thought of a monastery in the hills near Kyoto in Japan, a country where deep encounter across boundaries is part of the religious culture. In the prayer hall of the monastery there stands as a focus for meditation a sculpture of the Buddha engaged in dialogue with Jesus. This, of course, is impossible historically, but is a fascinating possibility in the realm of the imagination. It seemed to come near to the spirit of some of the discussions between this disciple of the Buddha and today's disciples of Jesus.

My reflection on this incident can stand for the whole chapter. Firmly rooted, we can be bold in our imagination, and take risks for Christ's sake. A good motto would be the Victorian hymn of F. Faber, also quoted in my book *Encounter in the Spirit*.[11]

> But we make his love too narrow
> By false limits of our own
> And we magnify his strictness
> With a zeal he will not own.

Preoccupation with sound doctrine and fear of syncretism can sadly block the Spirit who blows where he/she wills, and who is prepared to say, 'not even in Israel have I found such faith … ' (cf. Luke 7:9).

Public occasions

These can be divided into two main types of occasion. The first, and easiest, are times of emergency. Recent examples are the aftermath of 9/11, the bombing of Afghanistan, the beginning of the second Gulf War and the Gujarat earthquake of 2002. It is important that there is an infrastructure already in place, such as a Council of Faiths or a Faith Leaders' Forum, which can quickly initiate a response of this kind (see pp. 39ff.). These occasions should have as high a profile as possible, with media coverage if it can be arranged, so that the solidarity between faiths can be demonstrated. There will always be those who suggest that religions are contributing to the problem; in some situations this may be the case but it is important to show that it need not be so. Public events need to be advertised quickly through the media and faith organisations. As many faiths as possible need to participate, each being given equal weight. This means the voice of Jains or Bahais is equal to Muslims or Christians, which can be humbling for the major faiths.

Careful preparation needs to be made. Time limits should be adhered to, which means giving less time than is available to each member, since most will overrun. It should be made clear that this is not a time for speeches, but for readings and prayer. At a prayer time for Gujarat, with the TV cameras present, a Muslim suggested that the earthquake was an act of God showing his displeasure at the extremism of political Hinduism. This embarrassed all, including the Muslims present. Political debate is for elsewhere. Realistically, we should not expect this type of media event to be a spiritual experience but rather a demonstration of unity. It is worth beginning the event by saying something like, 'We welcome you to this occasion, when each faith will offer its prayer for peace. We ask you all to respect those prayers, and join in if you feel able.' No one's conscience is then being trampled upon.

More profound have been two other occasions. On the eve of the second Gulf War, we called a Jewish/Christian/Muslim prayer meeting in a church hall. About sixty people attended. It had a great effect on us all, as prayers and readings were offered, both formal and informal. We ended by offering the peace to each other, and sharing a common prayer, which we read out from a card from Pax Christi (see below). It was moving to see the Imam holding his card with a Christian neighbour. With all the tensions that exist between Muslims and Jews over Palestine, the event had a second level of meaning. Though we may not prevent war, this kind of event can help to keep the peace locally. In the hall, there was a large cross. No one asked for it to be removed, and we would not have done so. It spoke strongly to me of the unspoken presence of the crucified one, suffering with our sinful world.

Another example of public solidarity took place after the destruction of the mosque in Ayodhya in North India, causing more than a thousand deaths there. There were also attacks on temples in the Midlands. We called all faiths together. At the meeting faith leaders shared their thoughts about the situation, followed by mixed faith discussion groups. Each group lit a candle for peace in India and the Midlands, and silence was kept. This was very moving, and was all covered live on Asian as well as English language local radio.

A recent prayer event for peace and reconciliation was occasioned by the visit to Leicester of twenty-eight Japanese people from Christian, Buddhist and Shinto faiths. They have visited a different city each year since 1945. They are mostly now old, and it was powerful to experience the Buddhists chanting at considerable length and the mysterious rituals of the Shinto faith, and hear the Bishop of Yokohama speak, translated into English by an old American missionary. People from the Jewish, Muslim, Sikh, Hindu and Bahai faiths all gathered together. The event, which took place in St Philip's Church, was deeply appreciated by elderly members, who belong to the generation which fought the Japanese. Explicit mention of the name of Hindu gods as part of the Hindu contribution did not spoil the generous spirit of the occasion. We had the Asian TV company MATV filming the whole event (see also p. 162), and they network their productions not only in Britain but also within India. Again, media involvement is important, not for its own sake, but because of the message it can give.

It is essential that these public occasions should be well prepared and sensitively guided, with people not being hurried but working within necessary time limits. However, there should be some freedom of the spirit; not all will follow the instructions given, and it is important to be relaxed about the outcome, since surely God appreciates the spirit of the occasion, not the letter of instruction. At the event I have just described, the Japanese arrived fifteen minutes late, and the Japanese Buddhists chanted for fifteen minutes, not three, against all stereotypes!

Another type of crisis is a sudden personal tragedy. A young person gets knocked over by a car and is clearly dying. A crowd gathers. We happen to be passing. Clearly, the person is Asian – we do not know the faith. We are asked to pray. What do we pray, and how? There is no time for preparation, we just have to react from our heart.

The second type of public occasion is one which occurs as part of a regular routine of events. Civic services are an example. We may, for example, be confronted by the challenge of an event at which there is a mayor of a faith other than Christianity present, necessitating the inclusion of prayers of other faiths within a Christian building. In a multi-religious city, it may be that prayers from various faiths should be included even if there is a Christian mayor. I was asked to supply a prayer to a Hindu, who had been asked to pray to support a Hindu mayor!

There are other occasions such as prayer for the millennium. In Birmingham, after all the faiths had prayed, the Bishop closed using a very neutral prayer. When he asked me afterwards what I thought, I reflected that other faiths had prayed in their own idiom, and he could have used a Trinitarian prayer without difficulty. Here again we see the problem of over-sensitivity.

Much more powerful were the prayers at the inauguration of the presidency of Nelson Mandela. He insisted that all the main faiths pray for the new South Africa, since all were to be key partners. Desmond Tutu concluded by offering a fully Trinitarian prayer, ending 'through Jesus Christ Our Lord'. Here it was entirely right to offer a full Christian prayer. What was clear was that the era of a country legally bound to the Afrikaans Church was over. The whole occasion was a symbol of the rainbow people of God.

There are an increasing number of occasions when prayers are being said jointly for state functions. In 2003 an Imam friend became the first Muslim to share in leadership of prayers in the House of Commons, along with a Christian priest and a rabbi. Other occasions have included a memorial service to those who died as a result of the tragedy of 9/11. To be included on local and national occasions is of more than symbolic importance. Prince Charles has expressed a wish, when king, to be known as Defender of Faiths, and not just Defender of the Faith. This may be unlikely to happen, but is seen by many as an honourable intention.

Another very significant occasion is the annual Commonwealth Service. This was mentioned specifically in the Open Letter alluded to above (see p. 94). One of the paragraphs states, 'We are deeply concerned about gatherings for interfaith worship and prayer involving Christian people. These include the Interfaith Commonwealth Day Observance in Westminster Abbey and such other events in some of the cathedrals and churches of England, whether they refer to Jesus Christ or whether such references are minimal or excluded.' It is a service attended by the Queen and instigated by her. The Dean of Westminster of the time was very hurt by this attack. He told me that he had no choice but to make it interfaith, since the Queen herself desired that it represent the diversity of faiths within the Commonwealth. The service is an occasion to celebrate the wonderful diversity within this remarkable, if unexpected, successor to the Empire. It represents a deeply Christian ideal about the breaking down of barriers between people. The letter went on, 'We believe these events, however motivated, conflict with the Christian duty to proclaim the Gospel.' I would argue that the very inclusion of people of all faiths within the heart of this ancient Abbey is itself a proclamation of the gospel of the love and openness of God. Jesus came to proclaim the Kingdom of God, a place of righteousness and compassion and peace, and that is the intention of prayers in this service.

On such occasions, careful preparation is of the essence, and the following kinds of issues need to be considered:

- What is the intention of the occasion? Is it essential that worship is involved?
- Will the possible benefits outweigh anticipated controversy?
- Is it a Christian service, in which other faiths are invited to contribute, or is it a multi-faith event?
- Where should it be held? If in Christian premises, why? If in a hall, why? If in a building of another faith, why? There may be a pragmatic reason, such as that the church has the best premises. It may be that it is an annual occasion and, if that is the case, why should it not sometimes be in a church? If it is in a church, it should not involve removing what can

be seen to some as offensive items (such as a cross), any more than Hindus would remove an image of Krishna. Nor should it involve covering anything up, as some, in my view, misguided Christians have done.

- Symbols should not be imported into a church. The emphasis should be, for all participants including Christian, on what is inclusive. I heard of one occasion on which the hymn 'What a friend we have in Jesus', with the words 'Precious Saviour, still our refuge ... ', was chosen. This may be fine for Hindus, but if Jews and Muslims are present, it is likely to cause offence, or at least an uncomfortable feeling.

- It should not be assumed that everyone is at the same place as the most enthusiastic interfaith leaders of an event. An aim should be to widen the circle of sympathetic persons, not to further reduce it, which means erring on the side of care rather than shocking people into conformity. The danger of an unseen divide between 'the enlightened' and others should be avoided at all costs.

- The eucharist is not a suitable vehicle for such a service. If all are invited to participate, of whatever faith, this may enable very liberal Christians to rejoice, and Hindus and Sikhs to feel included, but it will alienate Muslims and Jews. Furthermore, it will overemphasise the fellowship aspect of the meal and separate it from the explicit witness to the saving death of Christ. Opening the eucharist up to others, even with the best of motives, only causes major stumbling blocks not just to people of other faiths, but also to some Christians, who participate and feel uncomfortable or just stay away.

- An event which drifts towards being 'new age' in nature, should also be treated with caution. In Birmingham Cathedral about ten years ago, there was a One World Week service with the theme of creation. Jonathon Porritt, from Friends of the Earth, was invited as speaker, and each faith given the opportunity to contribute. The controversy was intensified when it was agreed that each person tie a ribbon round the wrist of their neighbour, which was linked explicitly with a Hindu ceremony of brotherhood and sisterhood. The priest blew a conch shell repeatedly as a sign of *Om* and chanted a Sanskrit chant, naming Hindu gods. Dance followed to celebrate creation. While all this may seem innocuous to many, the preparation was not careful enough, and this resulted in uniting opposition to the New Age with opposition to interfaith prayer and worship. One deanery officially boycotted it, and some picketed it. It was not good for the cause of interfaith dialogue.

A second area is where people of other faiths come to Christian worship, and I list here some opportunities and cautions:

- It can be very powerful to invite someone of another faith to speak within a regular Sunday Christian worship service. In practice, this has normally been a Jew or a Muslim, but it could be extended to other faiths. The talk can focus on a particular subject, or, in the case of a Jew, on a particular passage of the Hebrew Bible. It is important that there is Christian input also.
- Intercessions and silence are an important part of any Christian worship and can be very moving when broadened to cover the concerns of those present from other faiths.
- In all Christian worship, it is probably helpful to preach or speak as though there were people of other faiths present. Many have become aware of the need to take care not to make inadvertent antisemitic comments. This is easier to avoid in preaching than apparently in some biblical texts! We also need to change our mindset with respect to other faiths, particularly Islam. We must avoid using intercession as a vehicle for preaching or giving unnecessary messages. For example, while on holiday in Northern Scotland in 2003, I heard a prayer both for the well-being of Christian Iraqis in the aftermath of the war and that other Iraqis might be rescued from a false prophet (Muhammad) and deceitful religious leaders (Muslim clerics).
- A colleague asked a Hindu group to come for midnight eucharist. To his amazement, fifty of them came on block. Some took off their shoes, some did not; some came for a blessing, others did not. The problem was that the congregation was not prepared for this sudden advent, and there was a mixed reaction to what was an amazing opportunity. The predominant emotion felt by the Hindus was a sense of holiness. Another opportunity is to invite a group from another faith to witness the eucharist, and to follow this up with discussion, during which it can be explained how this rather mysterious occasion links with the heart of Christian theology.
- Our church buildings are great assets, particularly if they have stained glass windows, statues, vestments, etc., which can be used as teaching aids. We can also explain Christian prayers, collects, etc., for *lex orandi, lex credendi* – what we believe is shown by our way of praying.
- Another opportunity is afforded when a couple who are not Christians choose to be married in church. All people have the right to be married in their parish church, whether they are baptised or not. This will usually mean a mixed-faith marriage, but in theory could include two Hindus or two Sikhs living in a village. By doing so they are opting for a Christian marriage, which will need to follow the liturgy of the church concerned. In the Church of England, this will mean receiving a

Trinitarian blessing, while the Methodist Church allows the use of the simple term 'God', as rings are exchanged. Further prayers and readings can be added from the other faith to enable the service to become inclusive, but the core needs to be Christian. Symbols can helpfully be included, such as breaking a glass, as in a Jewish wedding, and arranging a canopy. A Brahmin convert told me about his marriage to an Irish Christian. His own family were reluctant to come to a church wedding. He encouraged the priest to use the text 'Perfect love casts out all fear', to reassure them there was nothing to worry about.

A third area to be considered is when Christians are invited to attend worship by another faith:

- We should be prepared and ready to do what is needed to show respect. It is essential that we take off our shoes, and I have had to ask some Christians not to come, if they are not prepared to do that. Those who object have claimed that doing this would mean acknowledging the reality of the deity being worshipped there. They would not accept that it is a cultural gesture shared with Asian Christians. Max Warren, who has a great understanding of mission as Christian presence, says:

> Our first task in approaching another people, another culture, is to take off our shoes, for the place we are approaching is holy. Else we may find ourselves treading on men's dreams ... We have to try and sit where they sit, to enter sympathetically into the pains and griefs and joys of their history, and see how those pains and griefs and joys have determined the premises of their argument. We have, in a word, to be 'present' with them.[12]

- We should not do things we are uncomfortable about. This may include such gestures as falling prostrate before the Guru Granth Sahib (the Sikh scriptures), because we feel we should do as Sikhs do, rather than showing respect by standing in front of the book before sitting down; holding our hands over the sacred flame, after it has been waved before a deity; and consuming blessed food. It may even include being asked to wave the flame before the deity ourselves, considered a special privilege for a Hindu, and therefore a sign that we are being honoured. Politeness should not lead us to cross a line that we do not feel happy about.
- We should be aware of Paul's teaching and respect the conscience of the weaker brother or sister (1 Cor. 8:7ff.; 1 Cor. 10:23ff.). This applies particularly to clergy, who can put pressure on lay people by doing things that they have come to feel happy about through experience. We should give space for people not to follow.

- Clergy need to remember, if they are with a group, that they are there as representative persons, and not just as individuals who are free to follow their conscience.
- Helpful intra Christian discussion can be held on texts such as those in Corinthians mentioned above, in which Paul speaks about his personal freedom to eat meat dedicated to idols, because those idols are nothing. Another interesting text for discussion is Jesus' words that it is not what goes into a person that contaminates, but what comes out (Mark 7:18ff.).
- When visiting a mosque, the situation as regards women needs to be explained carefully beforehand. If Christian women are welcome, and not Muslim women, then that needs to be talked through. Some Christian women may not want to attend out of what they see as solidarity with their Muslim sisters. If they go, they can raise questions afterwards, but should not go resenting what they will experience.
- Christians should also have explained to them that joining in the bodily gestures in Muslim prayer, which is one of the five pillars, is tantamount to becoming a Muslim. It is the equivalent of taking the eucharist. Muslims are likely to be embarrassed rather than impressed with such a well-meant action of solidarity. What will be appreciated is visitors sitting at the back and quietly respecting what is seen and heard. Christians can be encouraged to pray in the heart.
- In a Sikh *Gurdwara*, sharing in the *langar* (meal) is an essential part of the follow up to worship. It is important that the guests enjoy a meal – it is not 'food dedicated to idols'.
- Visitors should leave plenty of time for a visit. The period afterwards, involving informal discussion, is a vital part of it. Visitors should be encouraged to ask questions frankly and openly. Most worship places of other faiths will have been visited by groups who will have asked almost any question they are likely to ask.
- As mentioned in chapter 1, I recommend giving a group a form to fill in after and not during a visit. It is very important to focus upon feelings, before, during and after a visit. It is feelings that normally greatly influence our intellectual response. We may feel a very warm welcome, which may conflict with preconceived and theological ideas. I recommend a group, with a facilitator, spends as much time in follow up, as they do on the visit itself.
- An invitation to speak in the worship of another faith should be considered as a very precious opportunity. It should not be exploited, nor should it be a time to be reticent about our Christian faith. It is a sign of trust. It is good to use the New Testament as a base for what one is

saying. I always took a small New Testament when I went to a *Gurdwara* in Sandwell. The teacher there gave an exposition of Sikh scriptures to the two hundred people who regularly attended. He always asked me to share something with the congregation, and I would use a passage of scripture around the theme on which he had been speaking. This was a wonderful opportunity, which depended entirely on the personal trust that had built up between us. He knew I would not exploit the situation. I have also been asked by Hindus to speak as part of what they have themselves called 'Mothers' Day', when many mothers do the *puja*. I was asked to explain the origin in Christian tradition. A colleague has also had the chance to explain Easter to a Hindu group.

A final area to consider is the use of church buildings. This includes those buildings that are still being used for Christian worship and those that are up for sale because they are redundant.

This has been an important area of Christian hospitality over the last forty years. As people arrived in this country, their energies at first went into getting a job, a property however small and bringing the family to Britain. Houses were used for worship, or warehouses and school rooms were rented. In time, churches were approached to offer prayer and teaching facilities, and often they were generous about this. The normal principle was that halls could be offered, but not the church itself, and that is a wise distinction. Some would rent for teaching or social functions, but not for worship, but the dividing line is not always easily drawn. Hindus often used church halls for festivals, which are both social and religious and a means of teaching the faith. Any problems arising from these arrangements have usually been about practicalities such as parking and clearing up rather than theological questions. When it has worked well, it has led to deeper understanding between the faiths.

Deeper questions arise when a church has to be sold. Denominations vary in how they deal with this situation. I was approached by some Hindus who asked me whether I knew of any Methodist church that was available. By the time I had made some enquiries, they said, 'Do not worry, we want to build a temple from scratch. Christians came and destroyed some of our temples in Sri Lanka. We do not want that to happen again.' The first two sites they found met with strong local opposition, both from those who did not want their neighbourhood disturbed and from those with Christian fundamentalist reasons. They found a third site. On this occasion the Christians were split between those, including the local bishop, who supported the project and those who opposed it on the grounds that they were 'taking our green fields', in fact reclaimed industrial land in a run-down area. I met the demonstrators and pointed out that, since in India Christians had been given many plots for churches by Hindus, was it not possible for us in the West Midlands to give one to them? Their reply was that this was England and not India! However, the urbane leadership of the temple, mostly doctors and engineers, eventually won over the locals, not least by offering them food and hospitality and showing patience.

It can be very disturbing for those whose family have worshipped in a particular church for decades or even generations, and held their weddings and funerals there, to find it being sold to be a temple. In Leicester, Indian Christian visitors have been particularly disturbed to find that the Baptist Church from which William Carey set out as the first Protestant missionary to India, has now become a Hindu temple. Some would much prefer that it had become a supermarket, bingo hall or flats than a temple. It is important to be very sensitive to these feelings when many Indian Christians have suffered greatly as a result of their conversion.

The Anglican church process for redundancy is very prolonged. Up till now, churches have not normally been sold to other faiths for worship. A great many factors need to be taken into consideration: church community, ecumenical partners, local authority, the wider community, the preservation lobby, those wishing to buy the church, their place in the community, proposed use.

Church buildings do not become redundant because locals are converting to Islam or Sikhism. It is because the demography of an area has changed and because the Church has failed to hold its own members, particularly the established churches. If a church has to go, is it better that it is used by a black-led church or by people of another religious faith, or that it is used for a secular purpose? That is increasingly the question before us.

Concluding reflections

Prayer, meditation and worship are at the heart of all religions. Here, and in social action together, we can most easily be seen as a hopeful influence in a world that is drunk on consumerism, power rivalry, the unhelpful aspects of globalisation and often violent religious rivalries. Meeting at heart level, and taking risks to do so, is at the centre of a journey to rediscover the Soul of Europe. This is something we can only do together across faiths. I went recently to a Muslim-Christian residential consultation on *ta-aruf*. This is a Qur'anic concept, from the following quotation: 'Oh, mankind, we have created of you male and female and have made you peoples and tribes, *that you might come to know one another*.' Prayer is the place where we can show to the world that we can indeed know each other and act accordingly.

Suitable biblical passages that can be used on interfaith occasions:

Many of the psalms, such as 8; 23; 33; 90; 103; 104; 139; 148
Proverbs 8
Leviticus 9:9–18
Micah 4:1–4
Isaiah 25:6–10; 40:10–17
Matthew 5:2–14; Matthew 6:25–34, and much of the Sermon on the Mount
Luke 1:46–55; Luke 10:25–37 (and many other parables)
Romans 8:18–27
1 Corinthians 13
Philippians 4:8–14
1 John 4:16–21
James 3:5–18
Revelation 21:1-8

A Muslim/Jewish/Christian prayer for peace

O God, you are the source of life and peace.
    Praised be your name forever.
We know it is you who turn our minds to thoughts of peace.
Hear our prayer in this time of trouble and anxiety.

Your power changes hearts.
Muslims, Christians and Jews remember and proudly affirm, that
they are followers of the one God, children of Abraham,
    brothers and sisters;
Enemies begin to speak to one another;
Those who were estranged join hands in friendship,
Nations seek the way of peace together.

Give to us understanding that puts an end to strife;
    mercy that quenches hatred,
and forgiveness that overcomes vengeance.
Empower all people to live in your law of love. Amen.

CASE STUDIES/QUESTIONS

1. Your church is set in an area that is fairly multi-religious, but without places of worship of other faiths. One early morning there is a terri-

ble fire in a house, and five members of a Hindu family, from three generations, are burnt to death. The effect is immediate on the whole city, with an enormous sense of grief beyond the Hindu community and much media coverage. You decide to open your church for those who wish to come and pray and light candles. Quite a number come, and because you have taken this initiative, they approach you to ask whether they can have the funeral services in the church, bringing along their Hindu priest. They do not have the space anywhere else, since this is the biggest building in the area. It is also, they feel, a holy place.

How would you respond to this request if you were the minister? If you were a member of the church committee? What considerations or cautions would come to the fore?

2. You are a Christian minister, and one day when you are in the market, a vendor approaches you and shares his problem. He and his assistants are Muslims and they have nowhere to pray, since the mosque is too far away. At the moment, weather permitting, they say their prayers on the pavement outside their shop. Your church is just across the road. He would like you to allow them to say their midday prayers each day in your church premises, bringing their own prayer mats. You say this must be brought to the church committee, though you personally have much empathy with the request, and there is a space outside the main church.

The committee turn the request down, however hard you try to persuade them. They say that a church is a church and not a mosque. Sadly, you inform the shopkeeper. Some weeks later there is an article in the local paper about how some of the market traders have been given a 'sanctuary' in the local library, so that they can pray indoors. The minister feels sad.

How do you react to this story? What would you have recommended and why?

3. You are a member of a Muslim-Christian dialogue group. There has been a discussion about some interracial tensions in the community between African-Caribbeans and Somalis. Discussion then moved to racism in general. At the end, you are asked to offer a prayer.

Compose such a prayer.

4. The child of a Christian family has been taken seriously ill. The neighbours are Hindus, and their children are very good friends with

this child. The father says he would like to go to the hospital to offer prayers for the child and ask his priest in the local temple to offer a special *puja* for the child to his own family god, Krishna. The father and mother of the sick child come to you and ask you for advice on how they should respond.

What do you say to them and why?

5. Some Muslims ask to use your church hall regularly for Qur'anic teaching for children, since they have no other facility nearby. It is put to the church committee, and various positions are taken in response. A further factor is that they ask, if permission is granted, for the cross on the wall to be removed or covered over.

How would you respond and why? Alternatively, if there is a group, play out a role-play with you as the chair.

6. The following was composed as an interreligious benediction by a Christian Professor to welcome the new President of Emory University (United Methodists) in the USA. He was asked to pray, not as a Christian priest, but on behalf of all the people of the university, of whatever faith:

> As a new chapter opens, a new flower blooms, and a fresh fragrance of novelty and expectation spreads, let us step into the future with confidence and hope.
>
> May our pursuit of excellence be complemented by our desire to care for each other! May our search after truth be accompanied by our appreciation of plurality and variety! May our works of beauty be sensitised by the ugly realities of suffering and pain! And may our acts of goodness be tempered by a deep sense of humility and grace!
>
> The One, The One, who is called by many names yet meets us as the nameless one, that One, may that one surround us, sustain us! Let it be so, let it be so! Amen.[13]

How do you feel about the content and phraseology of this benediction? Do you think the priest should have agreed to do this in the first place?

5. PASTORAL ISSUES

As people live alongside each other in a multi-religious society, it is inevitable that a whole range of issues arise. This will happen less if people of different faiths live in totally separate compartments, as is true in some parts of the country. In some cities, Muslims, for example, live in almost entirely Muslim areas, their children attend almost entirely Muslim schools, employment is almost entirely within Muslim enterprises, shops and doctors in the area are all Muslim, and so on. In such circumstances the issues of living together with other faiths do not arise. Nevertheless, this kind of polarised context produces its own community issues. Parallel to this, there are many all-white communities, monochrome in ethnic background and also often in class, whether on housing estates, on wealthy suburban avenues or in comfortable rural commuting villages, in which the same kind of mono-cultural, mono-religious daily experience becomes the norm. Such polarised areas breed a culture of fear, ignorance and a readiness to accept the stereotypes presented by the media, whether through the press or through books, films, television or radio.

There are also areas where Hindus or Sikhs are in the majority, but historically they are few in number, and they are decreasing. Economic success and a willingness to travel to temples and *Gurdwaras* mean that Hindus and Sikhs are moving in increasing numbers into suburban areas and districts beyond the city boundaries. In the Jewish community, while Orthodox Jews like to live within walking distance of their synagogue and consequently there are areas where they are in the majority, generally they are scattered among the general population, and this applies even more to Liberal adherents. Likewise Buddhists, whose *viharas* and communities are often in rural areas, such as those found in Scotland, Wales or the north of England, can be found anywhere. Although some Muslims live together in particular areas, this is by no means true of all. Wealthier Muslims travel to mosques from their homes in all parts of the cities. As Muslims move into an area in large numbers, there is sometimes an element of 'white flight', and even 'Hindu flight'. But it is never total, and some white people remain, frequently the elderly. Interaction, albeit it often minimal, between the communities occurs in the encounters of daily life.

Schools can be monochrome, reflecting local communities, though the teacher body usually brings more variety. In several of my local junior schools, the children are nearly all Asian Muslim, but the teachers nearly all European white. The head of RE in one of these schools is Christian, while the head of RE in an Anglican secondary school, with nearly all white pupils, in a nearby market town is Muslim. The same is not true of the expensive private schools. The Asian zeal for private education and their willingness to pay for it, as would happen in the sub-continent, means that the major faiths are well represented at these schools.

Universities and colleges of further education are increasingly places where people of different faiths meet. As student numbers in universities grow towards the government's 50 per cent target, more and more people of all faiths are studying together. Interaction takes place at all kinds of levels, even if many Asians are day students and go back to their family home at night. Sixth Form colleges also provide such opportunities. Interaction is high in the professions and public service work. Business also necessitates interaction, though this can be more limited than one might expect. In Leicester, for example, there is a largely white Chamber of Commerce and an Association of Asian Businesses. Local politics, community work, issues of common concern, and social and sporting activities are further areas of interaction.

In this chapter, I will be looking at issues that arise as a result of people of different faiths living alongside one another in a multi-faith society. For a Christian, responding to these situations is part of the imperative to love our neighbour, whatever their background. Though there is a special obligation to those who are 'of the household of faith' (Gal. 6:10 KJV), the command does not stop there.

The care of converts

Whether we seek it or not, conversions to Christianity happen, as the Spirit blows where the Spirit wills. Conversions also happen in the other direction, as Christians, nominal or active, become Muslims, Buddhists or members of the Hare Krishna movement, etc. How are we to approach the pastoral care of converts to and from Christianity? What we need to be clear about is the enormous step that is involved for the individual or family concerned. The following definition from my book on conversion, *The Church and Conversion, A study of conversion to and from Christianity in the Tamil area of South India* (see Bibliography), which was formulated as a result of studying more than a hundred cases, highlights the importance of this:

> Conversion is a process, including a personal decision, taken alone or as part of a group, to centre one's religious life on a new focus, which one believes is more liberating, in every aspect of that word, and closer to truth. This involves a change of identification within oneself and normally a change of outward affiliation to a new community, which will affect one's life at various levels, 'body, heart, mind and soul', and to tangible change of behaviour and religious practice.

An appreciation of this will help us towards an appropriate sensitivity, even though we may ultimately rejoice at the courageous step someone is taking.

Converts away from Christianity

This is a very difficult area. All religions find it problematic when people leave their faith. They find the reasons hard to comprehend, they feel a sense of betrayal, and they are often paralysed in knowing how to respond.

A black churchwarden, who has a deep faith, enabled his son to become head server. One day the young man announced that he had become a Muslim, explaining that this was part of affirming himself and his African roots. He had taken the new name Ibrahim. He had found the church racist, and was determined to follow a faith that respected his integrity. The father wanted to resign from his post as churchwarden, feeling he could not face the shame. His anger was immense. Should he take some action and, since violence was not an option, what could he do?

A congregation member explained that her daughter had come across Buddhists at university and had decided to convert. It became clear that the mother was unable to distinguish between becoming a Buddhist and becoming a member of an extreme sect. It took a long conversation to dispel her ignorance and lessen her fears. I even said that if a member of my family, who was not a practising Christian, became a Buddhist, I would be glad that he or she had at least found a religious faith. Much more difficult was another situation. An Anglican woman asked to see me because her marriage was in danger. Her husband had joined a Guru-led sect called Patmos, which was consuming a large amount of his time. She was desperate about the hold of the faith on him: it appeared to have become more important to him than his marriage. The leaders of the sect were suggesting that she should also convert, or that he should leave her. How do people distinguish between what is dangerous, what they can live with, and what can be rejoiced in? How are families to respond?

Love, forgiveness and grace are at the centre of the Christian ethic. We should encourage the family to love that person, whatever he or she appears to have done. Conversion is a test of how far that love goes, and continuing to show love can be a witness to others. On marrying a Muslim a Christian woman became a Muslim. The fact that her strongly practising Christian family stood by her evoked astonishment. While some Muslims said that this just showed the permissiveness of Christian faith, one man remarked that he had something to learn from such an attitude.

It is important too that the church help the family. One way is by explaining the other faith to the family and, if necessary, dispelling stereotypes, particularly of Islam. If the local minister or lay people cannot help, then the assistance of a local interfaith adviser should be sought. Above all, contact with the convert should not be broken. Such a step only prevents any possibility of a way back, as well as making it difficult to provide support if the convert becomes lonely.

More positively, and probably only after some time, converts who are former Christians can play a constructive part in interfaith dialogue, but only if they have not been driven into a corner. Often converts can take an extreme position against their previous faith, but where this has not happened, we can seek for opportunities for involvement, which is also an appropriate form of acceptance.

Any future involvement may depend on how far they have been made to feel guilty about letting down their parents, who did their best to pass on the Christian faith. Making people feel guilty is only likely to create disruption of relationship. A far more positive response is likely to be elicited by taking the position, 'I am not happy with what you have done, but I would like to hear why you have done it. Tell me about your new faith, and those you worship with. I love you anyway and will pray for you.'

A television documentary told the story of some Texans who had converted to Islam. Most had been fundamentalist Christians, and part of the attraction of Islam was its definiteness. Although their families were very hurt, on the whole they stayed together and joked about whether the convert was more likely to convert the parents, or whether the prayers for the return of the convert were more likely to be effective! One mother asked to attend Muslim prayers with her daughter. Looking awkward, she put on a scarf and gingerly entered the mosque. After witnessing the prayers, she expressed a new respect, though remained as clear as ever that salvation depended on holding her view of Jesus! She showed great love by doing this at all. Her Christian faith was displayed, both by what she said about Jesus and also by how she displayed his love in her actions.

Converts to Christianity

The act of converting to Christianity from no religious faith is difficult enough. As well as changes of belief, it will mean changes of lifestyle and will deeply affect the convert's family. At the very least, Sunday mornings will change; at the very most, everything will be transformed. Conversion from one faith to another will be all the more profound if a change of culture is also involved. In India or Pakistan, most conversions have been group conversions, involving family members, or at least part of a village. Here, in accordance with Western individual choice, it is normally an individual who takes this great step. For the lone convert, used to living within a close family structure there is the potential for isolation.

The decision to undergo baptism should be taken by the potential convert him- or herself, and not by the clergy. The decision will have to be lived with for life, while the minister is likely to be transferred in a year or two. It can be tempting for the minister to wish to rush a convert, in an eagerness to baptise from another faith. But if there is a cross to carry, it is the convert, and not the minister, who will have to carry it. It is the pastoral task to enable the potential convert to see all possible implications, short and long term. It may be worth painting a worst-case scenario. It does not matter if some of the negative possibilities do not occur. The pastor, if – and only if – it is appropriate, might visit the family of the potential convert to try to allay some of their fears. Where there is a prior relationship, the pastor might talk to the priest or Imam, though only, of course, with the convert's permission.

The convert should be encouraged to express his or her anxieties, but in a context in which the appropriate teaching is also given, ideally in a group rather than just with the minister on his or her own. It is the whole congregation which receives the convert, and a support group is needed. A natural group such as a Bible study or a house group can fulfil this need, and should include members, if there are any within the church, from the convert's background. But the welcome should not be excessive, since it can create false expectations, leading to disillusionment. Nor should the pastor ask the convert to give his or her testimony on each and every occasion. This makes it very hard for the family and appears to rub their noses in what has happened. St Paul, according to Galatians, had fourteen years of quiet after the Damascus Road experience. Sometimes a convert is not even given fourteen days!

Conversion usually happens when a person is in a place of dis-ease. This may be a natural consequence of his or her stage in life – most individual conversions happen between the ages of eighteen and thirty, a time of experiment without responsibility, for example when students are away from home. It is not then surprising that all religions put a great effort into their operations within the university world. In part they are seeking to provide pastoral support to their adherents at a potentially confusing stage in their lives, but there are also groups whose driving force is evangelism and who seek to convert those of other faiths or none, particularly Muslim and Christian. Dis-ease can, of course, also occur at many other times of life – as a result of being hospitalised or undergoing a prison term; at times of family break-up, bereavement, unemployment, long-term illness, or a love affair taking someone away from home. Recent immigration is another situation of vulnerability, particularly for those who are refugees.

A key question is what must be discontinuous and what can be continuous with the earlier life. There are no easy answers. Each person, family, religion and context is different. The pastoral needs of the individual should be a prime consideration in any decision, which should be taken by the convert, not the minister, who should only facilitate. Conversion is always a process, and what may be right in its immediate aftermath may change in the course of time. In many cases, the convert initially wishes to make a complete break, indicating a change from darkness to light. Indeed, such a change may be forced upon the convert by leaders in the former religion or family. Converts often quote the text, 'No one who puts a hand to the plough and looks back is fit for the kingdom of God' (Luke 9:62). But as time goes by, there may be some healing, some reviving, of natural ties. For pastoral reasons, that can only be encouraged. Converts then need to be helped to re-evaluate how far they can now take part in family events, which are an inextricable mix of culture and religion (for example, marriages and funerals), whether actively or passively. If asked, a pastor can provide advice, but should leave the decision to the people concerned. It is they who will bear the guilt, either of being absent at a key family occasion or of feeling they have betrayed their new faith.

A survey of Asian Christian converts undertaken in 1992 revealed that out of every ten Hindus who enter churches and can be counted as 'converts' in any one year, seven have walked out by the next year. The Alliance of Asian Christians was established to counter this reality, and there has probably been some improvement since then. There is also no reason to think that the situation as regards Sikhs or Muslims is any different. This rate of reversion is higher than I met in South India. Of the 5,400 Asian Christian on the Alliance's lists, 80 per cent were converts. Twelve per cent of new believers are Muslims, and the number is rising: this figure is clearly much higher than that found in India or Pakistan.

When conversion begins with an individual, the man may take the lead, but it is more often the woman who does so. Women may feel a sense of vulnerability within their culture. When a woman becomes a Christian, her husband does not necessarily follow, though her children may. When a man converts first, his wife will almost certainly follow. There are a number of factors which encourage conversion: the possibility of independent living, a pattern normal in the host culture; the smaller independent nuclear family; widespread higher education for women as well as men; mobility and financial independence. Where whole families do convert, it is usually person by person: mother, father, children, grandchildren in turn.

Women from other faiths who live in Great Britain often feel trapped by the cultural expectations of their extended families, at variance with goals encouraged by their education here and seen in their white contemporaries. Such women may feel accepted by Christ who they understand is calling them to freedom, and then face struggle at every turn. Moreover, such converted women are no longer willing just to accept their lot. Many husbands discourage their wives from becoming Christians because being a Christian gives them some status, as well as a resistant streak. Where both convert together, the situation is much more stable. Punishment from the community more often takes the form of ostracism than violence. Beating can be used to stop women going to church. However, the strength women gain from their faith may make them calmer and more full of hope, enabling them to bear suffering in the belief that one day their husband may change.

Statistics show that a large proportion of converts come through evangelical churches of various kinds, while those in the established churches tend to be second- or third-generation Christians, or more, having already been converted when they arrived from India. Asian Christian churches have been necessary in this generation not least for linguistic reasons. In the future they may remain for cultural reasons. They are often much divided. In Wolverhampton in 1998, for example, there were seven churches for just over 500 people. Countrywide only one in four South Asian Christians were Christians before coming to Britain, and this quarter is only reached because of the substantial numbers of South Indian and Sri Lankan Christians who have immigrated.

Identity questions are central for South Asian Christians. Where do they belong? At one level they have left their past behind; they have obeyed the text, 'Come out from among them' (cf. 2 Cor. 6:17). But often they do not feel accepted by the English Church. Culturally they remain essentially in continuity with their past, their association with their compatriots of other faiths being closer than their bonding within the Church, which theologically includes them with European Christians. In which direction will their children go? Will they even know the language and culture of their Indian background? It is often young Westerners who find themselves fascinated on a visit to India, while those young people of Indian origin are not enamoured at all. Moreover, living in the West means that they find themselves expected to think in an individualistic way – 'I' and not 'we' – which leads to a potential generation clash, not least about religion and church attendance.

Asians often feel the lack of community in church life within the mainline churches and find themselves part of two cultures. The main church group may be warm and accepting to a point, but it does not provide the closeness of cultural bond which permeates every aspect of their life at home and beyond.

Further questions relate to the way culture and religion are seemingly so bound up. Is it possible to discriminate between the two, so that a group of converts can be encouraged to retain appropriate elements of their own culture? The tendency is to err on the side of being overstrict, lest there be any trace of syncretism. Such an approach often ignores how much implicit syncretism there is between Christianity and Western culture. Are we ready to listen to the recent convert challenging our Anglo-Saxon understandings and practices, with the freshness of new faith coming out of a very different culture? Or do we give the impression subconsciously that our faith is more enlightened because of its Westernised clothes, and that the convert will benefit by quickly adjusting to our practices?

An example is the consumption of alcohol or beef and pork. St Peter declared all things clean (Acts 10:9–16), but if a convert eats pork (in the case of Muslims and Jews) or beef (in the case of caste Hindus), this makes him or her ritually unclean in the eyes of his or her family. The same applies to drinking alcohol. As Christians we do not have to do everything we are permitted to do. I had a student in India who came out of a village Hindu background. He told me that when he became a Christian he began eating mutton, but when he came to the seminary, he felt fully free, and began to eat beef! Somehow he had the feeling that doing so made him a superior Christian. Higher caste Hindus already look down on Christians as a 'low' community because of the predominance of converts from so-called untouchable communities. These additional factors will only confirm them in their view that Christianity is an unsavoury religion that encourages bad habits in every direction.

Another specific issue is food offered to idols, which may arise if a convert still relates to a Hindu family. He or she may be served *prasad*, food brought from the temple. For the liberal Western Christian, eating such food is not a problem. It shows respect for the giver, and St Paul made it clear that whether or not to eat such food is a matter of personal conscience (1 Cor. 8:8). But Paul also says that we should not offend the conscience of the weaker brother/sister. Here the weaker brother/sister may well be the convert.

A high degree of pastoral sensitivity was shown by Leslie Brown, former Archbishop of Uganda and Bishop of Ely, when he was Principal of the Kerala Seminary in South India. In the college chapel there was a crucifix behind the altar, and the eucharist was celebrated facing eastwards, which meant the celebrant raised the host to the crucifix. Leslie Brown noticed that one new student did not take communion. The student explained that he was a Hindu convert and he could not abide eating bread that in his heart he felt had been offered to an idol. He knew with his head that the crucifix was not an idol, but it reminded him too much of a Hindu idol. The Principal asked him, 'Would it help if I put my back to the crucifix and faced the congregation when I lift the host?' The student said it would. When Leslie Brown was later involved in the drafting of the Church of South India Prayer Book he cited this incident as instrumental in the requirement that celebration should be westwards facing, which has now come back to the Western Church!

For converts the 'good and bad occasions', as Indians call them, of birth, marriage and death will raise specific issues. In some cases the trauma involved in the break caused by their conversion will mean they are not invited on these occasions. Those who are invited may seek advice as to how they should respond. For some a simple rule may be helpful, such as that they are free to participate in social occasions, but should keep away from any religious ceremonies. However, this may be easier said than done, since it may be difficult to draw a line between the two. Another option is to have a more open approach, determining that out of love for the family, they will do all they can do with a clear conscience. Occasionally families may allow a Christian prayer or reading, if they respect the convert's position. Some Hindus have put off being baptised at all until after the death of their parents, so important are the Hindu rituals required to ensure the soul is safely set on its way. This applies particularly to the elder son, although he may be able to delegate his duties to a younger brother. But if he is the only son, the problem is particularly acute. Others may do what is necessary, but feel great guilt. Pastoral care then requires the kind of sensitivity that enables individuals to forgive themselves and to feel forgiven by God. Such action, they need to be helped to see, is not a real backsliding. A Brahmin convert in Britain lived fully as a Christian here. On returning to South India on a visit, the first time after he had become a Christian, he could not face telling his wider family, and therefore went through all the Hindu rituals. By the time of his next visit back, he had the confidence to own up to his new faith.

A Hindu convert, married to another Hindu convert who was a pastor, had not been able to have children after several years of trying. Her family insisted she go to a particular fertility temple. She herself had been conceived, in their eyes, as a result of rituals undergone there. Torn between her loyalty to Christ and honouring her father and mother, she decided to pray in her heart to Jesus that he would both protect her as she went through the rituals and also remove her barrenness. This she did, and the result was the birth of a child. All were satisfied that their prayers had been answered!

I know of a converted Sikh who is more ready to take part in family functions than his wife, who feels she is not strong enough to do so. I know of another Sikh who retains his silver bangle, one of the five Ks (key Sikh symbols), as a mark of cultural and not religious identity. Other Sikh converts would be horrified at this.

The celebration of festivals is another place of challenge. Here it is hard to generalise. Some families will be sensitive and not expect their Christian relative to join in the religious side: indeed, they would be surprised if they did. Others may see it as a test, through which they hope to demonstrate that what has happened is not real and that loyalty to the family comes first. In reality, it may be almost impossible to unravel the cultural from the religious, as, for example, is clearly the case with Christmas. Some celebrations can be Christianised in the mind, as for example, *Diwali*, the beautiful festival of lights, with Jesus Christ being thought of as the Light of the World behind all these lights.

Overall, this task of differentiating between culture and religion is one of the hardest for the convert. In India there is a tradition of placing beautiful black and white or coloured decorations – *rangoli* – on the ground outside the house. Some have Hindu religious connotations, and generally they are thought to ward off the evil eye. Can this practice be continued by a convert? Should the decorations be Christianised, with the drawing of a fish or a cross? Hindu married women put a red spot – *puttu* – on their foreheads. Can the convert continue doing this or not? Roman Catholics traditionally have carried the practice on, but other Christians have not, with some being strongly opposed to it. For the latter it is a sign of being a Hindu. Who is right? A pastor to Indian converts in Britain told me that he advises people to do only what is in accordance with the Bible. But the Bible has nothing to say on so many of these things, certainly not about red spots!

In most cases, at the beginning, the attitude of converts to their former religion is largely negative, but in time they may find a more balanced view of past and present. Many can accept that knowledge of God had been there in their former religion, and links are often seen between the Old Testament and their culture. Many converts come to a place of concentrating on the full salvation experienced in Christ, rather than on deriding the former faith – that of mother and father – from which they gained a knowledge of God. An even smaller minority may wish to be known as Hindu Christians or Sikh Christians.

The absence of a liturgy for 'engagement' occasions has been mentioned to me as a difficulty for converts since, in Asian culture, this is considered as important as marriage. Pradip Sudra has written an engagement liturgy, in which engagement is seen as a foretaste of marriage, as the Holy Spirit is the foretaste of heaven.

Marriage leads some converts back to Hinduism, since Christian marriage partners are often not available from within their caste communities. There is a need for marriage brokers in this context, a strange concept for European ministers, but understood by Asians. Marriage partners are sought from the same language area and the same caste. I heard of one case where a marriage could not be arranged because a convert would not speak of his caste background on principle. When the Christian religion is added as a condition, choice can become quite limited. This may even be true amongst *dalits*, the so-called untouchables. In Britain, far fewer converts, in proportion, are *dalits* than in India where they dominate the Christian Church. The majority of converts from Asia within Britain are of caste background, since those from scheduled castes (i.e. the lower castes) did not normally emigrate. Exceptions are those from the Punjab, where there have been a significant number of conversions.

In cases of relapse it is not normally theological difficulties that are the cause. Ex-converts continue to hold Jesus in affection, but their problems have usually been with the church or with overwhelming cultural issues. Eurocentricity has an inhibiting effect on Asian Christians and on potential converts. The challenge to change applies as much to the church a convert enters as to the convert him- or herself. The pressure to conform to a culturally alien church community may prove too much. There may be a real or perceived lack of acceptance in a mixed or mainly white church, so that the convert can feel intense loneliness even in a supposedly warm and charismatic congregation. The convert looks different and is different. Depending on their personality, it may take ten to fifteen years for converts to gain a mature understanding of the Christian faith. They often need support for years, particularly if they are on their own. If maturity is to be achieved, Asian leadership may be vital. This is exemplified by the experience of a couple converted from Sikhism who have been Christians and readers in their Anglican parish for many years. During that time they built up an Asian Fellowship which met each Sunday afternoon and in various house groups and Bible study groups during the week. Eventually they found this difficult to do in their Anglican parish, where they felt the cultural gap was, in the end, too great. Within the main church, Asian numbers were too small to influence policy, only ever fifty out of 300, and the majority rarely allowed worship to be significantly influenced, in the couple's opinion. Opposition was subtle, but the question of whether the worship was relevant to the Asian members was seldom discussed. People liked the reputation of having Asians in their congregation, including a number of converts, but their general view was that non-English services were not necessary because language was gradually becoming less important as an issue. The church never took the radical step of asking what they could do to help a significant group of thirty or forty of their members. As a result, while some of the Asians became 'white' Christians, the professionals often wishing to identify with the host community, the poor, who could not articulate their needs, really missed worship in their own language and style. Since the mainline church could not respond to their needs, the Asian Christians became part of a community where they could find such support. At first sight it may seem to be the converts or their leaders who are to blame for dividing the church, but more sober consideration may lead us to the conclusion that the church failed the converts and left them with little alternative.

CASE STUDIES AND QUESTIONS

1. A young Hindu woman begins attending your church. She enjoys the worship, and attends a prayer meeting. After several months, she asks whether she can be baptised. How do you respond to this question? What questions do you ask her? How do you decide whether to proceed, and what steps do you take?

2. A member of your congregation wishes to talk with you. You learn that her daughter, who is currently living in India, has begun to follow a Hindu Guru. She had no religious faith previously, but has now begun to live very simply and devotionally, and to show a new commitment also to attending church with mother when she comes home. The mother is confused and does not know whether to welcome this or not. The daughter also says that she has fallen in love with a Hindu follower of the same Guru. How do you respond to this anxious mother?

3. A woman from a Muslim family is attending your church regularly. Some want to approach her to take baptism. A debate ensues amongst those who know her. Prepare a role-play about the situation, and the different positions that might be held. Bring her in during the middle of the scene and allow her to respond from her position.

4. A Muslim man and his wife take baptism, but wish to keep their baptism secret. The wife wishes to continue to wear a scarf, and remain in contact with her family and community, whenever she returns to their neighbourhood. Is it valid to be a secret Christian in this way?

Marriage between Christians and people of other faiths

Marriage or long-term relationships between Christians and people of other faiths are becoming increasingly frequent and many readers will have met such couples. There are various reasons for this increase. The age profile of those of other faiths from South Asia, which is where the majority originate, is younger than the general population. They are becoming more settled and geographically gradually more diffuse, leading to fewer community restrictions. It is now much less common for brides to be brought from Asia, and mixed-sex schooling and, above all, college education bring young people of different faiths into daily contact. Despite their increasing prevalence, cross-religious marriages may still mean total separation from the community, particularly for Muslim women.

Such marriages may happen anywhere in the country. The issue often presents itself in relationship to people of Asian background and I will concentrate my comments on this kind of marriage. The aim is neither to advocate such marriages nor to discourage them, but to point out some of the issues involved to ensure sensitivity in our dealings with them. This has also become a very topical subject, as its frequent appearance as a theme for TV and radio programmes demonstrates. Protecting couples from unnecessary publicity is also a role we have!

Preliminary comments

Every marriage is unique, and this is equally true of a marriage between a Christian and a person of another faith. We must look at each case in turn. We need to distinguish between a marriage that involves crossing cultures as well as religions and a marriage across religions within the same culture. Examples of the latter are a European Buddhist marrying a European Roman Catholic, or a Tamil Christian marrying a Tamil Hindu. Interdenominational marriage – for example, between an Irish Roman Catholic and an Anglican – can, on occasions, cause the couple to face some of the issues we will look at. Previous experience in assisting such marriages can be a help to clergy involved with cross-religious relationships. Marriages between committed Christians and those who are strongly atheist or indifferent to religion also bring their own issues.

There can also be culturally diverse marriages within the same faith, for example, a Palestinian Christian marrying a European Christian or Indian Hindus marrying across caste, such as a Brahmin marrying a *dalit* (so-called 'untouchable'), which raises huge issues. This can also be an issue for Asian converts to Christianity who marry someone from a different caste. A local Brahmin told me that he would find it very difficult if his daughter married a Hindu *dalit* because of the different 'culture'. He would prefer her to marry a white Christian. Four out of ten relationships or marriages involving Afro-Caribbean Christians are now cross-cultural, according to the study *Ethnic Minorities in Britain* published by the *Policy Studies Unit* (1997). This compares with the figure of approximately one in ten for Asians. As regards Muslims, acceptance depends very much on the family background. For some it would be deemed totally unacceptable; for others, although they had not experienced it personally, it would be acceptable in theory. Others can give several examples of cross-cultural marriages from their extended families. Imams too would vary in their experience and in the pressures they would apply upon prospective couples in an effort to make them conform, even beyond Islamic regulations. Perhaps the same range of attitudes can be found across Christian families.

Where people marry from two different religions, they may decide to remain in those two religions or, out of religious conviction or a desire to strengthen the marriage, they may decide that one should convert. My experience is that it will usually be the woman who converts, perhaps out of a sense of obligation or of love. But, in the heart, there may have been no real conversion. In this case, there may be a sense of incomprehension or isolation and, if the marriage subsequently gets into difficulty for other reasons, an area for revolt and assertion of a right to religious freedom. This is less likely to happen if the 'converted' person was not a strong believer before.

The issues will vary depending on which two religions are involved. If a Muslim is involved, no choice can be expected for children. They have the 'right' to be brought up as Muslims. A Muslim man is allowed to marry a Jew or a Christian, i.e. a person following a 'religion of the book', and his wife has the right to practise her faith. But the reverse is not allowed, and a non-Muslim man is expected to convert before taking a Muslim bride. It is vital that both parties know these non-negotiable requirements, and anyone advising on such marriages needs to make them clear. Having said this, marriages against the rules do take place, and when they do, it is difficult for the couple to remain in touch with the wider Muslim community or with the extended Muslim family. In the case of other religions, different issues may arise. When, for example, a high caste Hindu Brahmin and a Christian marry, the couple has to work out how they will manage the consumption of meat, particularly beef, and the drinking of alcohol. A Jewish/Christian will face similar questions over food laws and the keeping of the Sabbath.

Some key issues
The issues raised in these marriages do not fall into neat categories but frequently overlap. Once again, we should not forget that we encounter couples and families, not isolated issues. For ease of reflection, I list six key areas of possible concern. As stated above, I write here primarily about those marrying across the South Asian/British European divide, which covers the majority of cross-religious marriages, but clearly other marriages will have their own set of issues which may be similar.

(i) Cultural
A number of cultural issues will arise in the majority of marriages across two different cultures. They can relate to food, how leisure and in particular holidays are to be spent, how a house is to be decorated, the kind of music and humour appreciated, and the place of hospitality (in India or Pakistan, guests are sacred and serving them is a primary obligation). Most important is the position of the woman: the kind of decisions she can be permitted to take, the clothes she should wear and the degree to which she can have an independent life and independent friendships. The question of *izzat* (honour) is very important. For example, a man should not lose face through his wife or children disagreeing with him in public, whatever happens privately.

(ii) Family
The way family issues are approached is clearly related to culture. Where two cultures are involved, they present an area of great potential difficulty and also the most important area of potential support. How does each culture view family? How are the various relationships seen within the family, both nuclear and extended? How is the family seen in relationship to the outside community? Where do paramount obligations lie? How is responsibility for the elderly seen?

There are many areas where tension may arise. One example is when family visitors come from South Asia: there may be an obligation on the wife to put most things on hold while they visit, which is difficult if she is working. The wife is traditionally seen in Asian culture to have left her parents' family and entered the extended family of her husband. In times of need and sickness that is where her obligation lies, and not with her own family. Different members of the family have importance at particular times – the husband's father, the mother-in-law or the eldest son. Life cycle events involve particular obligations. Questions of dowry may also arise.

Questions related to children also need to be considered carefully. Traditionally, producing children, especially a boy, is the great test of the success of a marriage. This brings particular pressures on a European wife. There will also be expectations surrounding how children should be brought up, and no shortage of advice! How much freedom should a child be given to study what he/she wishes, to choose a career, to choose a partner? Should they learn an Asian language? Should they attend mosque school, as well as day school? As teenagers, should they be allowed to do as their peers do, particularly with regard to drinking, clubbing, friendships across the sexes? Should they be allowed to choose their religion, whatever the view of the father, or to have no religion at all? How far should they relate to the land of their father's or mother's origin, to Pakistan or India or wherever?

(iii) Community

Through marriage two families unite, and behind them are two communities. In the case of a Christian/Sikh couple, for example, the Christian community may be very loose, if it exists at all, whereas the Sikh community may be quite close, with strong expectations of the way life is to be lived. Matters may be taken as community concerns that, in Western society, are considered private. The Muslim husband in a Muslim-Christian marriage may, on occasion, put community affairs before wife and family. The mosque community is difficult for a European woman to penetrate. If she goes to community gatherings, she may feel an outsider and be expected to be with the women, whose language she does not speak. If she does not go to such gatherings, she may spend much time on her own. She may also find her husband's opinions on social, political or religious matters being influenced by this community. She may disagree with him privately but be under strong obligation not to disagree with him publicly. For her husband's sake she may be expected to wear particular clothes within his community. The husband may or may not help in the house but, if he does, she should be ready to be especially thankful and to express her gratitude, since it is not expected within Asian communities. These pressures can also exist between an Asian couple of different backgrounds. I have been listening to a 'modern' Muslim woman who is married to a Sikh, for whom the pressures are becoming too much. One of the symptoms is that she is not expected to express an independent opinion. Her family are saying, 'We warned you'.

There may be unstated pressures from both communities to show that a cross-cultural marriage cannot work, even if the woman tries especially hard and converts to her husband's faith. People are waiting to say, 'I told you so'. These pressures are considerable if the family remains in Britain, but they will increase dramatically if they decide to return, say, to a Muslim country.

(iv) Law

The legal status of the marriage may be questioned if the couple have married overseas and return here, or if they have married here and then go overseas to a Muslim country. There can be real fears about losing children if the marriage breaks down. In such circumstances there is a clear clash, in the Muslim-Christian case, between Western law that normally gives custody to the mother, and Islamic law where the Muslim father will have definite priority. If the marriage breaks down overseas and the mother wishes to return to Britain, will she be able to bring the children with her? There are also questions related to other wives. For example, in a case known to me, a Christian woman who is the second wife of a Muslim, having married in a mosque, has no legal rights under British law, should the marriage run into difficulties. The prime interest of Islam would be to ensure that her young son is brought up as a Muslim, not to protect her as estranged wife. In London Shia Islam has recently begun to offer special contracts, whereby the husband waives certain rights, for example, regarding the children, and also agrees to have only one wife.

(v) Race

At all levels of society racism exists to varying degrees and is likely to be faced by the couple and their children, if they have married across race as well as religion. We should also note the kind of prejudice provoked by 'Islamophobia' and antisemitism, which may include attitudes displayed in the media as well as in society. A white person married to a Muslim, who had converted, told me that she found the period after 9/11 very disturbing. It caused her to reflect deeply on the nature of a religion that could do such things, and she felt very aware of how people were looking at her, wearing her scarf. Children in a mixed marriage may not be clear about which race or religion they belong to. They may blame their parents (subconsciously) for who they are, and on occasions may need specialist help to work through their confusion.

(vi) Faith

In a religiously committed couple, there may be clear issues related to very different understandings of doctrine, theology, spirituality and worship. These may centre on the understanding of God and of Jesus Christ, but equally significant is the range of areas that are considered as relating to faith. Whereas most religions see their religion as a whole way of life and religious obligation covering all its aspects, many Christians compartmentalise their religion to a narrow field of experience. In Islam, obligations like prayer and fasting, mosque attendance and celebration of festivals take on a very high priority. There may also be differing views of the nature of marriage: in Buddhism and Islam it is, for example, a contractual affair between two people and two families; in Christianity it is essentially a sacrament or covenant celebrated before God. Each faith will vary in how much pressure it exerts upon marriage partners to convert. From a faith perspective, there will be little such pressure in a Buddhist-Christian or Hindu-Christian marriage, for example, though there may be other pressures, social or otherwise.

Support for cross-faith marriages

What kind of support can be offered to couples who make the decision to marry across religion?

(i)   It is vital that, if possible, couples contemplating such marriages are helped to be honest with each other about the kind of issues we have considered above. Sadly, statistics show that 'love conquers all' is not likely to be enough in Muslim-Christian marriages, for example, since a large proportion break down. It is crucial that the couple look beyond the wedding day to consider how their life together will be shaped, including the way children will be brought up. The couple should also be clear about their religious expectations (for example, a Muslim man who has practised little before marriage may become much more pious, partly to prove himself within his community). If the Muslim husband-to-be, whatever the Qur'an says, expects that his wife will convert and conform outwardly at least as a Muslim, he should be honest about his intention. Then the wife-to-be can make an informed decision.

(ii) It is helpful if parents and siblings are involved in discussions concerning the marriage, since its success or otherwise may depend on their attitudes, which initially may be fear or prejudice. A practising Christian woman told me that, when she found her daughter was to marry a Muslim, she discovered prejudices she never dreamt she had. Parents may be particularly anxious if they know their child intends to convert to the future spouse's religion on marriage.

Support will be needed through all the normal ups and downs of married life as well as through the kinds of issues mentioned above. There can, on occasions, be a rich reward. One parent told me that she had been more cared for by her daughter and son-in-law than she could normally have expected.

(iii) A couple from different religions may ask to marry in church. There is a legal requirement to allow an Anglican church to be used for such a marriage, if they live in the parish even if the individual priest is not happy about it. Moreover, the number of such marriages may increase, since new legislation under preparation stipulates that 'significant connection' from one of the couple is sufficient. The baptism of either party is not required. However, there is a requirement to follow the authorised service, which is not only Christian but includes the Trinitarian formula at the sharing of rings and the final blessing. A careful explanation of what is required helps the couple make their own decision as to whether to proceed, and may provide an opportunity for Christian witness to them. If they decide to go ahead, the challenge is to meet what is required by the Church and, at the same time, to provide an ethos that enables the couple and their families to be comfortable, perhaps through cultural additions to the service or through appropriate prayers or readings, for example. Each case is different and, if there is doubt, advice should be sought. There are published Bishops' Guidelines (see Bibliography). Other Churches take a more relaxed approach, such as the Roman Catholic Church which follows specific regulations set down in the various European National Bishops' Conferences in accordance with the Papal letter *Matrimonia Mixta* (1970), and the Methodist Church, whose service book allows the word 'God' to be used, rather than the Trinitarian blessing.

Preparation for the marriage may also be used to raise some of the general issues related to a cross-religious marriage and, if appropriate, further advice can be sought. Resources include the Diocesan Inter-Faith Adviser or suitable individuals in the other faith. As an alternative to a church service, a Registry Office wedding followed by appropriate blessing ceremonies in both religions can be suggested. For example, two hospital workers were marrying across faith in a

Registry Office. The Imam would not bless the marriage unless the Christian wife converted. The Muslim bridegroom refused to allow his future wife to be put under such pressure. The hospital chaplain agreed to bless the marriage in the chapel and used appropriate inclusive words.

It is important to fit the approach to the couple who are preparing to marry. A Christian white woman was marrying a Brahmin who had become a Christian. The conversion had brought the family much anguish, and reconciliation had been slow. But the extended family agreed to come to the church wedding. The couple asked the priest to preach on the text 'Perfect love casts out all fear'. In a wedding blessing, between a Muslim and a Christian, the priest offered this prayer informally at the beginning:

> In your being together, two cultures, two forms of religion meet. From afar they seem like a world of difference, nearby it is love for each other, which finds a place of discovery in the search for similarities, and a challenge to make your distinctiveness creative in small and large matters. In this service, where you ask a blessing from the God of all beings, from Allah the merciful, you want to say to each other: we will try with all that is in our power, to love each other, to be true to each other, and each to accept the other as he or she is.

It would be a great help to have a network of advisers with appropriate training in the cross-cultural and cross-religious areas. Particular skill is needed in distinguishing between those normal problems which any marriage faces and those that can be attributed to its cross-faith nature. Another source of support is a mixed-marriage group. This may be an informal group set up by two or three couples who have a natural affinity, or it may have been set up for the purpose through an organisation (see Resources section). We should also note that each marriage is different: because one marriage has faced a particular problem it does not follow that another will.

Final reflections

It is possible to see mixed marriages as a symbol of hope in a divided world, a sign of a more accepting, harmonious and healthily pluralistic future. This they can certainly be and bring much happiness. But they can also be the source of much misunderstanding and misery if the only thing holding the couple together is romance.

An Asian psychiatrist in Birmingham, who is much versed in the issues involved, writes,

> Such relationships take courage and a broad outlook to break artificial boundaries of race and culture and conservative views. The ultimate winners are two individuals and their love for each other and commitment to live together. At the same time, we should not forget the very high divorce rate of such marriages, and the real problems associated with such unions.

And a Jewish-Christian couple comment:

> Diane and I remain in a marriage that is full of discovery and learning. I hope that we are honest enough to recognise the difficulties and brave enough to explore them. I am not sure that the church or orthodox Jewish opinion knows quite what to make of this 'experiment'. It is no 'experiment' for us. Just two lives working with an ordinary happy marriage, to try and witness to the way of the Kingdom, a marriage in which God has sprinkled an extra little spice. I do hope that in the years to come, the spice will not only enrich us, but will contribute more fully than we feel allowed at present, to interfaith education and dialogue, between Church and Synagogue, Jew and Christian.

Perhaps we can hope the same for Christian and Muslim, mosque and church, and for other religions too.

CASE STUDIES AND QUESTIONS

1. When your daughter, who is at university, returns for the vacation, she says that she has met a Muslim man, whom she wishes to marry. How do you respond? What questions do you ask? Would you feel the same if it were your son who wished to marry a Muslim young woman? (Please answer honestly!)
2. You are a minister or adviser. One of the families in your congregation has a daughter who has married a Pakistani Muslim. She is a Christmas and Easter churchgoer, but was clear at the time of her wedding that she wished to remain a Christian. However, she comes to see you one day and says that pressure is being put on her, partly from her husband and partly from the wider in-laws, to convert to Islam before she has children, so that the family will be unified. They feel they are already losing face within the community. How do you respond to her? What if she were from a churchgoing family, but never came herself because she is an agnostic?

3. What readings/hymns/prayers would you suggest for the wedding of a Christian marrying a Hindu?

Asylum seekers and refugees

Ten years ago, there would not have been a section on this subject. At that time the numbers of asylum seekers and refugees coming to this country were much lower, but over the last decade, until 2004, numbers have risen considerably, partly because of the apparent increase of disturbed situations in the world, and partly because relatively more people are seeking a home in Britain. This does not mean that a vast proportion of the world's refugees come to Britain. Far greater numbers seek refuge in countries like Tanzania, Iran and Pakistan. But what has changed is that it has become a major political issue in Britain and throughout Europe. There are a number of reasons why immigration has become such a political hot potato. First, there has been a media campaign waged by certain popular newspapers which have become obsessed with the issue. Second, it has become a political tool used by opposition parties to put pressure on government whom they urge to 'get a grip on the problem'. Third, there is a perceived unfairness in a benefits system which is regarded as giving priority to those who come new to the country at the cost of communities of British citizens who have suffered deprivation over a number of years. Fourth, there is a perception that those entering
the country are coming in under a false pretext, exaggerating the dangers from which they are fleeing, when in fact they are really economic migrants.

All this may be true, but why include the topic here? The reason is that perhaps seventy per cent of refugees are Muslims, from North Africa and countries like Iran, Iraq, Afghanistan, Somalia and Turkey (Kurds). In addition there are Tamil Hindus from Sri Lanka, large numbers of Christians from Zimbabwe, Congo and other African countries and elsewhere, and small numbers from other faiths. The high percentage of Muslims is latched upon by the media and used as a stick to beat them with: 'Muslim countries are all disturbed dictatorships. Their people come here, because they cannot live there. Then they make all kinds of demands for rights here. We are in danger of becoming a minority within our own country.' The last statement is nonsense: at the time of the last census in 2001 Muslims made up 1.6 million of Great Britain's total population of 55 million. Although this figure for Muslims may be an underestimate, since it does not take account of illegal immigrants and others who were afraid to register, it does give an idea of the percentage of Muslims within the population. While Muslims are concentrated in certain areas where they are in the majority, across the country those naming themselves as Christians still constitute 72 per cent of the total population.

What then is the pastoral role for Christians in the face of this real, if often exaggerated issue?

To begin with, we should be unapologetic about the biblical imperative to offer support to the 'stranger'. In the Old Testament, it is repeatedly made clear that the Jewish people had a special obligation to care for the alien and the foreigner within their midst, which equalled the requirement to care for the widow and the orphan. The people of Israel were especially judged when they failed in this obligation. This care was to be an expression of their thankfulness for the way God had looked after them when they were aliens in Egypt. In the New Testament, in the parable of the sheep and the goats in Matthew 25, the nations are judged by how they cared for the homeless, the hungry and the thirsty. A parable such as the Good Samaritan has an obvious relevance (see Luke 10:29ff.). In addition Matthew's account of how Mary, Joseph and Jesus became political refugees in Egypt, out of fear of Herod and his persecution of the innocent, has a disturbingly modern feel (Matt. 2:13–15). Even St Paul, we read, spent fourteen years in Arabia after his conversion (see Gal. 2:1).

Granted we have an undeniable obligation, how can it be carried out? Clearly circumstances vary, and this is not something Christians can or should undertake on their own. One avenue is volunteering through statutory bodies such as Refugee Action, through local authorities, or through the Red Cross and other charities who play key roles. But in addition Christians can make an important contribution by working together, ecumenically wherever possible. For the refugee, it is a human being first, and a Christian second, who is helping them: it is not an Anglican or Baptist. Pastoral support can be given through regular visits to asylum centres. In Leicester, there is an International Hotel, which houses single asylum seekers for months while they are waiting to be placed around the country via the government's dispersal scheme. Sunday afternoon visits take place each month. Individuals can be taken out to homes for meals, and they can also be invited to church social functions. Some may ask to attend worship, even on occasions Muslims. Special gifts can be given at Christmas or other times. Clothes and other necessities can be collected.

In addition there is the key role of advocacy: providing a voice for individuals who need it. This may be related to their wish to study or upgrade their qualifications, or a need to find housing when their asylum has been granted, or providing support when they go to a tribunal and speaking for them. It is not a easy role, and it is time-consuming. It may, however, make all the difference to their case. This is obviously a time for clergy to wear their collar. But it is also a role which lay people who have the time can fulfil – ideal for those who have taken early retirement. It is important that the advocate knows the person well, has had the opportunity to talk directly with the individual's lawyer, and is convinced about the validity of the case. I took up the case of an Iranian. I was clear about his circumstances, the dangers he was in, and his burning desire to study and work professionally. He loved Iran and would never have left, if he had had a choice. Once I appeared at the tribunal, the case was immediately decided in his favour, without my speaking at all. My earlier carefully written submission was considered enough. On another occasion, I was asked to speak for a second Iranian. I had much sympathy for him and his family, but somehow his story did not add up. I did not know him well enough to vouch for him. I advised him to be honest in the tribunal, but did not offer to come with him. It would be wrong to use our influence inappropriately.

Another type of advocacy is campaigning for better conditions for asylum seekers and the safeguarding of their legal status, which has become more and more important in recent years, as the Home Office has tightened regulations year by year in an effort to prove they are tough on asylum. Some of the decisions have been very harmful to the security, health and well-being not just of the asylum seekers but also of their children. It would not be helpful for me to comment on individual decisions and regulations, since they are changing all the time. If they were specified here, they would probably have been toughened further by the time of the publication of this book – although on occasion the government is forced to relax them as a result of a European human rights ruling or high court decision within Britain. One of the biggest problems is ignorance, and a Christian volunteer can help greatly by being up to date with regulations, so that ways to provide support can be found within the law. In Leicester, there are at least three centres run by the churches, which act as pastoral and advice centres.

One vital area is the education of church people on asylum issues, so that they may distance themselves from the more extreme views around and understand enough to pass that understanding onto others. Another is political lobbying to change more extreme regulations, by well-researched argument rather than merely prejudiced assertions. Actual stories can help here, to enable officials and politicians to understand the consequences of decisions.

In terms of direct interfaith aspects, Christians are likely to find that some Muslim asylum seekers wish to know about the Christian faith. They may be motivated by an academic interest or by a real empathy for what they have experienced from Christians, whether within their homeland or after they entered Britain. This provides a major challenge and opportunity. Clergy and lay people should be appropriately cautious, without 'quenching the spirit'. Each story will be different, and motivation is a key area, as is family situation, likely consequences and immigration status.

It is crucial that any individuals who eventually seek baptism are not doing so because they think, rightly or wrongly, that it will improve their chances of staying in Britain. This does not mean there are not mixed motives – there always are in any human decision. Indeed, it was with mixed motives that people came to Jesus to seek help. Usually they wanted a personal benefit, particularly healing. Asylum seekers often need deep healing. But to become a follower of Jesus, much more was required, in particular a desire to begin a new life, transforming all dimensions of their existence.

A great many of these enquiries come from Iranians. Many have had contact with Christian groups in Iran, whether open or underground. Amid all the political pressures there is clearly a spiritual awakening taking place in Iran. Those coming here are usually part of various political opposition groups, and often associate oppressive political structures with an oppressive Islamic state and oppressive clergy, who have removed the possibilities of freedom and participation in the future of their country. Most of them are professionally trained and feel deeply frustrated, politically and religiously. Hence they arrive in Britain with a longing for a better Iran, but at the same time feeling that political Islam has been responsible at least partly for the history of their country over the last twenty or more years.

On their arrival in this country they are suddenly free to test out a new religious as well as political and professional future. They find clusters of Iranian Christians, most of them recent converts, who suggest that their experience has been good. They are scattered among several communities, loyal to their receiving church, and otherwise come together for Iranian events and services. Some have remained warmly received enquirers. Others have gone further and taken baptism after a period of preparation. This important step should not be rushed. They need to talk through how their new faith relates to Islam, which they should be encouraged to see as a positive background. They should also be encouraged to keep in contact with their families in Iran, and not to announce their new step in an email or by phone. It is a deeply serious step, and one that should normally only be revealed in person. I know a convert who made arrangements to meet his family members in Turkey.

The testimonies of asylum seekers as they take baptism – which they can be encouraged to give publicly – can be very powerful. Here is an edited extract from the testimony of an Iranian woman, who is now a deputy churchwarden:

> I am the lost sheep that was separated from its herd for many years. Words cannot express my happiness, as new birth takes place. The story of my beloved country and its kind people would take a long time to tell, with its rich natural resources, culture and beauty. It is now in the hands of oppressive rulers ... Kind and hard-working people seem to be destined for gradual death. I have been thirsty for the righteous words of Jesus from an early age, but I have always had to hide my feelings. If any born Muslim wants to move towards Christianity, he/she is asking for trouble, if not for a short life. Even research about the true Islam is not possible in Iran. All that is possible is obedience to fanatical rules. We left our homes and our jobs to seek refuge from fear, and driven by spiritual need. We are very happy to have found a new home, new faith, peace and safety. I thank my kind Muslim husband who has left me free to find my own way to God. I thank you, my Christian brothers and sisters, for accepting us with open arms, and showing such love and kindness. I ask you to pray for me, and for my country, that one day all its people will be freed from the rule of cruel people.

In these kinds of testimonies, there is much about freedom, life and fellowship. There is a turning to Jesus, without a rejection of the God of Islam, who is common.

Another area in which pastoral care can be given is in the support of marriages between asylum seekers of different faiths. Their common experience of exile, persecution and discrimination can override differences of faith, with surprising results. Two cases have come to my notice. One is an Afghan Muslim man who has married a blonde Catholic from an ex-Soviet republic. Neither has converted. The other is that of an Afghan woman who has married a Serb orthodox man. They also remain in their own faiths, but she has totally cut herself off from her family, here in Britain and back in Afghanistan. The binding together of exile, in this second case, has not transcended the rules of Islam (see p. 128–9).

How have British Muslims responded to the challenge of refugees and asylum seekers? In only a limited way. This may be because those fleeing here have suffered from Muslim regimes and do not want to have much contact with local mosques and Muslim communities, even though they may go for prayers. Or it may be because of the economic and social pressures in areas of high Muslim concentration. An empathetic Muslim woman told me that Islamically they have a strong sense of responsibility, but when they feel the doctor's surgery and the school becoming over-crowded, they find it very difficult. They also get bound up in the climate of fear generated by Islamophobia which becomes even more pronounced against Muslim asylum seekers. Such hatred makes all Muslims easy targets. More is done by Christians because Muslims already often feel overwhelmed by the problems they face and cannot cope with yet another one. Another Muslim commented that his community thinks that the government carries the primary responsibility to sort out the problem, and many hold asylum seekers and refugees to be scroungers. They are much better at sending containers of food and other necessities to fellow Muslims overseas than giving them support here. He is sad to say that there are limits to inter-Muslim solidarity!

The challenge for Christians is how far they can enable their work to become ecumenical, not just between churches but across faiths. Such collaboration can be an important symbol to society and to the asylum seeker, but it is not easy to achieve.

CASE STUDIES/QUESTIONS

1. Prepare a speech to be given to your church council making a case for why they should make a grant to the asylum seeker project in your town. You anticipate opposition from a member who feels strongly that they should not help Muslims like this, but rather should care for their own poor.

2. What are the key questions you would ask a Muslim asylum seeker who has been attending your church, if he or she asked for baptism?

6. COMMUNITY AND SOCIAL ISSUES

All major faiths have at their heart a commitment to love God (or, in the case of Buddhism, perhaps ultimate truth) and 'love our neighbour as ourselves'. Our neighbours are those who live next door to us, and those who live around us, and beyond that, those who come to live amongst us from around the world, and ultimately, all humanity, wherever they live. However, this love must extend beyond individual goodwill and deeds of kindness and be shown in corporate action and in developing community. This chapter looks at how this can happen and how Christians can be involved in these wider spheres. Such action, of course, is not new. In the middle of the nineteenth century Charles Kingsley, when asked to pray for those dying of cholera and typhoid in Victorian Birmingham, replied that he would do that only when the municipality agreed to pay for a new drainage system which would cure the water problems. What is new is the challenge to take action alongside other major faith communities and not just as Christians.

Since September 11, 2001 there has also been a dramatic change, at least in intention, in the encouragement from government for religious communities to play their part in community cohesion (the generic term) which underlines most of these issues. Central government has grasped the importance of the contribution of faith communities, and its various departments are expected to take faith issues into account.

The MP John Battle was chosen to be Adviser to the Prime Minister on faith communities. As a committed Roman Catholic, he is well aware of the important contribution of faiths in his locality. An example he gave in my hearing was of how Muslims have driven loan sharks out of his South Leeds constituency by encouraging Islamic banking. The social fabric of Leeds would collapse if faith communities suddenly withdrew their voluntary work. At the same time, those of faith are needed not just for their work but for their prayer. For this to be effective, however, they have to be deeply involved in dialogue together. Dialogue needs to take place between people of faith, people of little faith and people of no faith.

The Government's task is to ensure that this emphasis extends beyond the Home Office, which now has a Faith Communities Unit, to all departments. Some ministers may come to this with a faith commitment, others because they recognise the pragmatic benefits. This is where 9/11 has had a strong effect. Local authorities also need to be challenged. A cultural change is taking place, but only slowly. Since the 1960s it had been increasingly hard for faiths to get public funding for anything they did. The public arena had become highly secular and talk of religion could easily be the kiss of death to an initiative. The word 'secular' here is used in a Western sense, where religion becomes a privatised affair, and public life is conducted with no spiritual or religious dimension. In more recent times a shift seems to be occurring towards the Indian sense of 'secular'. India is one of the most highly religious countries in the world, but it has a secular constitution. This constitution recognises the right of all faiths to practise, preach and propagate their faith, but the state is neutral between religions. In Britain today, faith communities are beginning to be seen as significant players. Where previously the Church of England was the only key voice, it now shares its significant role with other churches and faith communities.

In 2002 the Local Government Association produced a report which encouraged local authorities to take action with faith communities.[1] It states that such communities are vital for 'good health, as providers of pastoral care, promoters of citizenship and community development, voices for social justice, and as a locus for gatherings of people in varying economic and social positions, of differing political views, from a range of ethnic backgrounds with shared concerns.' The danger is that faith groups are seen by local governments as providing them with an easy way to opt out of their social duty. Some authorities are generous in their funding while others are niggardly, and the difference does not necessarily depend on the size of the faith communities. This is acknowledged in another report, in this instance compiled by the Office of the Deputy Prime Minister, which states, 'the government's recognition of the faith communities' significant neighbourhood renewal and social inclusion role has yet to be reflected fully in local practice. The broad picture is patchy with enthusiasm in some areas matched by apparent reluctance to involve faith communities in others.'[2]

Granted that this is the case, we will now look at a number of significant issues.

International issues

The twenty-first century, far from ushering in the peace on earth many prayed for on millennium night, has seen an increase in violence. And far from this being taken out of the sphere of religion, as might have been expected in earlier decades, religious passions seem inextricably linked with international conflicts. We may or may not agree with the thesis of Samuel Huntington that today's conflicts are centred primarily on the clash of civilisations, in particular that between the West and Islam (see p. 160), but we cannot deny that there is a religious dimension to most if not all conflicts today. As mentioned in the Introduction, Rabbi Jonathan Sacks has wisely commented that if religion is not part of a solution, it will be part of the problem.[3] And that is our choice.

It is easy to list recent conflicts of this kind: Chechnya, Afghanistan, Iraq, Israel/Palestine, Gujarat, Kashmir, Sri Lanka, North East India, Pakistan, Indonesia, Kosovo, Northern Ireland, Nigeria, Sudan. These are just the most prominent ones, and more will no doubt have been added by the time this book is published. No individual, no matter how influential, is able to resolve any of these conflicts (though most of our major religions were formed by individuals who have changed the course of history!). However, what each of us can do is to work together to show that religions can react to events together, and can act as moderating and reconciling influences, rather than inflammatory ones. Some initiatives, involving Christians, have been taken at a high level. Canon Andrew White has taken considerable personal risks in acting as a peace-making envoy in the Middle East, in Nigeria and in Iraq, rather as Terry Waite did some years ago. The Alexandria initiative, which was launched by the previous Archbishop of Canterbury, has been an attempt to foster understanding between Muslim, Jew and Christian in the Holy Land. The al-Azhar Dialogue in the famous University of Egypt is another project between Muslim leaders and the Anglican Church. Muslim and Christian scholars have also come together to discuss the scriptures, and these conferences have been held in Canterbury, Qatar and Georgetown, USA, and a further one is planned for Sarajevo in 2005.[4] The conference in Qatar took place even as the bombs were falling in Baghdad. The Barnabas Foundation concentrates on the plight of Christians persecuted in Muslim lands. This is an important cause, but it needs to be balanced with understanding of Muslims here, and also with awareness of Muslims persecuted in Muslim lands. The Network for Interfaith Concerns of the Anglican Communion (NIFCON) promotes understanding, including that of conflict and reconciliation, across the Anglican Communion.

At the same time, we need to address the question of what can be done at a more local level about these mega issues, bearing in mind the high degree of solidarity felt by religious people for their co-religionists, particularly by Muslims. They see themselves as one community, the

Ummah, across the world, as symbolised by the image of Muslims together at prayer in an identical fashion across the world and by the *Hajj* pilgrimage.

How are we to react at a local level to ongoing conflicts around the world? How can we respond sensitively in highly charged situations in ways that can help to keep communities together in times of deeply held difference of view? Through experience gained in recent times in connection with the conflicts in Israel/Palestine, Gujarat and Iraq, the following pointers have proved helpful:

- Prior relationships are vital to ensure a sensitive and quick response. They should be across as broad a network as possible, including the faith leaders of the groups mentioned in chapter 2 on structures, but also, beyond them, to key secular groups such as the media, the police, local councillors and Members of Parliament. Crises may create relationships, but that is not ideal. An exception seems to have been 9/11, which proved to be a catalyst for the development of numerous local structures.
- Face to face meetings, the telephone and e-mail communication all have their place. Again, if structures are clear beforehand, more effective action can be taken. A list of key contact persons within each faith can be drawn up. These individuals can then contact their own significant members, who can cascade any message more widely.
- Speed is of the essence, if the media are to be interested in the responses of faith leaders. And radio, TV and local newspapers are the surest way of enabling news and sharing statements. The Asian media, as well as the English media, should not be forgotten. It is good to have a press officer available: often this can be the Anglican Press Officer, who should be invited to all important meetings.
- Statements are a useful tool for expressing the views of faith leaders, and these can be sent to the media, but also to government officials, Members of Parliament and, on occasions, to appropriate leaders overseas. Such statements must be written with great sensitivity to ensure they are inclusive. Here is an example on the Israel/Palestine question, agreed by leading members of three faiths:

> We are all religions who have our ancestry in Abraham and believe in One God. We respect each other's sacred scriptures and the commitment there to peace and justice for all people, regardless of race, creed or culture. We all have holy sites in Jerusalem and the surrounding areas, which have been places of pilgrimage for centuries. Sharing this common ground, we commit ourselves to do all we

can to support movements for peace and justice in the Holy Land. We deeply regret all loss of life and destruction of property, and have a special concern for innocent Palestinians and Israelis who have died in the recent conflict and for their families. We call on the international community, and our own government, to fall behind efforts made by the United Nations, the European Union, the United States and Arab nations, to bring their influence to bear on the government of Israel and the Palestinian Authority to bring about a permanent ceasefire. We ask for the implementation of United Nations resolutions that would lead to the formation of a Palestinian State and also to the full and permanent recognition of Israel, and the rights of all peoples in the region to live in peace and security.

In Leicester, we pledge ourselves to work for the continuation of the good relations that exist between our three communities and not to allow disturbance elsewhere to lead to fear or suspicion between us. We all oppose discrimination and violence, based upon spurious religious or political grounds or inflammatory media reporting. We pledge ourselves to remind our co-religionists of the sufferings experienced by all communities, not just our own, and to oppose extremists of all kinds including those within our own community. We remain hopeful that peace and justice will eventually come to this troubled part of the world, in spite of the present impasse.

- It is good to come to agreements about some general principles. One decision we have made in Leicester is that an attack on one of our faiths should be seen as an attack on us all, whether it is a building or a person that is a victim. How we then act together depends on the circumstances, but this gives each faith the security that they can bring to others their concerns when they have been hurt. This principle was elucidated after 9/11, when local Muslims were being insulted, and women were often afraid to put on their scarves for fear of being singled out. Sikhs also were being victimised, since many people are ignorant of the difference between faiths. This has been applied too when there have been attacks on synagogues, and Muslim leaders have offered to escort Jews home from Sabbath services. When Muslim graves have been repeatedly desecrated, support has been shown by Christians and Jews. When, in the aftermath of the Gujarat civil strife, Hindu shops were being accused of making sweets using urine, Muslim leaders gave full support to the local hygiene officer as he informed local Muslims that this story was complete fabrication. These are some examples of the working out of this principle, which its agreement in advance can make possible.

- It is good to establish procedures, with the police, for rapid reaction response to any potential terrorist incident. Wherever this happens in the UK – and London is the most likely target – there will certainly be immediate implications for other places. We have established a network of contacts, which will ensure that a meeting can be called at twenty-four hours' notice, so that the police can communicate with all faith leaders their concerns and how they can best help reduce tensions. It is noteworthy how the police see the faith groups as a significant component of any such response.

- Faith groups in any city are a touchstone of international opinion. From within their membership they have networks spreading throughout the world. This also makes them especially sensitive to violence and accident wherever it is happening in the world. If the rapid response of faith groups to emergency can include the raising of relief funds and gifts in kind, this makes a considerable impact on the community. In Leicester, for example, very large sums of money were raised for the victims of the Gujarat earthquake and in Birmingham for the relief of those suffering and dying in Bosnia. The Birmingham Sikh community also raised a large sum of money for the victims of the Rwanda genocide, though no Sikhs were involved. If the money donated comes not just from the community that is touched by the suffering, but from across faith communities, it speaks a loud message. Christians may well be in a good place to initiate such gestures of support.

- Christian leaders, and especially the bishops, are seen to have an influence out of proportion to their actual power. The bishop can speak for the wider faith community, and not just for Anglicans, or indeed other Christians. The Archbishop of Canterbury nationally is in the same position and, in recent years, his influence with other faith communities has grown rather than lessened, though he may have considerable difficulties within his own communion. Rowan Williams' small book about the destruction of the Twin Towers, which he witnessed,[5] led a Muslim who read the book to remark that this man must be Archbishop of Canterbury. He gained considerable credibility for his stance on the Iraq war, as did many bishops at a local level. It was partly because of this that the Iraq war of 2003, which could have created considerable tensions in local communities, has not had major disruptive effects within communities. The majority of Christians were recognised as being against the war, which was demonstrated by their willingness, following many of their bishops and other leaders, to march in solidarity with Muslims and secular groups.

- It should be remembered that it is as faith groups that we react to international events, and therefore prayer and vigil should be part of our response. (See p. 102 where I talk about the importance of enabling prayer publicly in face of major crises.) Speed is of the essence, and it is vital that demonstrations of unity are given media coverage in situations where many will expect communities to be divided.

• Though much can be done at a higher level, any ordinary congregation can engage in prayer and other appropriate action with a congregation of another faith nearby. Actions such as the people from a mosque coming across to a church to offer prayer and condolences, or vice versa, in the face of a crisis, can have a major effect.

• As Christians we should be ready to explain with clarity our theological and biblical response to these major events. For example, how do we relate these questions to the just war theory? How do we help congregations reflect about the fact that violence is often being perpetrated in the name of religion, or of factions within religions?

Education issues

This major area can be divided between school education, further and higher education and seminary education. Much of what follows applies principally to Muslims, who have the most distinctive approach. But there are also sensitivities related to other faiths. All I can do is give a brief introduction to the issues, as likely to be experienced by Christians.

Education of children

Amongst the other faith communities in this country there are a high proportion of young people, particularly in the Muslim community. The latest census figures show that a third of all British Muslims are under fifteen years old, and another 18 per cent are aged between sixteen and twenty-four.[6] Concern has long been expressed about the special needs of children of various faiths in schools. Much work has been done within local authorities and SACREs (Standing Committee on Religious Education). Guidelines have been produced, such as 'Guidelines in meeting the religious and cultural needs of Muslims' which was formulated by the Muslim Liaison Committee in Birmingham and revised in 1999. It covers food, dress, sex education, relationships between boys and girls, sports and changing facilities, appropriate fund raising, etc. At a more profound level, there is a strong feeling that Muslim contribution to the development of many aspects of the curriculum is almost ignored. Typical is this statement:

Thanks to the knowledge and the intellect of the Muslim scientist we were able to benefit from mathematics, anatomy, chemistry, philosophy, astronomy ... In other words, thanks to Islam, knowledge was preserved, further developed and passed on, and this is without any doubt one of the important treasures of Islam.[7]

The transmission of such knowledge is a religious duty for Muslims, and it is often felt that the schools do not aid them in making this contribution. They would value a greater involvement in open discussion of citizenship, democracy, values, history, as well as recognition within the curriculum of the Muslim contribution to science and the arts. There needs to be extensive discussion within the education system about what it means to be British and Muslim, European and Muslim.[8]

As Christians, how can we help? How can we be sensitive to the issues?

Anglican schools vary in their admissions policies and how they operate in terms of their Christian emphasis. Village schools have a natural catchment area and are likely to have few children from other faiths. In the cities it is a different story. In Birmingham, for example, some Anglican schools have nearly a 100 per cent Muslim intake because their catchment area covers a largely Muslim population. Muslims often opt for a church school rather than a secular one, since they favour religious values and ethical discipline. Talking to me about the value of church schools, one Muslim quoted Jesus' words, 'By their fruits you shall know them'! In the case of church-run girls-only secondary schools, the Muslim intake may be very high. Questions then arise about governance, and clearly there can be parent governors for a church school who are Muslim, if they are elected to the post. The link with the church may be hard to sustain in terms of the traditional role of hosting school services. Assemblies become a further issue, as does access for Muslim clergy to lead prayers or teach, particularly in secondary schools. What does it mean to run an explicitly Christian school in such circumstances? One answer is to say that those who send their children there know the ethos of the school, and that this will be spelled out in the offering of Christian teaching and worship. Others offer a more sensitive approach, which may well then raise the question: what is the point in running such a school? Is offering a service to the community in a poor area enough?

Some other church schools achieve high educational standards, and people of other faiths will seek ways to gain admittance for academic reasons. Roman Catholic schools normally not only have a strongly Catholic ethos, but also clear limits on non-Catholic pupils. St Philip's Sixth Form College in Birmingham was run by the Oratory. Numbers of Catholic students dropped below a critical number, though the school was run very effectively as a multifaith school. After a long and public battle, the Oratory fathers closed the school and then reopened it firmly re-establishing its Catholic ethos. Such public conflicts often result in church schools gaining the reputation of being anti other faiths.

The existence of church schools, and the long history of Jewish schools, has led to an increasing wish for the establishment of Muslim schools. There are very few Hindu schools, and little demand for them, since Hindus make their way very effectively through the state system, or use private schools, and reach a very high educational standard. They do not see the school as the primary place for their religion to be expressed. The same applies to Sikhs. However, there are now hundreds of private Muslim schools, and these vary in quality. There is a growing desire for more of these to gain voluntary-aided status, which will give them state funding but will also mean that they require more regulation. Up till now only a handful have been recognised. If a case is being made in a particular area, the support of church leaders may be significant. Anglican leaders have on the whole taken a supportive role. If Anglicans have many schools in an area, should not Muslims be supported in their desire for at least one state-supported school? At heart level Christians may not like the thought of Muslim schools, which can easily seem divisive. Some Muslims agree, feeling young Muslims can feed better into society if they have studied in integrated schools. In an Islamic school, even if there is a more ethical ethos and Islamic education can happen in school hours, they will have to work hard at integration with the wider community. But some would claim that church schools face these very same issues. In terms of justice and equity the matter would seem to be clear.

In Birmingham, the former Bishop gave strong support for a state-supported Muslim secondary school, and this is now operating well. In Leicester, an Islamic Academy for Girls already gets outstanding results. The atmosphere is disciplined and friendly, and for this reason a number of non-Muslims teach there, even though their pay is lower than it would be in the state sector. Their application for voluntary-aided status included a clause allowing up to 25 per cent of the children admitted to be non-Muslim and for them to have access to religious education from teachers from their own tradition. This application received support from the Bishop. It was, however, turned down. The Principal intends to try again, when certain conditions have been fulfilled. The fact that the Church is giving continuing moral support has been significant.

There are many state schools, which are de facto Muslim schools. This is true in the case of three large junior schools near to where I live. One has one white child, the second has one white child who is a Muslim, and the third has less than ten white children. The teachers are mainly white.

An important function of such schools is to expose the children to the tenets and practice of other faiths, including Christianity. They are unlikely to have this opportunity outside the school, since they live in an area that is nearly all Muslim, and time outside school is spent in *madrassas* (after school classes, see p. 152), or in the Muslim community. Nearly all children go to *madrassa* for up to two hours a day. In this type of school the RE teacher plays a critical role, and there is great potential for a Christian teacher. One such teacher enabled groups of clergy I brought to the school to engage directly with the children. The children were taken to the local church and answered a quiz about what they could find there. Some had never been in a church before. The same children were given free reign in the classroom to ask questions of the clergy. These required careful answering, in terms understandable to ten-year-old Muslims, and gave natural opportunity for the Christian faith to be talked about. These were some of the questions that were asked:

- Where is Jesus now?
- How and why did the Christian religion begin?
- Where are the nails of the cross, the spear and Jesus' cloak?
- What do you *do* as Christians?
- What do you believe happens after death?
- Why are there four Gospels? Why do they not say the same thing?
- Why did the Romans not believe in one God?
- What does an evil spirit look like?
- What does it mean to say Jesus is a 'lamb'?
- If Jesus was the Son of God, why did God not protect him?
- Do you believe in what all the prophets said, or just Jesus?
- Do Christians pray? How many times a day? How long each time? Are you punished if you do not pray? Why do you sing hymns?
- Do you go on pilgrimage? Do you fast? What are your festivals?
- Why are churches only open on Sundays?
- What is that white thing round your neck? What made you become a priest? Can you marry and be a priest? Can women be priests? Do you live at church? What does a priest *do*? How do you pay for your food? What languages do you have to learn to be a priest? Do you have a boss as a priest?

A further initiative taken by this same RE teacher was to arrange an e-mail link with a Roman Catholic school in a suburban area. Questions were asked over e-mail, such as what does it mean to eat the body and blood of Christ! A joint sports day was arranged, so the two groups could meet. She also arranged for a group of parents and a group of young people from different faiths to go as a team to visit schools and enabled a group of the minority Christians and Hindu pupils to talk about what it felt like to be in a predominantly Muslim school. They mingle well at school, but little outside, and are likely to go to different secondary schools.

The secondary school which most of these pupils go on to, is located nearby. The Principal is a Muslim woman. She told me that there is little framework of faith amongst the small proportion of 'Christian students'. She spoke about one student whose mother had died suddenly. The girl had no place to put her grief, no spiritual dimension within which to reflect, no concept of prayer or heaven. The Principal found herself, as a Muslim, trying to supply that for the girl, in her own terms! A Christian teacher – of evangelical background – says that he loves teaching there, describing it as 'such a relief' after being in a 'normal' secondary school. Here the students know where to place ideas about God and faith and are interested in his Christian ideas.

It will be helpful to add some further explanation about *madrassas*, the centres for after-school education run by mosques or other Muslim organisations. Their curriculum is traditional, including learning the Qur'an by heart, some Arabic and Urdu language, learning about the prophet Muhammad, and the Muslim way of life and Muslim history. The centres are unregulated and can vary enormously. Some teachers are well trained, others are volunteers. Some classes take place in overcrowded buildings and have very much the same feel as they must have in Pakistan, with rote learning, the use of the stick to ensure progress or attention and little English language being used. Others are now well organised, with English the medium of instruction and consideration being given to what it means to be British and Muslim. Similar methods are employed to those used in schools. Pupils are eager to attend and enjoy an atmosphere conducive to learning.

If there is a *madrassa* in the area, it is worth trying to arrange a visit since the pupils will normally be receptive to being asked questions. This can be a means of allaying fears that these schools are terrorist training camps in disguise. Though we may find the methods used and the amount of time children spend in them questionable, they are also a challenge to us to think about how seriously we take the education of Christian children. A constant concern for those who lead the schools is the question of how far children can be held beyond a certain age. For reformist leaders, it is an urgent task that the schools become places pupils like to be. But even when this intention is pursued, it is an open question as to how far it will be possible in the future to hold the youth within the community. It is in no one's interest that the proportion of disaffected young Muslim people should continue to rise. It is such youth who are likely to become attracted to extremism. Attempts are now being made by enlightened local authorities such as Watford, Birmingham, Manchester and Leicester to work co-operatively with such schools and to offer programmes of assistance. They also have the advantage, appreciated by some authorities, of keeping children off the streets!

Hindus and Sikhs have also initiated training programmes for their young people. These are less frequent, perhaps on Saturday mornings, or through intensive summer camps. While within the British context it has become necessary to teach the faith intentionally, in India it is picked up through community and family living and through temple life. Here, it will not happen without direct programmes. Consequently, the training of teachers has become an important issue. The normal role of the priests is not to teach, but to lead ritual. Their training has normally been in India, but there are now one or two centres in this country, such as the ISKON (Hare Krishna) Centre near Watford for Hindu priests at *Bhakti Vedanta*. Visiting gurus and others from India, who come on speaking tours, provide occasional lectures. There is a need for Hindus who can give proficient, regular teaching. Sikhism has a more developed teaching process and is probably more ready to provide such support. Hinduism, traditionally, is a religion which is caught and not taught.

Further and higher education

There are a number of reasons why this is a very important sector. Government policy in at least the last fifteen years has been radically to increase the size of the higher education sector. When I was at university in the 1960s, 5 per cent of people went on to higher education. Current policy aims to achieve 50 per cent, and this is nearer to being achieved than many other government targets. The further education sector is also enormous, with the detaching of many sixth forms from schools contributing to its growth. In Manchester 185,000 students are taught in higher and further education. In many of our cities this sector competes with the National Health Service as the largest employer.

It is an area of growing ethnic and religious diversity. Institutions vary, but in further education Muslims are over-represented in proportion to the population. The proportion of Hindus going on to higher education is greater than that of the white community, and numbers are rising fast. In addition, there is a great drive to attract overseas students, many of whom are from Muslim and other backgrounds.

There is a growing profile of people of other faiths within the institutions. Muslims are no longer willing to be taken for granted, and other faiths want to show that they are not willing to be ignored, just because they appear, as they say, 'to cause less trouble than Muslims'.

Being a student at university is a window of opportunity. It is a time when students are less under the control of their families or their local communities. The amount of freedom is more limited for those who attend further education since it is by its nature local. The proportion attending local institutions is high from other faiths. The motivation for white parents to send their children to local universities is usually financial, while Asian parents hope thereby to keep control, particularly of girls, for a little longer. Nevertheless, it is a time when opinions are formed or progressed, and where experiments in lifestyle can be extended. It is an impressionable age, when peer group pressure is high. It is likely to be foundational, not just for a person's career, but also for their religious or non-religious outlook. Soon after leaving universities, the students of Asian background at least are likely to get married. Many will be employed locally, and barriers may return.

In higher education, the level of religious practice tends to be above average, but it is often prey to excess zeal and sometimes extremism. Religious groups may try to take advantage of the vulnerability of young minds, their displacement from the home environment, their uncertainty about the future in a very competitive world, their growing enslavement to debt, crises about personal relationships and issues of alcohol and drugs. They see a field ripe for the winning of converts, and most inter-religious conversion takes place between the ages of eighteen and thirty.

It is where issues of secularism and faith are most likely to be fought over. Some universities were originally religious foundations, such as Oxford and Cambridge, while others like Leicester have had an aggressively secular history in recent decades, with the theology faculty being abolished and the chaplaincy being placed deliberately outside the campus. Things are changing, however, and three of the local further education colleges now have half-time chaplains. There are increasing demands for chaplains from other faiths, raising a number of questions which I will address later. But, from the institution's point of view, having a positive approach to all faiths can be seen, at the least, as a useful recruiting tool.

Universities are historically places for pushing out the boundaries of thought, and this should especially be true in the religious and spiritual sphere. People of faith can learn from each other and can learn from the way religions have historically treated each other. High on their agenda should be the issues of social cohesion, the common good, international understanding and conflict resolution, as well as those of theology, the study of the scriptures and spirituality. Universities can also be key places for interfaith dialogue, if the atmosphere and the leadership are right. The role of the university is becoming increasingly functional, with research, output, career development and numbers of students the important ends. The religions together can offer something counter cultural that suggests that the dimension of life they represent is not an optional concern for a few, but can provide an alternative world view which at least should be given a hearing. This can increasingly be better done, and with more integrity and strength, if they work together, rather than in competition.

What then are some of the practical challenges that those working in these sectors face?

- Thought needs to be given to how the well-established role of the Anglican chaplain can best be used. Although they are recognised by the universities, these posts are usually financed by the Church and thus frequently vulnerable, since sector posts are an easy place to bring cuts. They have a breadth of role which needs to be re-affirmed. This includes extending the opportunities by making room for usually part-time chaplains from other denominations. But increasingly the role should include the perhaps interim task of providing a gate for other faiths to come through. Encouraging developments in this direction will often make the chaplain unpopular amongst some conservative Christian staff and students.

  I was recently interviewed about doctrine and scripture, along with an Imam friend, by a Muslim-Christian audience of about a hundred. I found myself under deep scrutiny, not from Muslim students, but from Christians, more concerned about my soundness or otherwise than having dialogue with the Imam. For such groups – and Christian Unions vary – the chaplain is there to minister to the Christian students, and, where possible, to seek for opportunities to engage in evangelism, implicit or explicit.

- 'Chaplain' is not a word found in the vocabulary of people of faiths other than Christian and so the concept needs to be explored and training offered. I am one of the Advisers for a Muslim Chaplaincy course established at the Islamic Foundation in Markfield, just outside Leicester. I was approached to offer this support, and now there are five Christians on the Advisory group from different sectors. The Muslim leadership recognises that the concept of chaplain is one from which they wish to learn. The traditional Imam is a teacher and a leader of prayer. The pastoral role is a key one in chaplaincy, and the training covers educational, hospital and prison chaplaincy.

- The provision of prayer rooms, *halal* or *kosher* meat and alternative entertainments to the usual diet of bars and clubbing, needs to be addressed. It is also important for the religious holidays of other faiths to be recognised, not only for Muslims but also for other faiths.
- Intentional programmes need to be developed. These can include dialogues and events, which are of interest to all faiths. Festivals can clearly be opened up to others, and awareness building days held, such as a common fast in Ramadan. Chaplaincy lectures can be on themes, which will attract a varied audience. Fundraising events can be done together, or work with such groups as asylum seekers or the homeless. Demonstrations can be organised together.
- Moderate groups need to be strengthened to avoid the dangers of extremism. There are extremist groups in all faiths. The Muslim groups tend to emphasise political causes and Christian groups a conversion agenda. They can give the impression that they are larger than they actually are, but small groups can have a disproportionate effect, just as used to happen with extreme Marxist groups infiltrating organisations. The Muslim groups have come to the public eye because of the issue of terrorism. But everywhere we need to be watchful, since recruitment now can lead to a lifetime of commitment to causes, which are a danger to the world as well as inter-religious harmony. The best way to oppose them is to strengthen the Islamic societies and other representative organisations. It has been well said that it is the responsibility of leaders of each faith to face down their own extremists. This also means Christians standing against inappropriate methods of evangelism or closed fundamentalist attitudes.
- The issue of Islamophobia needs to be named and addressed (also see pp. 160f). The university cannot be isolated from the rest of society, of course, but many Muslim students can personally testify that since 9/11 they have been subject to increased racism. Chaplains can play a key role in enabling such issues to be examined. But there can also be a kind of 'religious people phobia', which makes it difficult, for example, for people to admit they are Christian. More open practice by people of other faiths may help the Christian to 'come out'. This is certainly a difficult area for the Christian in the vast further education sector.

In an important lecture delivered at Downing Street in March 2004, Rowan Williams emphasised that religious education should not be about including atheism, but about religions being purified by atheism. It should be an opportunity to explore alternative religious beliefs and spirituality and examine the validity of any religious belief. This can be aided by evaluating the critique of these religions by atheists such as Philip Pullman and Bertrand Russell. He added that those who believe in a mortal God who can win or lose power, will have a religion saturated with anxiety – and so with violence. The wrong kind of God is dangerous, and the Archbishop quoted the Zen Buddhist saying, 'If you meet the Buddha, slay him.' The university can be a place where false and dangerous gods can be cleansed, not just by atheist critique, but by the critique of other faiths than our own.

Seminary education

The education of clergy is critical for the future of relationships between faiths. Traditionally this has been undertaken as if they were in a cocoon and their own faith was the only one in the world. As late as the early 1970s, that is how I was trained. The only reason we learnt about Judaism was because Jesus and Paul were Jews. But we did not meet living Jews or read about contemporary Judaism. Nor did it ever strike me that I myself was a quarter Jewish. I really only began to learn about other faiths in the parish in which I worked in the West Midlands, where I lived among 'immigrants', as they were known pejoratively, from India and Pakistan. They were not seen as Hindus, Muslims or Sikhs. My real education was gained through becoming a missionary in South India and later through teaching in a college where training in religions and interfaith dialogue was part of the bread and butter of the syllabus, and all students were exposed to practical engagement across faiths. The education provided was theological, dialogical and practical.

On my return, I taught at Queen's College, Birmingham and later became Principal of the West Midlands Ministerial Course at Queen's College Birmingham. A programme of interfaith education was introduced, as part of which an exposure programme was developed within the faith communities of Birmingham. A regular dialogue group enabled many students to become involved in systematic dialogue with Muslims.[9] As part of the restructuring of the syllabus, interfaith perspectives were included within a thematic section of the course – concerning God and creation, Christology, the Holy Spirit, perspectives on pastoral care, ethics, mission and spirituality. At Selly Oak, we established the principle that wherever possible, it was people of other faiths who taught their own faith, and Christians taught Christian responses to those faiths. Action/reflection was the general principle of educational methodology – either direct involvement or reflection on the previous engagement of class members.

This level of education on interfaith perspectives was unusual in terms of initial training for ministry. Attempts have been made since then to require at least some exposure, theological reflection and teaching about another religion, usually Islam or Judaism or both. The intention may be there, but syllabus overcrowding, lack of appropriate staff resources or lack of imagination may mean it does not happen.

The same is likely to apply in continuing ministerial education, when even those coming to live and work in multi-faith areas may have had minimal if any preparation for this. Arising out of the Presence and Engagement process (see chapter 2) new centres have been established in Leicester and Bradford (see Resources section). The training of lay people is equally, if not more, important.

From the Muslim perspective, little has yet happened to enable Muslim students to experience Christian teachers. To date, the majority of British Imams have been trained elsewhere, in the Indian subcontinent, Egypt and Saudi Arabia. They often have little English and teach as if they were in the subcontinent. This does not mean they teach 'terrorism' or 'extremism', as many think. Rather they teach the traditional faith in the traditional languages, usually Urdu and Arabic. There is little or no con-textualisation to the British or European setting. They teach as for a majority Muslim community within a minority context. They offer what they have learnt in their seminaries. A recent study of the training of Imams in Britain, which was undertaken by Jonathan Birt and Philip Lewis, reveals a similar picture.[10] There are, they have discovered, at least twenty-five seminaries in Britain. Sixteen of these are dominated by the conservative *deobandi* tradition (Dar-al Uloom) within the *Wahabi* school. Five follow the *barelwi* tradition which is rather more open, influenced by Sufism, but they bring even more Imams from overseas. The roots of 74 per cent of British Muslims are in South Asia and are predominantly linked to these two traditions.[11]

The Birt and Lewis report suggests that a movement towards change is proceeding slowly as adaptation takes place within the British context. It is being given a cautious but clear lead by graduates from the leading seminary in Bury, whose founder, Sheikh Yusuf Motala, has enormous influence. It concludes:

> Developments have been encouraged by the Deobandi elders, who have always married religious conservatism with pragmatic engage-ment … In the long term, the most interesting question is to what extent imams exposed to a new professionalism – in terms of new social skills, a public service ethos and distinct intellectual formation in western institutions, whether university, teacher training college, or chaplaincy training centres – will form a critical mass able to influence and shape the religious formation in the *dar al-ulums*

themselves ... Such, arguably, is the precondition for developing a new hermeneutic equal to the task of engaging confidently with contemporary challenges.

Often postgraduate training, perhaps in Egypt or at the School of Oriental and African Studies in London, encourages younger Imams, fully loyal to their tradition, to suggest changes appropriate to context. One of these suggestions is the use of English at all levels. Training needs to be given for a world in which particular attention must be paid to the majority faith. As yet there has been little direct engagement with Christians, but there are exceptions. The Islamic College of Dr Zaki Badawi in London regularly has lectures from Christian scholars. I have been invited to speak at the Shia College in London. And a small breakthrough took place in Leicester recently when, facilitated by a British Asian Imam, I was invited to one of the two *Dar al-ulums* in the city. It was suggested that I go with two Christian clergy, one of whom should not be white, to show that Christianity is a world faith.

These are small beginnings. It is to be hoped that in future years such interaction will become a standard part of training within both communities. These questions do not yet arise for Hindus and Sikhs, who do not have seminaries in the same way. But if they begin to develop such institutions, then the lessons learned by other faiths will need to be considered. Being essentially inclusive faiths, however, the lines are not drawn in the same way and the problem of isolation is less acute. Many Buddhists who train to be monks and teachers will have been Christians and, thus, naturally think of their faith within this context and in an inclusive way.

The media

The majority Christian community depends largely on the media for their perceptions of other faiths. This is where they get their stereotypes, since many have never consciously met Hindus, Buddhists or Muslims. Their general impression is likely to be that the Hindu, Sikh and Buddhist religions are good, that Islam is a faith to be wary or afraid of, and that Judaism is acceptable as a religion since it encourages full integration into British life. This last perception has been rather rocked by the actions of the present government of Israel, but most can distinguish between British Jews and Israel.

Buddhism will be known as the religion of some famous converts and of the saintly Dalai Lama, and for the fact that it lies behind the increasingly popular pursuit of meditation as an antidote to the stresses of modern life. Likewise, Hinduism is linked with yoga and the faith's colourful festivals, which are often covered by the media, whether TV or local newspapers. Apart from the occasional reference to a corrupt guru or to aberrations in the politics of India, generally it has a good press, and the achievements of its followers in British life are increasingly reported. A recent television programme exposed some of the more dubious sides of the Sai Baba movement, followed by many British Hindus, but this did little to shake the faith of his followers. The image of Sikhism is of a responsible, industrious community getting on with life and making progress. The murder of Indira Gandhi and the storming of the Golden Temple are now twenty years ago, and the more militant side of Sikhism is largely forgotten, even if part of the ethos of some *Gurdwaras*.

The area where issues related to the media really bite, is in relationship to Islam and Muslims. It is through the power of the media that the hypothesis developed by Samuel Huntington, who sees a clash of civilisations between the West and Islam, has become for many a self-fulfilling fact. He expresses his thesis thus:

> The underlying problem for the West is not Islamic fundamentalism. It is Islam, a different civilization whose people are convinced of the superiority of their culture, and are obsessed with the inferiority of their power. The problem for Islam is not the CIA or the US Department of Defence. It is the West, a different civilization whose people are convinced of the universality of their culture and believe that their superior, if declining, power imposes on them the obligation to extend that culture throughout the world.[12]

There are many flaws in this generalisation, not least the diversity of what is meant by the West, or Islam, and the lack of appreciation of the importance of economic and cultural factors among others. No doubt there are cultural and religious factors in many recent wars. But are such factors the primary issue? And some clashes in Africa seem to have no religious element, as, for instance, the terrible civil wars in Congo, Sierra Leone, and Darfur, Western Sudan. There is also a superficial identification of the West with Christianity, though the majority of Christians are no longer in the West. But it has suited the popular media to play up this thesis, since it seems to bring explanation to a muddled world and provide an enemy to be named.

In the Listening to Muslims project, established by the Archbishop of Canterbury in 2003 at Muslim request, the area of negative perception of Muslims was among the six issues highlighted on the visits to five areas of England. It will also be one of the topics to be addressed in a new Christian-Muslim National Forum, which is currently in preparation. It is closely linked to the phenomenon of Islamophobia, which was investigated in the Runnymede Report published in 1997 by the Rowntree Foundation – long before 9/11. It highlights the way that, even within more balanced articles, negative images often come to the fore.[13] Islam is easily seen as monolithic and the extreme voices who claim to speak for Islam, such as Al Muhajiroun or Hizb ut Tahrir, are often the ones given media time or quoted in the press. Journalists and reporters may not check who is in the mainstream. The Runnymede Report uses the following distinctions to analyse how Islam is viewed:

- as monolithic and static, or as diverse and dynamic
- as 'other' and separate, or as similar and interdependent
- as inferior, or as different but equal
- as an aggressive enemy, or as a co-operative partner
- as manipulative, or as sincere
- whether Muslim criticisms of the West are rejected or debated
- whether discriminatory behaviour is defended or opposed
- whether anti-Muslim comments, stereotypes and discourse are seen as natural and 'common sense', or as problematic and to be challenged
- whether account is taken of the fact that Muslims have limited access to the media, or whether unequal freedom of expression is recognised.[14]

Responsible bodies such as the Muslim Council of Britain have found it difficult to get a hearing in the popular press, though this is improving. Islam is often portrayed as: divisive, with its adherents living in self-selected ghettos; foreign; possibly disloyal in a crisis to Britain; anti modern, particularly in relationship to women, but perhaps also in its emphasis on prayer and discipline as a way of life in a society in which outward expression of religion is counter-cultural. It is also represented as inherently violent in its rhetoric and actions, however much Muslims assert that the taking of innocent life is deeply anti-Islamic and appropriate Qur'anic verses are quoted to back this up. 'Fundamentalist' is often used to describe Muslims, in opposition to those who are 'moderate'. This is hard for Muslims to understand because they all consider that it is a good thing to be rooted in the fundamentals of faith.[15]

Some of the media coverage is very responsible; some is dangerous in its bias and thrust. There seems to be an obsession with Islam, which the volume of stories and programmes reflect. Every angle is covered: international, European, British and local. Television and radio programmes cover a fascinating range of subjects. There have been some fine documentaries examining Muslim faith and history and providing contextual studies of Muslims in Britain. Issues such as the *hijab*, *hajj* and *Ramadan* have also been covered. Muslims, as well as people of other faiths, give a Thought for the Day on Radio 4's *Today* programme. There has recently been a late-night series of television programmes called *Sharia TV*, which have hosted debates amongst British Muslims, including one about Christianity and relationships with Christians.

At the local level, it has been my experience that radio stations will readily include items of debate between people of faith, if we call them and offer to make the contacts. They are particularly interested in interfaith initiatives. I have found the same to be true of Asian TV. The Leicester-based television company MATV produces programmes which are net-worked throughout the country and watched by most British Asians, and are also screened in India. I have taken part in long discussions on air – up to half an hour – with a Muslim, a Hindu and a Sikh on topics such as terrorism and security.

In an age when the tabloids are seen as influencing the results of general elections, the power of the press cannot be overestimated. Because their editorial bias is much more obvious than that expected from either television or radio, they can easily whip up hatred against a person or a faith. This is usually directed at Muslims or Islam. There has been plenty of scope for doing this at an international level since 9/11, but it was also true well before, with the Taliban, reactions to Salman Rushdie, suicide bombing in Palestine, etc. But so often Muslims are blamed for anything done by one of their people, in a way that does not happen with other faiths. Christians are not blamed for the actions of George Bush, nor Catholics for the IRA, nor Hindus for lethal suicide bombers amongst Hindu Tamils in Sri Lanka. But the media easily scapegoat the British Muslim community for what happens in a distant part of the world, or British Muslim Imams for an extremist like Abu Hamsa. *Jihad* is seen purely as an aggressive war concept. On the Internet, the word was being bandied about as part of a recent by-election campaign in terms of a *jihad* against Labour because of its involvement in the Iraq war. The idea of the greater *jihad* being the spiritual fight within to follow the true path is unknown or ignored. In another emotive area, the media can give the impression that all asylum seekers are Muslims.

Muslims are blamed for terrorism wherever it occurs, and their attempts to distance themselves from such actions, and to condemn them utterly, are hardly reported. The Muslim Council of Britain has produced a well-documented and extensive study of Muslim reactions to 9/11, and those of the media and other influential groups. It records wide and unambiguous Muslim condemnation of the attack on the Twin Towers, which it regards as 'simply evil and criminal'.[16] Nevertheless, in late 2002, *The Church of England Newspaper* published a full-page article with the headline 'Why don't Muslims condemn terrorism?' I wrote a full-page reply, 'Muslims have condemned terrorism', which documented statements which had been made at local, national and international level. But the problem remains that the media only report what they want to.

These comments should not be seen as blanket condemnation of all the press. *The Sun* itself printed a characteristically large headline post 9/11: 'Islam is not an evil religion'. Papers such as *The Independent* and *The Guardian* give much space to Muslim writers and a fair presentation of the issues for British Muslims, as well as covering the numerous international issues involving Muslims.

Islam is newsworthy, and that is why it is rare to find a week, often a day, when there are not several articles, and numerous news items, relating to Islam or Muslims. Indeed, there is often more coverage of Muslims, a minority, than there is of Christians, and vastly more than of Hindus, Sikhs, Jews and Buddhists, whose numbers in total are similar to that of Muslims. However, it can be argued that there is a higher media interest in religion in general because of the high profile Islam has brought to faith, and because Islam does not allow religion to be confined to the religious slot in a newspaper, or on radio or television.

It is worth getting hold of some publications written in English by Muslims themselves. Examples are *Q News, Emel,* described as a Muslim lifestyle magazine,[17] and the free paper found in mosques *Muslim News.* There are many websites also available. The best way to counter Islamophobia and media distortion is to make our own judgements by meeting with Muslims, by doing our best to educate ourselves about Islam, and by discovering what Muslims are saying about themselves.

Social and community involvement, regeneration, work with the poor

Typically, people of other faiths have come to Britain either with the push factor of persecution in their own country, or the pull factor of filling a gap in the economy in Britain, or both. The Jews are an early example. Recent migrants have come partly because of post-colonial tribalism, nationalism and power seeking in Asia, the Middle East and elsewhere, and partly because of economic opportunities for a better life, filling gaps in the labour market either as unskilled labourers or highly skilled staff particularly in the fields of medicine or information technology, or to invest large amounts of capital to the benefit of the British economy. The result of such migration is that the disparity between the rich and the poor seen in society is mirrored by most faith communities. This means there is the world of difference between poor Muslim communities in Oldham or Burnley, and the affluent suburbs in West London where Hindus live, or rich Arab communities in Central London. In any city, the gap will be clearly visible.

There are also great differences in political contexts. In the Northern cities, the British National Party (BNP), which, as we have seen, deliberately targets Muslims, is a force to be reckoned with. The law at present allows such groups to pursue their religious hate policies. Race legislation protects Jews and Sikhs, but not Muslims or Christians. An attempt to bring in a law based upon religious discrimination failed in the House of Lords in 2001 and was reconsidered again in 2004. Practicalities of enforcement stand in the way of legislation, as much as any matter of principle. At present, the BNP can only be banned on the basis of likelihood to cause civil disturbance.[18] Their presence in other parts of England is currently only patchy, but there is a need to be wary everywhere.

The best counter to all forms of extremism is economic regeneration and social cohesion. This does not mean integration that suggests that we are all the same. Rather it involves the affirmation of what is distinctive, and what each can contribute to the common good.[19] This can be worked out by faiths separately, or by faiths together. There needs to be a common commitment to the wellbeing of the country in which people are settled. The second and third generations know no other home. Working out what it means to be British and Hindu, British and Sikh, British and Muslim can best take place in situations in which there are few economic pressures and disparities, and in which there is a general sense of harmony. White Muslim converts (or 'reverts'), white ISKON (International Society for Krishna Consciousness), devotees, or European Buddhists are playing a part in this. Such integration also flourishes when the political leadership of a city represents the different communities, both in the ruling party and in the opposition, and councillors are seen to represent all in their ward, and not one ethnic or religious community. These are signs of political maturity.

Communities across the board face the challenge of engaging its richer citizens in the taking of some measure of responsibility for those who are left behind. All the religions are clear in their ethics that the poor and out-siders are the special concern of God. Social projects are one way of doing this, and it is moving to see, for example, the Hindu community caring for their elderly through lunch clubs. They meet together for a Gujarati meal and spend the afternoon talking, singing *Bhajans*, or hearing a religious talk. Sikh men may play cards. Respect for the elderly remains a given, for cultural but also religious reasons. Whether this will break down in future years depends much on education today, community cohesion tomorrow and resistance to the strong individualism of Western culture. It will also depend on how far groups can maintain the best of their religious and cultural norms, while not allowing them to become claustrophobic, preventing young people having at least some of the freedom that they are claiming for themselves. Numerous films, plays and novels about family life highlight such clashes between generations, values and religious norms, one of the most prominent of which is *East is East*.[20]

It is essential is that the emphasis on regeneration does not leave out spirituality. Human communities are places where God's spirit can be at work. This side of the equation is symbolised by the following story told by John Battle, about whom I spoke at the beginning of this chapter. At a meeting between people of faith within his poor constituency, one of his Roman Catholic colleagues shouted out, with great passion, 'My life in this area is like the River Ayre. Most of the river is choked with filth – old tyres, Morrison's shopping trolleys, plastic bottles, old glass, even the occasional body! That is like my life most of the time in this city. But occasionally, if I go a little higher up, clear water flows down, a fresh and crystal stream out of the Dales. That is like my life when it is in touch with the God who is always with me, even in the filth. That is when I am sure I am surrounded by his love and forgiveness.' This is a dimension we also need to bring to the city, a gospel of reconciliation and love, of prayer and of hope.

The police, crime, security and prisons

Since 9/11, much discussion has centred round the security of faith communities. This is a particular concern in relation to Muslims, but also to others who find themselves caught up in what seems an increasing cycle of violence on our streets. There are all kinds of rivalries and tensions – whether between white and black, white and Asian, Afro-Caribbean and Somali, Pakistani and Indian, intra Sri Lankan. In all these conflicts race, culture and religion are factors. Add into the mix the element of asylum seekers, and the police have a very complex job in enabling community cohesion, especially since drugs, alcohol, prostitution and guns increasingly exacerbate the problem.

Attacks have been made on religious buildings, predominantly mosques and synagogues, but also occasionally on Hindu temples, as well as on Jewish and Muslim graveyards. Churches are also vandalised but this is usually pure mindless vandalism or theft-motivated crime. On occasions where attacks are clearly religiously or racially motivated, such incidents need to be handled with great care. In Leicester, when Muslim graves were desecrated for the second time in three months, the police called a range of faith leaders, including Muslims, together. This resulted in a non-Muslim offering to put in CCTV cameras free, and the local authority arranging for the repairing of fences to be speeded up. Muslim leaders agreed that the perpetrators were yobbish young people who happened to be white. In this way a potentially explosive incident was handled without further trouble.

Issues related to the operation of the antiterrorism acts can be very explosive. Community education is vital. The police can best operate if they have strong community contacts, including, for example, a Muslim adviser and close contact with the faith communities. Often local police may try very hard to build up trust, only to find stop and search operations have affected members of the community in ports or airports. Time and time again people are arrested and then released without charge, which creates a feeling of victimisation. Nor does the continuing imprisonment without trial of terrorist suspects in Guantanamo Bay and Belmarsh help, since all are Muslims. But local liaison with faith leaders can enable difficulties to be anticipated, and potentially difficult situations to be managed smoothly, even where necessary actions have to be taken.

Much can be done to reassure communities. A senior police officer in a multi-faith area, who at an earlier stage in his life had begun training for the Roman Catholic priesthood, has made an effort to learn some phrases from several Indian languages. These he uses to such effect that his efforts have been reported in the local paper! He makes time to attend worship centres and to talk with the worshippers after prayers. He says that few officers have done this – many have never set foot in a mosque, and often not in a church. All officers in these kinds of areas are now being challenged by the Chief Constable to do the same. Specific training is given to police officers about cultural awareness, and how to behave when entering the house of a person of another faith, especially when a woman is there on her own. Women police officers have a special responsibility in such situations. In police stations, space is given for Muslims to pray at the appointed times. Care is also taken in providing appropriate food. This is seen as a right, not an inconvenience.

In situations where what is going on is not appropriately equitable, where unnecessary force is used, where appropriate suspicion about terrorist activities drifts into paranoia, a strong gesture of interfaith solidarity can be made by not leaving it to the community affected, usually Muslims, to have to make complaints on their own. A good principle to establish together is that an attack on one faith, whether it is on buildings or people, is an attack on all. This applies both to the attacks of criminals and of racists, but also in circumstances in which the police act without sensitivity. While understanding for the difficult task the police have to do on behalf of the whole community should always be expressed, there are times when voices should be raised: these will be remembered for a long time if we voice concerns on behalf of another faith community. Where things improve, it is also important to express our appreciation. It should also be remembered that the police administer the laws passed by Parliament and carry out the instructions coming from the Home Office. They cannot be held responsible for everything that comes out of Whitehall.

It is also important is to support the police in their attempts to attract more recruits from various faiths. This is not easy, since careers in business or professions such as law and medicine are considered more prestigious. But nothing gives greater confidence to people of faith than to find their adherents are confidently part of the police and other bodies responsible for law and order. The same applies throughout the system, for example, to magistrates and others within the legal profession. It is important, too, that there are judges from the various faiths. At the Council of Faiths we have recently had visits from the crown prosecution service, a judge and the leader of a commission which investigates complaints against the police. This shows the seriousness with which the faiths are being taken. So also does the production of a training video in Birmingham about the various faiths, well made and largely being introduced by people of those faiths. Sadly, despite the fact that ignorance of Christianity is enormous, it does not feature.

Another sector of enormous concern is the prison service. There has been a steep rise in the number of Muslim prisoners, many of whom are young people. Although this rise is in proportion to the numbers of Muslims in the population, it contrasts with low figures amongst Hindus, Sikhs and others. Hence, most of the issues once again concern Muslims. There are now directives which make sure their religious needs are addressed, with the provision of prayer rooms, halal meat, Friday visits from an Imam and provision for the keeping of Ramadan. This has all been strengthened since the appointment of a Muslim Adviser to the Home Office. Key now is the provision of Muslim chaplains, and the course mentioned above in relationship to higher education focuses on prisons also. There is a long tradition of Buddhist and Jewish chaplains. The Muslim situation is being addressed both by sessional provision, where numbers are low, and by full-time chaplains where numbers warrant it. It is routine for chaplains to see prisoners when they arrive whatever their faith. I heard a story about a white young man who served a sentence, was released, re-offended and returned. On returning to the same jail, his immediate request was to see 'the Paki Chaplain', because he really listened!

It is important that Christian chaplains are also trained to relate to a multi-faith situation within institutions. Such training gives them the confidence to treat as colleagues and equals those chaplains appointed by other faiths. Times of special concern, such as when there is a death in the family of a prisoner from another faith, may have to be handled by a Christian chaplain, since often no Hindu or Muslim chaplain will be available as they may cover many prisons. Quality listening and showing unconditional respect will be valued, whatever the faith of a person, or the dilemmas of life they are facing.

Chaplains should also take any opportunities available outside the prison to help to educate their community, since it is when people – whether adults or youth – leave prison that the community becomes a key element for the future prospects of the released person. This applies particularly with other faith communities, who may well have more contact with a released prisoner than the churches.

Health issues and funerals

Most of what is of concern here is shared across all faiths – good hospitals, sufficient doctors, appropriate care in the community, and so on. But there are particular issues for various faiths. For both Muslims and Jews, the provision of circumcision on the National Health Service is one example, to avoid people resorting to back-street practitioners. Muslim women will often wish to be seen only by a woman doctor and to wear long gowns for X-rays. Good appropriate food for hospital patients is a further need, with vegetarian food available for Hindus who request it. In the Leicester Royal Infirmary, after three years of negotiation, it has now been agreed that the seal on meal packs can be broken at the bedside, to make clear there has been no cross-contamination. Places for prayer are especially important in a hospital, for staff as well as students. If there is a traditional Christian chapel, can this be adapted? If so, how can it accommodate the needs of Muslims wanting a plain room and those of Hindus who require artefacts? In the case of a new facility, the provision of a table and a cupboard, in which Hindu images, a statue of the Buddha, a cross or crucifix could be stored, could solve the problem. A comment/prayer book for the use of patients and families placed in the chapel/prayer room can be a very helpful guide to the best use of the facility. Training for nurses in how to deal with the sensitivities of different groups of patients has been introduced but not across the board. The need to open up sensitive taboo areas such as that of HIV/Aids with particular communities is becoming an imperative, as they remain in denial.

The way hospitals deal with deceased patients and their families is of vital importance. This is of course a time when the bereaved are at their most vulnerable. There are strict rules about what should be done with a body in Islam, and these should be known and adhered to if at all possible. It is the relatives, for example, who should wash the body. Most sensitive is the question of post-mortems. Post-mortems which involve cutting into the body are of great concern to relatives. So also is the normal requirement that the funeral takes place within twenty-four hours, which will usually be prevented by a post-mortem. It will require great patience to explain that cause of death must be established before a body is released. One example of the difficulties that can arise is the death of a ninety-year-old woman in hospital. It took five hours for the coroner to take the body. Meanwhile forty relatives were becoming very agitated, and the police had to be involved to stop them seizing the body. Incidents can also happen when people are trying to return a body of a loved one to India or Pakistan, without completing the necessary formalities. In such situations the mediation of the chaplain can be sought, or if there is no chaplain, of a local Imam. Sensitive hospital staff can also be of great help. Other faith communities will also have their concerns, and a leaflet listing these can make things much easier for staff. Leicester Muslims have produced a booklet *Dying and Deceased Muslims: a guideline for hospitals*. Education is necessary for three groups of people: the Muslim public, Imams, particularly those from overseas, and hospital staff. At a recent training course for nurses in Leicester, ten were expected, and seventy came!

Chaplaincy in hospitals has traditionally been an Anglican preserve, with sessional chaplains from other denominations. In recent years, the involvement of other faiths has advanced rapidly, encouraged by some enlightened Christian chaplains and by hospital trusts and the NHS. In some places there are now full-time Muslim chaplains, who will minister to their own people but also need to be trained to respond sensitively to those of little faith from the Christian community or those of no faith, who may ask to talk to them.

Mention should also be made of the various questions associated with funerals. In my locality there is a Muslim Burial Council which has negotiated facilities for deaths to be registered and funerals to be conducted at weekends. They also help with practical matters, such as facilitating the sending back of bodies to India and Pakistan and explaining to relatives that they should wear gloves for washing bodies to avoid contagion. They now work in co-operation with their Jewish counterparts. Hindus are finding things more difficult. They want a special facility for conducting cremations and, above all, a funeral ghat, where they can scatter ashes into flowing water. Both requests have been continually frustrated locally, and the community has been vociferous in its opposition to these demands. Christians can encourage sensitive support for these kinds of needs.

Gender and family issues

It is difficult to know where to place this section, but it needs to be in the book as it is a major area in which Christians encounter patterns of life in other communities that raise important issues and can cause misunderstandings.

This is an area in which stereotypes abound: Muslim men are seen as women oppressors; no matter what their faith Asian women are seen as submissive, spending their time making tasty food that requires hours of preparation; children are seen as being brought up to conform; arranged marriages are assumed to be forced marriages. Many of the questions relate, again, to Islam, which is the area on which I will concentrate.

Unlike temples, *viharas* and *Gurdwaras*, most mosques are not open to women in this country. This fact can be covered over by any number of reasons: women are relieved from the duty of going to the mosque; women can better pray at home where they can be an example to their children and teach them to pray; women will distract the men; the mosque does not have adequate facilities; it is cultural, but that is how it is; women can come, but they don't come. Some Muslim women themselves are raising questions also, asking why, since women and men worshipped together in the time of the prophet, they do not do so now? The prophet is reputed to have said that, if women want to go to the mosque, they should not be prevented and they should be actively encouraged to do so at the festival *Eid*. In London, most mosques have a section for women, why not elsewhere? Arab and Pakistani mosques are more likely to have this facility than Gujarati mosques. Many women are content; others are saying there should be a choice everywhere; a third, small group are becoming quite militant.

Christians also raise concerns about how women dress. The scarf – *hijab* – is questioned and the *nikab* or *burka* (full cover) is viewed as oppressive and even sinister. What is not easily understood is that, though some are forced to wear these head coverings, most choose to do it as part of their identification as Muslims, and some men are not themselves happy that their wives go that far. Of course, Muslim girls may well be dressed in a very modern way, with high heels visible under their *burkha*. The increasing use of these clothes in recent years indicates in some cases that Muslims have felt more secure in Britain, while in other cases the opposite, depending on the person. They have also refused to be cowed by the fact that since 9/11 they have become easy targets and have continued defiantly to wear the *hijab* or *nikab* – some have even begun to wear it. A Turkish woman told me that she had come to Britain because she had not been allowed to wear a *hijab* while working for the government in relief work amongst the Kurds. A British young woman said that the scarf liberates her to be herself, as she rejoices at being British and Muslim. Another asked the question why a woman in a scarf is taken as being oppressed, while a woman in a bikini is seen as liberated. Liberated for what? An academic Muslim woman, Nushin Arbabzadah, comments that the wearing of the *hijab* is discussed in a confused manner, with no distinction being made between its use at a personal level of choice, at a sociological level as identity marker, or at a theological level as mandatory for Islam.[21]

Another stereotype is that most Muslim men are polygamous. Certainly, four wives are permitted in the Qur'an, but there is the key proviso that the man must be able to treat each exactly equally. A very rich man may be able to do this, but not many men fall into that category: more than one wife is the exception rather than the rule. Within Britain polygamy is not, of course, allowed legally. Some mosques, though not all, will perform ceremonies for second or subsequent marriages but they have no legal status. The second wife is in a similar position to a woman with whom a Western man has an affair. I was approached for counselling by a Christian woman, living in a village, who said that her husband, whom she had married out of love at a mosque, had a first wife in the city. He lived half the week with each. Now that she had given him a child, he was insisting on her becoming a Muslim, which she was not prepared to do. She was in great turmoil, since he was threatening to take away her young child.

Another issue is whether Muslim youth are happy to live according to the same values as their parents. This is a more contentious issue among Muslims – 60 per cent of British Muslims are below thirty – than among Hindus or Sikhs, who are freer and offered more choice. In their case the kettle lid is jammed on less tightly, and so will not explode so easily. Between the ages of five and twelve Muslim children are normally happy to go to the *madrassa* – they have no choice anyway. But from twelve or so onwards it is different. Some stick strongly to traditional faith and family values, such as those young men who are *hafiz* (know the Qur'an by heart). One known to me works at the constabulary, wearing full beard and Islamic dress. His department manager, who is a Christian, gives him every encouragement to be what he wants to be. She is an example of someone who accepts 'the other'. But many other young people disregard traditional values. There is real potential for a clash between the two, which the mosques and the Imams are ill equipped to deal with. They have no training or experience of counselling parents or youth. It is no longer enough for them just to lead prayers. Guidelines are needed on very difficult areas such as sexuality, though the tradition is that sex education only leads to promiscuity.

There is also a wide range of issues facing Muslim girls living in a Western culture. At the extreme end of the scale there is a need for helplines and safe houses. In some places the Muslim community is thinking the difficulties through; in other places this is seen as only encouraging indiscipline. The general attitude is that if girls are allowed to do higher education, they should do so from home. This is not normally because they are not trusted, but because it will give them greater protection. There is an Asian saying, 'When a girl goes out on her own, a pair of devils walk behind her.' The recent increase in drinking, drugs and crime amongst the Muslim community, has only led to greater constraints. A community leader commented: 'The community urgently needs to invest its time in providing advice centres with a religious ethos, in areas such as wife and child abuse, marital difficulties, HIV/Aids, family planning (as with the Roman Catholics, not permitted, but much used) etc., not pretending these things do not happen. Recreational and sports facilities are also needed, and not just mosques and religious education centres.' The problem is that, though it is comparatively easy to raise money for the building of more and more mosques, financing social and community centres and projects is seen as a much lower priority. This means Muslim areas are very sensitive to government and local authority cuts.

By comparison, the Hindu and Sikh family structures seem much looser. Women and men mingle together in the places of worship, though normally men sit in one section and women in another. But no eyebrows are raised if husband and wife come together and sit together. Clothing is very colourful – as are the festivals, where new clothes are de rigueur and shown off in public. Hence the enormous sales of saris in many of the Asian areas of our cities. I am reminded of the huge contrast between the streets of a Hindu-dominated South Indian city, and the sombre feel of Lahore and, even more, the almost totally male streets of Peshawar on the north-west frontier.

Freedoms such as these seem to express a rejoicing in the freedom offered in the faith: to believe or not believe, to choose from within beliefs, and even to be eclectic with other faiths. Such a faith suits the postmodern world in which the young are being brought up. A young Hindu commented on the Christians he had met at university, 'I feel excluded by them, though I have attended the Christian Union café several times. They do not want to acknowledge commonalities, or respect differences as valid. I attended the adult baptism of a friend, and saw how, in a discussion over lunch, searching questions were bypassed. But I understand that many are new Christians, insecure in faith.'

However, at a social level, Hinduism is much more conservative than at first appears. It has survived for thousands of years, because of the social hold it has on its adherents. This is particularly asserted through the caste and wider family system, and centres on marriage. A typical comment of an educated young Hindu woman might be: 'I expect to marry within my own caste, and in any case a vegetarian Hindu. For God is in all things. We will then enjoy the same values, festivals, way of life, and I will avoid hassle with the family.' And of a young Hindu man: 'My caste is only a label and creates no barriers, but gives me a community, and networks where I feel fully at home. I would marry any Hindu, and would receive a helping hand from my parents, if needed, in choosing a partner. Culturally I am proud to be of Indian birth, because of what my ancestors have achieved, but what I have to offer should be given by me as a British Hindu, and my wife should come from here.' Of course, there are an increasing number of interfaith marriages, which are love marriages. They are not easily absorbed, within high caste families in particular, but in the end, acceptance usually comes, particularly when grandchildren are born. Often the Hindu or Sikh family would rather a marriage with a white Christian than with a Muslim or a *dalit* ('untouchable') Hindu.

Concluding challenge

I end with a challenge from a leading younger Muslim academic, offered to Muslims, but important for all of us to hear:

> Muslims are now part of the West so the discussion is not really between 'them' and 'us', but between 'us' and 'us', amongst ourselves, with our common humanity. Talk of 'clash of civilisations' in this context is not only dangerous and irresponsible (for the false fault-lines it perpetuates), it is also foolish...Muslims living in the West may not agree with certain material motivations in the West or the way the family is being neglected, and on these issues they may stand together with many of their fellow citizens of Christian and other faiths, and non-faith backgrounds. Muslims living in the West may take issue with the current state of social and international justice, and they would, again, stand with the majority of their fellow citizens. On concern about the environment, again Muslims would

stand with the people. It may be possible that in each of these cases 'the people' would be different groups.[22]

He calls for the description of our Jewish-Christian European heritage to become Jewish-Christian-Muslim European heritage. This is a positive suggestion. But as a person concerned with Christian interaction with all faiths, being inclusive of all faiths is an important priority. It is easy for 'religions of the book' to be seen as forming an exclusive alliance. This would be far from the intention of this author. But we need to avoid this danger in others' hands. It is the common spiritual heritage of humanity that can be offered together for the new Britain and Europe, with these three faiths playing a special and interrelated part. Nor should we be apologetic about the predominant historical role of Christianity, nor slow to critique the mistakes it has made.

CASE STUDIES/QUESTIONS

1. What are the two key community needs in your area? How would you work at enabling those needs to be addressed by more than your own Christian community?

2. You are in hospital, and your bed is next to a Muslim's who is agitated because he wants to say his prayers regularly. He is able to get around, but has seen only a Christian chapel. He sees you have a Bible and knows therefore that you are a Christian. He asks your help in what he can do. How do you respond?

3. There is an article in the local newspaper, with the headline 'Islam, a dangerous religion'. It is written after a major terrorist incident in Europe, where Muslims are suspects, and instructs readers to be wary of all who follow this faith. This agitates you, and you feel you must write a letter to the Editor for publication. What would you write?

4. You have a church voluntary-aided school in the parish. Ninety per cent of the children belong to other faiths, mainly Islam. You are on the Board of Governors of the school as the church representative. The Muslim representatives say that the school is too Christian in its practices: assemblies should not be so Christian in ethos; more Islam should be taught; an Imam should be invited in on Fridays; there should be several Muslim teachers and, if possible, a Muslim headmaster. How would you respond to this shopping list of requests?

5. A Hindu is sitting next to you in the day room in a hospital. He tells you he has just received news from the doctor that he has incurable cancer, and only a few weeks to live. He does not know where to turn, and has turned to you. He wants to know what will happen to him

when he dies. He is frightened, and needs to talk to you. How do you respond?

6. A group of Muslims come to your church and witness the eucharist. After the service, you meet for a discussion. How do you explain to them the meaning of the eucharist? Which parts would you pick out to highlight and why? Would the explanation differ if you had a group of Hindus in front of you?

7. How would you respond if a Muslim asked you whether you were a Christian first or British first? How would you expect them to respond to the same question, whether they were a Muslim first or British first?

CONCLUSION

More than twenty years ago, Bernard Nicholls, CMS Secretary for Community Relations, wrote a pamphlet entitled *Dear Mary*. It is written to an imaginary Mary living in Bournemouth (apologies to those readers from Bournemouth for this stereotyping!). It is subtitled 'A letter to a friend, and it might be you'. It purports to answer a letter in which Mary has declined the Secretary's offer to speak in Bournemouth, because 'It's not our problem'. The pamphlet quotes politely 'no man is an island entire of itself' (John Donne) and the parable of the Good Samaritan, and then expresses sadness that, while Mary is interested in far-away people of different cultures and faiths, she does not want to find out about the growing multi-faith society in Britain. He writes of a parish in a white area supporting a missionary project in Pakistan, but who 'are effectively unaware of and unconcerned about the Christian implications of there being perhaps a thousand or more Muslims from Pakistan within the boundaries of another parish within the same city'. He points out the opportunities available twenty miles away to encounter people seen as 'the other', and suggests that, by deliberately rejecting any contact with the minorities living amongst them, people such as Mary may trap themselves into becoming disadvantaged, and thus deprive themselves of the enrichment that relationships with people of other cultural and religious backgrounds can bring.

Such people are not in reality 'the other': 'they are here because we were there.' As an industrialist put it, 'we asked for hands, and they came as people.' Bernard Nicholls writes of social mobility, particularly amongst the young, and how the tourist trade brings people of all faiths to every part of Britain, with the result that the world has got much smaller over the years. (I think of pulling up in a picnic spot in Perthshire last year, and finding ourselves next to what proved to be a Jain family from West London, who immediately offered us their Jain-style chapattis and curry. All we could offer in return were oranges – a kind of sacramental sharing.) Nicholls comments, 'A Christian in Britain may find himself ill-equipped for creative response to circumstances and challenges that may suddenly

come upon him if he has never reflected upon the fact and the implications of cultural and religious pluralism' (sexist language indicates the
date of writing).

Things have changed over the years since this pamphlet was published,
but not as much as we might like to think. Certainly opportunities for
contact have grown greatly. Moreover, there has been an enormous
increase in the number of people who travel for holidays to countries
where by far the majority of people belong to other faiths. Opportunities
can unexpectedly arise in such contexts if we have our eyes open, and we
see ourselves as visiting people, not just buildings or beaches, and can
make the connections with our life in Britain. Diane Johnson, initiator of
the Women's Dialogue Group in Leicester, describes a moment of charismatic calling on a package tour to Turkey, four years before she moved to
Leicester:

> We visited the great mosque at Bursa. As we were shown around, we
> became aware of a woman coming quickly towards the party across
> the floor of the mosque. We thought that someone wasn't covered
> enough. But the woman came straight towards me, stroking my
> hands and arms and face, weeping, and speaking words of recogni-
> tion and joyful greeting. I found myself with tears in my eyes. It was
> a most extraordinary experience and the rest of the party were
> amazed. I had no idea what it was all about.

Five years later – four days before 9/11 – she was being instituted to a
Leicester parish when another Turkish Muslim woman, wearing a head-
scarf, appeared at the service and afterwards invited her home: thus began
a journey together with Muslim women for Diane. At the same time, this
Turkish woman, whom it is extremely likely will always remain a devoted
Muslim, began her own journey. She came to love the peace of a church,
where she could pray when excluded from mosques. She asked to go to a
place of retreat. And then she wished to learn more of the Bible. I invited
her to join a course named Exploring Christian Life and Faith in the same
church. I expected her to come to the two biblical modules. In fact, she
came for thirty weeks, and became beloved by her fellow participants from
all kinds of theological persuasions. She appeared on the register as
'observer', but her new friends requested that I change her status to 'par-
ticipant', for this is what she was. At the end of the course she spoke in the
cathedral in front of the bishop about what she had learnt from her fellow
believers. I had never shaken hands with her, but I gave her a lift home
from the cathedral and, as she was leaving the car, she held out her hand
to me. I said, 'I should not shake your hand.' She said, 'Please do, as a

brother before God.' Another one of those sacramental moments that come so rarely.

This young woman told me that some of her Muslim friends criticise her for spending time with Christians. 'They may convert you,' she was warned. She replied, 'Well, if they do, they do. There is only one God, and if my faith is weak, then I may be converted if that is the path for me!' This conversation mirrors the talk that some of us have with our Christian colleagues, and I answer similarly that Christ does not need protecting, nor does my Christian faith.

These stories are about conversion. There are others in which people have actually changed their allegiance. Some happen through intentional evangelism, far more through circumstances or people, where life touches life unexpectedly. I have written much in this area.[1] We do not need to be apologetic about how our sharing of the good news of Jesus Christ in word or action can lead to people wishing to become his disciples (bearing in mind all that I have written in the section on the care of converts, see p. 116f.). People of other faiths are not normally reticent about those faiths' virtues: why should we be, provided we can also each be self-critical of the way followers of our own faith often behave? I attended a dinner, which was preceded by many speeches given by the staff of a Muslim seminary to a wide range of guests from the wider community. All the many speeches, recitations or prayers were clear about the spiritual heart of Islam and its virtues as the way of life. No one was called to convert, but it was very clear that the good news was being shared. The same would also apply to those who speak of their Buddhism and offer their practices of meditation. There may be no explicit call to conversion, but what is said is deeply attractive to those who are lost and seeking a spiritual home. This book, therefore, should not be seen as a clarion call to dialogue at the expense of appropriate Christian witness. The call to conversion to new attitudes to people of other faiths, which it surely is, does not rule out a response to those who seek a new centering in Christ and a transformation of their lives as part of the Christian community. It is not a question of dialogue or mission, friendship or evangelism. We are called to live our lives as faithful Christians, wherever God places us, and if this is alongside people of other faiths, we cannot tell where that will lead, for us or for them. The love of God, shown in Christ, will surely know no bounds in reaching out to those who live lives in surrender to him and embrace those of all faiths or none. It is good that more become his explicit followers, so that there are more to live out his gospel explicitly. But there will always be many others, some of whom we have met in this book, who long for a new world and believe that we will have more success in bringing this into being if we work together rather than apart. A Muslim issued a call for us to move, as Christians and Muslims, from tolerance to friendship to unity. This applies across all faiths and is a call to conversion.

Such a conversion movement has been illustrated often in this book. I end with two more examples from the local church level, and then with prophetic words from three great leaders of our time. I preached in a local church on a white working-class housing estate on the theme of our relationship with people of other faiths, those who live in another part of the city, and who on the whole, because of traditional attitudes, do not feel at home in the kind of area in which these people lived. I was then asked to come and lead a Bible Study for an ecumenical afternoon group, Anglican and Roman Catholic, and the priest asked me to bring into the discussion how Muslims see Jesus and Mary. We looked at Acts 17:16ff., and how Paul was willing to begin from the scriptures of those he was talking to. I then gave them sheets on the Qur'anic passages on Mary and Jesus. They were much engaged in both discussions, held in a dialogical way. At the end, I said that I was telling them about the Qur'an, but it would be much better if they could meet and talk with an Imam. The priest asked if they would like to go to a mosque and then have a discussion. All agreed with enthusiasm. We fixed a date immediately, redeeming the moment. They had come a long way to bridge a significant divide.

The second example is a postscript to the story about the multi-faith keep fit class mentioned right at the beginning of the book. One of the Christian members, Sheila, died at the age of seventy-five. She had always been outspoken about her strong Christian convictions, that no one comes to the Father except through Christ. On hearing the news of her death, those of all faiths were very upset. The Hindu leader said, immediately, that there should be a minute's silence. A Sikh man then suggested that they should all show some token of their appreciation of the deceased. They all signed a card, with the words 'God bless you, rest in peace', and a collection was raised for flowers to be sent to the church. During the quiet time at the end of their exercises, the Hindu group sang softly together in honour of Sheila, and all joined in with the Amen. The Age Concern Centre had begun with real anxiety about how to hold together people of all faiths in one institution. There has been a corporate journey of conversion here. A Christian member told me that, as a result of being in this community, she now stands up to her Hindu neighbours who say they hate Muslims: 'Why hate Muslims? There are good and bad in all communities. We should not hate, but love people of all faiths.'

This book is written as a challenge for us to do just that. We are fortunate to live in times when there are outstanding religious leaders deeply committed to their own faiths, but who radiate an openness to others. Often they have gone through their own journeys of conversion. I end this book with quotations from a very special trinity of such persons: one Jewish, one Buddhist and one Christian. They will stand for other such leaders I could have added from the other faiths we have considered in this book. Their words are placed here as beacons of hope, which is the sentiment I wish to leave with readers, who will be well aware, as all are who have lived through the last decades of the twentieth century and the early years of the new millennium, of the destructiveness of the violence perpetrated in the name of faiths. This awareness applies to these three also, who have felt personal anguish as a result. The Chief Rabbi, Jonathan Sacks, represents all of us in his reaction to this continuous violence. On the *Today* programme's Thought for the Day on 7 September 2004, speaking about the massacre of children and school teachers at a school in Beslan in the Southern Caucasus – how quickly perhaps we forget these tragedies as the media moves us on to the next one – he quoted a verse from Genesis, written in the face of primeval evil, 'And God regretted that he had made man on earth, and it grieved him to the core' (Gen. 6:6). Then he commented tellingly that we have heard much in these past years about nuclear, chemical and biological weapons of mass destruction, but all along we have been looking in the wrong direction: 'the greatest weapon of mass destruction is the human heart.'

But we end with the challenge to hope and to openness of attitude. On this theme, Jonathan Sacks draws lessons from his own early experience:

Many years ago when I was a student, I met one of the great rabbis of the twentieth century. At that time I was at a crossroads in my own religious development, and I asked him the following question. 'I would like to become a more committed Jew, but I also value the world outside – the great music, art and literature whose inspiration is often drawn from quite un-Jewish sources. Must I make this sacrifice? Is religious commitment exclusive?'

He replied with a parable: 'There were once two men who spent their lives transporting stones. One carried rocks, the other diamonds. One day they were given emeralds to carry. The man who had spent his days carrying rocks saw emeralds as just another heavy weight, a burden of no intrinsic value. The one who had carried diamonds recognized emeralds as another form of precious stone, different, but with their own distinctive beauty. So it is with faith. If your own faith is nothing more than a burden, you will not value the faith of others. But if you cherish your faith, you will value other people's faith also, even though it is different from your own. You will know that faiths are like jewels. One is especially your own, but all are precious.'[2]

We hear now from the Dalai Lama, whose goodness, lightness of touch, sense of humour, revealed in the endearing chuckle as he speaks, and his personal commitment to his Buddhist faith within the suffering of his people, has become a beacon for many far beyond his Tibetan people. The last sentence here perhaps sums up the purpose of this book:

> The important point to keep in mind is that ultimately the whole purpose of religion is to facilitate love and compassion, patience, tolerance, humility, forgiveness and so on. If we neglect these, changing our religion will be of no help. In the same way, even if we are fervent believers in our own faith, it will avail us nothing if we neglect to implement these qualities in our daily lives. Such a believer is no better off than a patient with some fatal illness who merely reads a medical treatise but fails to undertake the treatment prescribed.
>
> Moreover, if we who are practitioners of religion are not compassionate and disciplined, how can we expect it of others? If we can establish genuine harmony derived from mutual respect and understanding, religion has enormous potential to speak with authority on such vital moral questions as peace and disarmament, social and political justice, the natural environment and many other matters affecting all humanity. But until we put our own spiritual teaching into practice, we will never be taken seriously. And this means, among other things, setting a good example through developing good relations with other faith traditions.

I end with Rowan Williams, who because of his personal commitment, his academic standing, his spirituality, the stance he has taken on certain issues, and the office he holds, has done more than anyone to bring interfaith concerns to the top of the agenda across the Christian community, and far beyond. He ended a major lecture he gave at Birmingham University on 'Christian Theology and Other Faiths' by saying:

> The Christian is struck and challenged by the fact that outside the visible fellowship of faith, lives are lived which look as though they are in harmony with the Christian universe – which give the right place to contemplation and joy, to self-forgetfulness and the awareness of gift. The theological task is not only to go on patiently carrying the implications of the Christian universe and reflecting on the sort of critiques I have sketched (in this lecture) but also to think about how such lives outside the frame are made possible and sustained. There is no quick answer to this, certainly no answer that

would justify us in saying, 'Forget the doctrine, all that matters is the practice,' since the doctrine is what nourishes and makes sense of the practice. Our doctrine is still in formation; and the question of how holy lives can exist outside our own tradition has throughout Christian history led to some of the most searching and far-reaching extensions of our language about the significance of Jesus ... we do not see others either as bad or unsuccessful copies of ourselves or as people who have a few casual variants on a shared truth. We have to see how very other our universes are; and only then do we find dialogue a surprise and a joy as we also discover where and how we can still talk about what matters most – holiness, being at peace, and what truly is.[3]

As I complete this book, the latest meeting of the al-Azhar/Canterbury dialogue, initiated by George Carey, Rowan Williams' predecessor, has just taken place in Cairo on the third anniversary of 9/11. Responding again to Beslan and other acts of terrorism, Archbishop Rowan says that, 'When the Christian, the Muslim or the Jew sees his neighbour of another faith following the ways of this world instead of the peaceful way of God, he must remind his neighbour of the nature of the one God we look to. Once we let go of justice, fairness and respect in our dealings with one another, we have dishonoured God as well as human beings.'[4] He goes on, 'If we do act in the same way as our enemies, we imprison ourselves in their anger and evil; and we fail to show our belief in the living God who always requires of us justice and goodness. Whenever a Muslim, a Christian or a Jew refuses to act in violent revenge, that person bears witness to the true God.'

Such unity in the call to goodness, justice and fairness is, of course, not limited to these three faiths, as the Archbishop would be the first to affirm. Nor is it just about the horrors of what is seen in countries far away from our own. This book is a call to seek for unity, goodness, fairness and justice, as we work together with people of faith in Britain and Europe. Rowan Williams ended his reflections like this: 'We pray that this willingness to stand alongside each other, as seen in Britain, will be shared in other nations.'

This final meditation written by a Hindu expresses the longings of all people of faith:

> Where the mind is without fear and the head is held high;
> Where knowledge is free;
> Where the world has not been broken up into fragments
>   by narrow domestic walls;
> Where words come out from depth of truth;

Where tireless striving stretches its arms towards perfection;
Where the clear stream of reason has not lost its way into the
dreary sand of dead habit;
Where the mind is led forward by thee into ever-widening
thought and action;
Into that heaven of freedom, my Father,
Let my country awake.[5]

I would add, 'Let my community, my country, our world awake.'
I end with two final questions for the reader:

- How do I think differently after reading this book? What will I do differently?
- How do I respond to the three major quotations here, in my thinking and in my actions?

Notes

Introduction
1. *The Dignity of Difference* (Continuum, 2002), p. 9.
2. Church House Publishing, 1995.
3. See my book *Does Theological Education make a Difference? – Global lessons from India and Britain* (WCC, 1999).

Chapter 1
1. Published in 2004 by the Inter Faith Network of the UK (see Resources section).
2. The story of the Birmingham group is recorded in my book *Encounter in the Spirit: Muslim-Christian Dialogue in Practice* (WCC, 1991).
3. Quoted in an article by Jonathan Romain in *The Tablet*, 24 July 2004, p. 13. See also Jonathan Romain (ed.), *Reform Judaism and Modernity* (SCM, 2004).
4. From an unpublished paper *On religious and intercultural dialogue*, available on the Internet: *interfaithinteraction@yahoogroups.com*, pp. 4 and 5.
5. Unpublished paper delivered at the annual convention for the Association for the Sociology of Religion, Atlanta, August 2003.
6. The quotations in the section are taken from an article by Austin Ivereigh entitled 'Chiara's Quiet Revolution', published in *The Tablet* on 12 June 2004.

Chapter 2
1. This analysis of the census figures is by Guy Wilkinson, convenor of the Presence and Engagement initiative, which comes under the aegis of the Inter Faith Consultative Group of the Church of England (IFCOG).
2. Church House, 2004.

Chapter 3
1. Adapted from Geoffrey Parrinder, *Avatar and Incarnation* (Oxford, 1970).
2. Quoted in *The Asian Faces of Jesus* by R.S. Sugirtharajah (Orbis, 1993).
3. From 'Once, Only Once' by William Bright, 1865.
4. Published in Madras, 1976, 1991. See also E. Sharpe, *Faith meets Faith* (SCM, 1977).
5. See *Love meets Wisdom* (Orbis, 1990).
6. In this section I draw extensively on the Church of England Doctrine Report, *The Mystery of Salvation* (Church House Publishing, 1995), Chapters 1 and 7.

7. Oneworld, 2000.

8. Taken from the Golden Rule poster by Paul Mckenna. Another seven religions are also included.

9. Hans Küng drafted the text of the declaration which was adopted at the second Parliament of World Religions in Chicago in 1993, 'Towards a Global Ethic, a Universal Declaration'.

10. Quoted in Alan Race, *Interfaith Encounter* (SCM, 2003), p. 124.

11. 1 John 4:18; 1 John 4:8; 1 Corinthians 13:13.

Chapter 4

1. Available on the Internet at www.cec-kek.org or www.ccee.ch p. 9. From *Living together with Muslims*, Evangelical Church in Germany, Gutersloh, 2000.

2. Bose meeting of the WCC, and the Pontifical Council for Interreligious Dialogue, 1997.

3. Pontifical Council for Interreligious Dialogue, *Pro Dialogo:* Bulletin 98 (1998/2), p. 240.

4. Quoted on page 11 of the Conference of European Churches' document.

5. The full text is in the Conference of European Churches' document.

6. Kenneth Cragg (ed.), *Common Prayer: Muslim-Christian Spiritual Anthology* (OneWorld, 1999).

7. Oxford University Press, 1985.

8. Throughout this section the Sikh scripture *Adi Granth* is abbreviated as AG.

9. Elizabeth Harris (ed.), *Paths of Faith* (Christians Aware, 2002). 10. SCM, 1978.

10. SCM, 1978.

11. CCBI Publications, 1991.

12. From Max Warren's preface to Kenneth Cragg, *Sandals at the Mosque* (SCM, 1959), p. 9.

13. Pontifical Council Document, p. 192.

Chapter 6

1. *Faith and Community: a good practice guide for local authorities*, LGA Publications (London, 2002).

2. *Involving Faith Communities*, Office of the Deputy Prime Minister, 2003. See www.urban.odpm.gov.uk/community/faith/involve/index.htm.

3. *The Dignity of Difference* (Continuum, 2002), p. 9.

4. Two books have come out of these dialogues: *The Road Ahead* (Church House, 2002) and *Scriptures in Dialogue* (Church House, 2004), both edited by Michael Ipgrave.

5. *Writing in the Dust: After September 11* (Eerdmans, 2002).

6. These figures are on p. 18 of an important report, *Education and Islam a new strategic report* by Maurice Irfan Coles, published by the Schools Development Support Agency, www.sdsa.net. I acknowledge drawing on this report in the following section. He develops a list of fifteen key strategic components of a new approach to Islam educationally (p. 20).

7. Salim Hassani, *One Thousand Years of Muslim History*, www.Muslimheritage.com.

8. Seddon, Hussain and Malik (eds.), *British Muslims: loyalty and belonging* (Islamic Foundation, 2002); T. Ramadan, *To be a European Muslim* (Islamic Foundation, 1999).

9. See my book *Encounter in the Spirit* (WCC, 1989, 1991).

10. Jonathan Birt and Philip Lewis, *The Pattern of Islamic Reform in Britain: the Debandis between intra-Muslim sectarianism and engagement with wider society* (2004), as yet unpublished, but with a mine of reflective information.

11. Figures taken from the 2001 Census.

12. Samuel Huntington, *The Clash of Civilizations and the Remaking of the World* (Viking, 1996), p. 217.

13. See the example given by Michael Ipgrave of a *Times* front page article in 2004, which reported well the way British Muslims have condemned terrorism, but at the same time printed a prominent cartoon of a small group of Muslims burning a Union Jack outside a mosque, in an unpublished paper 'Images of Islam in the British Press' (2004).

14. Runnymede Trust, *Islamophobia, a challenge for us all* (1997), p. 5.

15. Michael Ipgrave has summarised these points from Runnymede, and updated them very effectively for the post 9/11 situation, in the unpublished paper 'Images of Islam in the British Press' quoted above. He also adds that in this sense he is happy as a Christian to be fully rooted in the fundamentals of Christian faith, though he is not in any sense a 'Fundamentalist'. The reader might also like to reflect on these terms.

16. Muslim Council of Britain, *The Quest for Sanity* (2002).

17. The July 2004 edition has articles on these kind of themes: torture, normalisation of Islam, the truth about Guantanamo, Euro football 2004, ID cards, the London Muslim Centre, Muslim marriage, university education, wind power, keeping fit, gardening, poetry of Portugal, street food, casual summer wear for men, spiritual lyrics, etc., www.emelmagazine.com.

18. In July 2004, the BBC screened a programme made by an undercover agent, exposing the viciousness and crudity of the BNP's attack on Muslims which was secretly filmed in meetings and conversations. The police are considering whether they can prosecute under present legislation.

19. See Seden, Hussain, Malik, *British Muslims between Assimilation and Segregation*, the Islamic Foundation, 2004 (www.islamic-foundation.com).

20. Directed by Damien O'Donnell (1999).

21. From a report on a conference organised by the British Council in June 2003, *Representing Islam*. She argues for the embracing of cultures, not for a dry and contextualised Islam, and warns against one cultural form of Islam being taken as 'Islam'. British Muslims should be encouraged to engage fully with the rest of society and not create their own ghettos, or allow such to be created around them. Narrowing the areas of interaction with British life, and constant explanations of rules and regulations only increases the suspicion of many that Islam is a 'dry, strict and sober faith'. For full text, see www. counterpoint-online.org.

22. Dilwar Hussein, article in *Emel*, July/August 2004, p. 16.

Conclusion

1. See *The Church and Conversion* (ISPCK/SPCK, 1997), adapted from my doctoral thesis. See also chapter on 'Freedom and Conversion' in *Free to Be* (DLT, 2002).
2. Jonathan Sacks, *Celebrating Life* (Continuum, 2003), pp. 159–60. This is a beautiful set of short pieces, on the theme 'Finding happiness in unexpected places'.
3. From *Sermons and Speeches*, Birmingham University, 11 June 2003. The whole lecture is available on www.archbishopofcanterbury.org/sermons_speeches/2003.
4. As reported in the *Church Times*' article by Rachel Harden, 17 September 2004, p. 8.
5. From *Gitanjali*, poem of Rabindranath Tagore.

Bibliography and Resources

Issues in interfaith relations

Ariarajah, W. *Not without my neighbour*, WCC, 1999

Harris, Elizabeth (ed.). *Paths of Faith*, Christians Aware, Leicester, 2002. Articles on faiths from the *Methodist Recorder*

Hart, David (ed.). *Multi Faith Britain*, O Books, 2002

Lamb, C., and R. Hooker. *Love the Stranger: Ministry in Multi-faith Areas*, SPCK, 1986

Thangaraj, M.T. *Relating to People of Other Religions*, Abingdon, 1997

General resources

Bowker, J. (ed.). *The Oxford Dictionary of World Religions*, OUP, 1997

(ed.). *Religions*, Cambridge Illustrated History, CUP, 2002

Crim, Keith (ed.). *The Perennial Dictionary of World Religions*, Harper and Row, 1989

Küng, Hans. *Tracing the Way, Spiritual Dimensions of the World Religions*, Continuum, 2002

Smart, Ninian (ed.). *The World's Religions*, CUP, 1998

(ed.). *Atlas of the World's Religions*, OUP, 1999

Wilson, Andrew (ed.). *World Scripture: A Comparative Anthology of Sacred Texts*, Paragon, 1995

Contemporary political/religious areas

Armstrong, K. *The Battle for God: fundamentalism in Judaism, Christianity and Islam*, HarperCollins, 2000

Esposito, John. *Unholy War: Terror in the Name of Islam*, OUP, 2002

Huntington, S. *The Clash of Civilizations and the Remaking of World Order*, Simon and Schuster, 1996

Jelen, Ted Gerard, and Clyde Wilcox (eds.). *Religion and Politics in Comparative Perspective*, CUP, 2002

Küng, Hans. *Global Responsibility: In Search of a Global Ethic*, SCM, 1991

LeRoy, Oliver. *The Failure of Political Islam*, I.B. Tauris, 1991

Marty, Martin (ed.). Volumes from the *Fundamentalism Project*, University of Chicago Press

McTernan, O. *Violence in God's Name*, DLT, 2003

Muslim Council of Britain. *The Quest for Sanity; reflections on September 11 and the aftermath*, MCB, 2002

Sacks, Jonathan. *The Dignity of Difference: how to avoid the clash of civilisations*, Continuum, 2002

Sedon, Mohammad (ed.). *British Muslims: Loyalty and Belonging*, Islamic Foundation, 2003

(ed.). *British Muslims between Assimilation and Segregation*, Islamic Foundation, 2004

Schmidt-Leukel, Perry. *War and Peace in World Religions*, SCM, 2004

Interfaith marriage

Alibhai-Brown, Yasmin, and Anne Montagu. *The Colour of Love*, Virago, 1992

Board of Mission, *Inter-Faith Consultative Group, Guidelines for the Celebration of Mixed-Faith Marriages in Church* (1992). This short publication contains the guidelines from the House of Bishops, as commended to dioceses.

Breger, Rosemary, and Rosanna Hill (eds.). *Cross cultural marriage*, Berg, 1998

Briggs, J. and L. *Jack and Zena*, Orion, 1997

Gajiwala, Astrid Lobo. *The Challenge of Being Different: a Hindu-Christian marriage*, Interchurch Families, Vol. 6, 2, 1998

Lamb, Christopher. *Mixed Faith Marriage, a Case for Care*, BCC, 1982

(ed.). *Marriages between Christians and Muslims: pastoral guidelines for Christians and Churches in Europe*, CTBI, 1997, reproduced in *Encounters*, Islamic Foundation, 5.1 (1999), pp. 63-106

Romain, Jonathan. *Till faith us do part*, Fount, 1996

Romarno, Dugan. *Inter cultural marriage*, Nicholas Brealy/Inter Cultural Press, 2001

Conversion

Forward, Martin (ed.). *Ultimate Visions*, Oneworld, 1995

Hefner, R. (ed.).*Conversion to Christianity*, University of California Press, 1993

Kose, Ali. *Conversion to Islam*, Kegan Paul, 1996

Krailshaimer, A. *Conversion*, SCM, 1980

Lamb, C., and M. Darrol Bryant. *Religious Conversion: Contemporary practices and controversies*, Cassell, 1999

Partridge, Chris, and Helen Reid (eds.). *Finding and losing faith: studies in conversion*, Paternoster, to be published in 2005

Percy, Martyn (ed.). *Previous Convictions*, SPCK, 2000

Rambo, L. *Understanding Religious Conversion*, Yale University Press, 1993

Romain, Jonathan. *Your God shall be My God, Religious Conversion in Britain Today*, SCM, 2000

Wingate, Andrew. *The Church and Conversion, A study of conversion to and from Christianity in the Tamil area of South India*, ISPCK, 1997

Interfaith prayer

Arai, Tosh, and Wesley Ariarajah (eds). *Spirituality in Interfaith Dialogue*, WCC, 1989

British Council of Churches.*Can we pray together?* BCC, 1983

Butler, Barbara and Tom. *Just Spirituality in a World of Faiths*, Mowbray, 1996

D'Costa, Gavin. *The Meeting of Religions and the Trinity*, Orbis, 2000

Hooker, Roger. *What is idolatry?* BCC, 1986

Inter-Faith Consultative Group. *Communities and Buildings: Church of England premises and other faiths*, Church House Publishing, 1995. A synod document (GS 1185)

'*Multi-Faith Worship*'? Church House Publishing, 1992. The report passed by the Synod

Klostermaier, Klaus. *Hindu and Christian in Vrindraban*, SCM, 1969, 1993

Pontifical Council for Religious Dialogue. *Inter Religious Prayer*, the Vatican, Current Dialogue Series, Bulletin 98, 1998/2. A systematic study of theology and practice, by a variety of authors from around the world

Practical aids

Appleton, George (ed.). *The Oxford Book of Prayer*, Oxford University Press, 1985

Braybrooke, Marcus. *1000 World Prayers*, John Hunt Publishing, 0 Books, 2003

Cragg, Kenneth (ed.). *Common Prayer*, a Muslim-Christian anthology, Oneworld, 1999

Faivre, Daniel (ed.). *Transcendence – prayer of people of faith*, Westminster Interfaith, 1994. Also, *Resources for Multifaith Celebrations*

Griffiths, Bede. *Universal Wisdom*, Fount, 1994

Theological questions

There is a vast amount of reading on these central issues. A small selection is given here:

Ariarajah, Wesley. *The Bible and People of Other Faiths*, WCC, 1987

Braybrooke, Marcus (ed.). *Stepping Stones to a Global Ethic*, SCM, 1992

Cantwell Smith, Wilfred. *Patterns of Faith Around the World*, Oneworld, 1998

D'Costa, Gavin. *Chrisian Uniqueness Reconsidered*, Orbis, 1990

Doctrine Commission of Church of England, *The Mystery of Salvation*, Church House, 1995

Dupuis, Jacques. *Christianity and the Religions: from confrontation to dialogue*, DLT/Orbis, 2002

Heim, Mark. *Salvations: Truth and Difference in Religion*, Orbis, 1997

The Depth of the Riches: A Trinitarian Theology of Religious Ends, Eerdmans, 2001

(ed.). *Grounds for Understanding: Ecumenical resources for responses to religious pluralism*, Eerdmans, 1998

Hick, John. *The Fifth Dimension: an Exploration of the Spiritual Realm*, Oneworld, 2004

An Interpretation of Religion; Human Responses to the Transcendent, Palgrave Macmillan, 2004 (and a series of earlier books around religious pluralism)

Hick, John, and Brian Hebblethwaite (eds.). *Christianity and Other Religions, Selected Readings*, Oneworld, 2001

Houlden, Leslie (ed.). *Jesus in History, Thought and Culture: an encyclopedia*, California, ABC-CLIO, 2003. Articles on Jesus within various faiths. Also on www.abc-clio.com

Knitter, Paul. *Jesus and the Other Names*, Orbis, 1996

Introducing Theologies of Religions, Orbis, 2001

Lockhead, David. *The Dialogical Imperative*, Orbis, 1988

McDermott, G. *Can Evangelicals learn from world religions? Jesus, revelation and religious traditions*, IVP, 2000

Pinnock, C. *A Wideness in God's Mercy*, Zondervan, 1992

Race, Alan. *Interfaith Encounter*, SCM, 2003

Robinson, John. *Truth is Two Eyed*, SCM, 1979

Samartha, S. *One Christ – Many Religions*, Orbis, 1991

Sanders, John. *No Other Name: Can only Christians be saved?* SPCK, 1994

Selvanayagam, Israel. *Relating to People of Other Faiths – Insights from the Bible*, CSS Books, 2004

Sugirtharajah, R. *Asian Faces of Jesus*, Orbis, 1993

Ward, Keith. *Images of Eternity*, DLT, 1987

Religion and Revelation: A Theology of Revelation in the World's Religions, OUP, 1994

Interreligious dialogue
General

D'Arcy May, J. (ed.). *Pluralism and the religions: the theological and political Dimensions*, Cassell, 1998

Cornille, Catherine (ed.). *Many Mansions? Multiple Religious Belonging and Christian Identity*, Orbis, 2002

Cracknell, K. *Towards a New Relationship: Christians and People of Other Faith*, Epworth, 1986

Justice, Courtesy and Love; theologians and missionaries encountering world religions, 1846-1914, Epworth, 1995

Forward, Martin. *Inter religious dialogue, a short introduction*, Oneworld, 2001

Griffiths, Paul. *Christianity through Non-Christian Eyes*, Orbis, 1990

Sherwin, Byron (ed.). *John Paul II and Interreligious Dialogue*, Orbis, 2000

Swidler, L. and John B. Cobb. *Death or Dialogue; from the age of monologue to the age of dialogue*, SCM, 1990

Swidler, L. *After the Absolute; the Dialogical Future of Religious Reflection*, Fortress Press, 1990

With particular religions:
Hinduism

Ariarajah, W. *Hindus and Christians, a Century of Protestant Ecumenical Thought*, Eerdmans, 1991

Bowen, Paul (ed.), *Themes and Issues in Hinduism*, Cassell, 1998

Coward, H. (ed.). *Hindu-Christian Dialogue*, Orbis, 1989

De Smet and J. Neuner, *Religious Hinduism*, St Paul's, Mumbai, 1996

Eck, Diana. *Encountering God: a Spiritual Journey from Bozeman to Banares*, Beacon Press, 1993

Fuller, C. *The Camphor Flame, Popular Hinduism and Society in India*, Princeton University Press, 1992

Griffiths, Bede. *The Marriage of East and West*, Templegate Publishers, 1982

Hooker, Roger. *Themes in Hinduism and Christianity*, Peter Lang, 1989
  Also his three booklets published by CMS, *Unchartered Journey, Journey into Varanasi, and Voices of Varanasi*
Klostermaier, K. *A Survey of Hinduism*, State University of New York, 1995
Knott, Kim. *Hinduism: a Very Short Introduction*, OUP, 2000
Lipner, Julius. *The Hindus: Their religious beliefs and practices*, Routledge, 1994
Little, Gwyneth (ed.). *Meeting Hindus*, Christians Aware, Leicester
Panikkar, Raimundo. *The Unknown Christ of Hinduism*, Orbis/DLT, 1981
Radhakrishnan, S. *The Hindu View of Life*, Macmillan, 1936
Sharpe, E.J. *Faith meets Faith, some Christian attitudes to Hinduism in the nineteenth and twentieth centuries*, SCM, 1997
Thangaraj, Thomas. *The Crucified Guru*, Abingdon, 1994
Thomas, M.M. *The Acknowledged Christ of the Indian Renaissance*, SCM, 1969
Wardell, M., and R. Gidoomal. *Chapatis for Tea: reaching your Hindu neighbour, a practical guide*, Highland, 1994

Islam

Ahmed, Kurshid. *Islam, its meaning and message*, Islamic Foundation, 1999
Brown, S. *The Nearest in Affection*, Trinity Press International, 1995
Chapman, Colin. *Cross and Crescent*, IVP, 1995
Cragg, K. *The Call of the Minaret*, 2nd edition, Collins, 1986
  Also many other books by Cragg, such as *Jesus and the Muslim*, and *Muhammed and the Christian*
Christians Aware. *Meeting Muslims*
Esack, Farid. *The Qur'an, Liberation and Religious pluralism*, Oneworld, 1997
Esposito, John (ed.). *The Oxford History of Islam*, OUP, 1999
Forward, Martin. *A Short Life of Muhammad*, Oneworld, 1997
Goddard, H. *A History of Christian-Muslim Relations*, Edinburgh, 2000
Hewer, C. *The Essence of Islam*, Many Books, 2002
Ipgrave, Michael (ed.). *The Road Ahead, a Christian-Muslim Dialogue*, Church House, 2002
  (ed.). *Scriptures in Dialogue, Christians and Muslims studying the Bible and Qur'an together*, Church House Publishing, 2004
  (ed.). *Bearing the Word: Prophecy in Biblical and Qur'anic Perspectives*, Church House Publishing, 2005
Lewis, P. *Islamic Britain*, I.B. Tauris, 1994
Machatsheke, R. *Islam: the basics*, SCM, 1995
Momen, Moolan. *An Introduction to Shi'I Islam*, Yale University Press, 1985
Montgomery Watt, W. *Muslim-Christian Encounters: perceptions and misperceptions*, Routledge, 1991
Nazir Ali, M. *Frontiers in Muslim-Christian Encounter*, Regnum, 1991
Sutcliffe, S. *Aishah my sister*, Paternoster, 1997
Wingate, Andrew. *Encounter in the Spirit, Muslim-Christian Dialogue in Practice*, WCC, 1991

Buddhism

Batchelor, Stephen. *The Awakening of the West; The Encounter of Buddhism with Western Culture*, Thorsons, 1995

Conze, Edward (ed.). *Buddhist Texts throughout the Ages*, Oneworld, 1995

Corless, R., and Paul Knitter (eds.). *Buddhist Emptiness and Christian Trinity*, Paulist, 1990

Derrett, J., and M. Duncan. *The Bible and the Buddhists*, Editrice Centro Studi, 2000

Gethin, Robert. *The Foundations of Buddhism*, OUP, 1998

Gross, Rita, and Rosemary Radford Reuther. *Religious Feminism and the Future of the Planet: A Buddhist-Christian Conversation*, Continuum, 2001

Hanh, Thich Nhat. *Living Buddha, Living Christ*, Routledge, 1995, and other books

Harris, Elizabeth. *What Buddhists Believe*, Oneworld, 1998

Harris, Elizabeth, and Ramona Kauth. *Meeting Buddhists*, Christians Aware, 2004

Harvey, Peter (ed.). *Buddhism*, Continuum, 2001

Kasimow, Harold, John P. Keenan and Linda Klepinger Kennan (eds.). *Jews, Christians and the Way of the Buddha*, Wisdom Books, 2003

Keown, Damien. *Buddhism, a Very Short Introduction*, OUP, 1996

Pieris, Aloysius. *Love meets Wisdom*, Orbis, 1998

Judaism

Braybrooke, Marcus. *Time to Meet; towards a deeper relationship between Jews and Christians*, SCM, 1990

  Children of One God: A History of the CCJ, Vallentine Mitchell, 1991

  How to understand Judaism, SCM, 1995

Cohn-Sherbok, Dan. *A Dictionary of Judaism and Christianity*, SPCK, 1991

  The Future of Judaism, T and T Clark, 1994

Friedlander, Albert. *A Thread of Gold: Journeys towards Reconciliation*, SCM, 1990

Guinness, Michele. *Child of the Covenant*, Hodder, 1985

Harries, Richard. *After the Evil: Christianity and Judaism in the Shadow of the Holocaust*, OUP, 2003

Kessler, E., J. Pawlikowski and J. Banki (eds.). *Jews and Christians in Conversation: crossing cultures and generations*, Orchard Academic, 2000

Küng, Hans. *Judaism*, SCM, 1992

Rittner, Carol, Stephen Smith, Irena Steinfeldt (eds.). *The Holocaust and the Christian World*, Kuperard, 2000

Romain, Jonathan. *Faith and Practice, a Guide to Reform Judaism Today*, Reform Synagogues of Great Britain, 1991

Rothschild, Fritz (ed.). *Jewish Perspectives on Christianity*, Continuum, 1996

Saperstein, Marc. *Moments of Crisis in Jewish-Christian Relations*, SCM, 1989

Solomon, Norman. *Judaism and World Religion*, St Martin's Press, 1991

Swidler, Leonard (ed.). *Bursting the Bonds: A Jewish-Christian Dialogue on Jesus and Paul*, Orbis, 1990

Ucko, Hans. *Common Roots, New Horizons*, WCC, 1994

Sikhism

Barrow, J. (ed.). *Meeting Sikhs,* Christians Aware, Leicester

Cole, Owen. *The Guru in Sikhism,* DLT, 1982

Cole, Owen, and P.S. Sambhi. *Sikhism and Christianity,* Macmillan, 1993

Nesbit, Eleanor, and Gobinder Kaur. *Guru Nanak,* Canterbury Press, 1999

Singh, Charanjit Ajith. *The Wisdom of Sikhism,* Oneworld, 2001

Narinder Mehat and Margaret Wardell. *When love prevails: a Sikh woman finds Christ,* Paternoster, 1998

Seva Singh Kalsi. *Simple Guide to Sikhism,* Global Books, Folkestone, 1999

Other Resources

Ahmed, Rumman and others. *Tools for Regeneration: a holistic approach for faith communities,* Faith Based Regeneration Network, Office of Deputy Prime Minister, 2004

CMS. *Dialogue,* a CMS study pack on Muslim-Christian Relations for small groups, including a video for four study sessions

Home Office. *Working Together: Co-operation between Government and Faith Communities,* Faith Communities Unit, 2004. This and the next reference are two of many reports, local and national, released since 9/11, and after the northern disturbances of 2001. They indicate the much increased involvement of central and local government with faith communities

Interfaith Network. *The Local Interfaith Guide,* 2003

Interfaith Network. *Inter Faith Organisations in the UK, a Directory,* 2004

Methodist Church. *Faith meeting Faith,* ways forward in interfaith relations, the Interfaith Office, Methodist Church, 2004. Resource for local Christians

MPA Council. *A Place of Refuge – a positive approach to asylum seekers and refugees in the UK* (Church House Publishing, 2005)

National Council of Hindu Temples. *Directory of Hindu Temples in the UK, 2004–6.* Available from Shree Sanatan Mandir, Weymouth St, Leicester LE4 6FQ, which lists the locations of the 141 temples in the UK

USPG, Methodist Church. *The Life We Share: a study pack on interfaith relations.* Includes the voices of people of various faiths on CD Rom

Weller, Paul (ed.). *Religions in the UK,* 2001-2003, University of Derby and Inter Faith Network. An indispensable reference book

Journals

Common Ground, produced by Council of Christians and Jews and available from them.

Interreligious Insight: a journal of dialogue and engagement, World Congress of Faiths, Oxford (www.interreligiousinsight.org)

Q News, a well-established monthly journal for younger British Muslims, challenging for all to read

Westminster Interfaith Newsletter, available from alfredagius@rcdow.org.uk, gives general news on interfaith activity, courses, etc. They also produce a range of very informative four-page leaflets for Christians engaged with other faiths

Jewish Chronicle (email webmaster@thejc.com)

Sikh Messenger (www.nsouk.co.uk)

Selected Organisations

Catholic Bishops' Conference of England and Wales
39 Eccleston Square
London SW1V 1BX

Centre for Interreligious Dialogue
Heythrop College
Kensington Square
London W8 5HQ

Centre for Jewish-Christians Relations
Wesley House
Jesus Lane
Cambridge CB5 8BJ
e-mail: enquiries@cjcr.ac.uk

Centre for the Study of Islam and Christianity
London School of Theology (formerly London Bible College)
Green Lane ·
Northwood · HA6 2UW

Centre for the Study of Islam and Muslim Christian Relations
and Asian Religion Centre
University of Birmingham
Elmfield House
Selly Oak Campus
Birmingham B29 6LQ

Christians Aware
2 Saxby Street
Leicester
LE2 0ND

Church of England Interfaith Relations Adviser
Church House
Great Smith Street
London SW1P 3NZ

Churches Agency for Inter Faith Relations in Scotland
Scottish Churches House
Dunblane FR15 0JA

Churches Commission on Inter Faith Relations
Church House
Great Smith Street
London SW1P 3NZ

Council of Christians and Jews
5th Floor
Camelford House
89 Albert Embankment
London SE1 7TP
e-mail: cjrelations@ccj.org.uk
website: www.ccj.org.uk

Derby Interfaith Centre
University of Derby
24 Kedlestone Road
Derby DE3 1GU

Edinburgh Centre for Muslim-Christian Studies
PO Box 23510
Edinburgh EH8 9ZA

Faith to Faith
Carrs Lane Church Centre
Carrs Lane
Birmingham B4 7SX
e-mail: office@faithtofaith.org.uk

Islamic Foundation
Ratby Lane
Markfield
LE67 9SY
e-mail: mihe@islamic-foundation.org.uk

Inter Faith Network of the UK
8A Lower Grosvenor Place
London SWIW 0EN
e-mail: ifnet@interfaith.org.uk
website: www.interfaith.org.uk

International Interfaith Centre
2 Market Street

Oxford OX1 3EF
e-mail: iic@interfaith-center.org
website: www.interfaith-center.org

London Inter Faith Centre,
125 Salusbury Road
London NW6 6RG

Connexional Secretary for Interfaith Relations
Methodist Church
Methodist Church House
25 Marylebone Road
London NW1 5JR

Oxford Centre for Hindu Studies
14 Magdalen Street
Oxford OX1 3AE

South Asia Concern
PO Box 43
Sutton
Surrey SM2 5WL

United College of the Ascension (USPG/Methodist)
Selly Oak
Birmingham B29 6RD

Presence and Engagement Centres:
The Bradford Centre for Dialogue and Diversity
c/o Diocesan Office
Kadugli House
Elmsley Street
Keighley
Bradford BD20 6SE

St Philip's Centre, Leicester – Study and Engagement in a Multifaith Society
St Philip's Church
Evington Road
Leicester LE2 1QJ

Additional helpful websites:
World Congress of Faiths: www.worldfaiths.org
International Association for Religious Freedom (IARF): www.iarf.net
The Good Web Guide: World Religions: www.thegood webguide.co.uk

Interfaith marriage support groups and information

Muslim–Christian marriage support group, run by Heather Yusuf, which also produces an occasional publication, available through email: heather@al-yousuf.freeserve.co.uk   See also website www.mcmarriage.org.uk

Churches Together website: www.safemarriage.org.uk

People in Harmony, based in Slough. www.pih.org.uk

General help, run by a Jewish/Catholic couple: www.dovetailinstitute.org

Index